Douglas Coupland

MANCHESTER
1824

Manchester University Press

Contemporary American and Canadian Writers

Series editors:
Nahem Yousaf and Sharon Monteith

Also available

Paul Auster   Mark Brown
Philip Roth   David Brauner

Douglas Coupland

Andrew Tate

Manchester University Press

Published by Manchester University Press
Oxford Road, Manchester M13 9PL
www.manchesteruniversitypress.co.uk

A catalogue record for this book is available from the British Library

ISBN 978 0 7190 7488 2 *hardback*
ISBN 978 0 7190 7661 9 *paperback*

First published 2007

Typeset
by Florence Production Ltd, Stoodleigh, Devon

For Michaela

Contents

List of abbreviations

AFAP   All Families are Psychotic
COG   City of Glass
ER   Eleanor Rigby
GIAC   Girlfriend in a Coma
GX   Generation X: Tales for an Accelerated Culture
HN   Hey Nostradamus!
JP   JPod
LAG   Life After God
MS   Microserfs
MW   Miss Wyoming
PD   Polaroids from the Dead
SOC   Souvenir of Canada
SOC2   Souvenir of Canada 2
SP   Shampoo Planet

Series editors' foreword

This innovative series reflects the breadth and diversity of writing over the last thirty years, and provides critical evaluations of established, emerging and critically neglected writers – mixing the canonical with the unexpected. It explores notions of the contemporary and analyses current and developing modes of representation with a focus on individual writers and their work. The series seeks to reflect both the growing body of academic research in the field, and the increasing prevalence of contemporary American and Canadian fiction on programmes of study in institutions of higher education around the world. Central to the series is a concern that each book should argue a stimulating thesis, rather than provide an introductory survey, and that each contemporary writer will be examined across the trajectory of their literary production. A variety of critical tools and literary and interdisciplinary approaches are encouraged to illuminate the ways in which a particular writer contributes to, and helps readers rethink, the North American literary and cultural landscape in a global context.

Central to debates about the field of contemporary fiction is its role in interrogating ideas of national exceptionalism and transnationalism. This series matches the multivocality of contemporary writing with wide-ranging and detailed analysis. Contributors examine the drama of the nation from the perspectives of writers who are members of established and new immigrant groups, writers who consider themselves on the nation's margins as well as those who chronicle middle America. National labels are the subject of vociferous debate and including American and Canadian writers in the same series is not to flatten the differences between them but to acknowledge that literary traditions and tensions are cross-cultural and that North American writers often explore and expose precisely these tensions. The series recognizes that situating a writer in a cultural context involves a multiplicity of influences, social and geopolitical, artistic and theoretical, and that contemporary fiction defies easy categorization. For example, it examines writers who invigorate the genres in which they have made their mark alongside writers whose aesthetic goal is to subvert the idea of genre altogether. The challenge of defining the roles of writers and assessing their reception by reading communities is central to the aims of the series.

Overall, *Contemporary American and Canadian Writers* aims to begin to represent something of the diversity of contemporary writing and seeks to engage students and scholars in stimulating debates about the contemporary and about fiction.

Nahem Yousaf
Sharon Monteith

Acknowledgements

My first debt is to the series editors, Sharon Monteith and Nahem Yousaf. I am very grateful for their interest in and support for this project from my initial proposal to the book's completion. The anonymous reader's report was also extremely useful. Thanks are also due to the staff of Manchester University Press and its board. I was able to complete the book with the support of a term's sabbatical leave at Lancaster University. My colleagues in the Department of English & Creative Writing have been unfailingly encouraging. In particular, I would like to thank Alison Findlay, Arthur Bradley, Jo Carruthers, Mike Greaney, Alison Easton, Tony Sharpe and Lee Horsley. Mark Knight and Thomas Woodman gave me invaluable feedback on my earliest work on Coupland and religion. Peter Francis, Patsy Williams and the staff of St Deiniol's Library provided an incomparable place to write and think during various stages of the book. Rachel Kitchen provided patient and eagle-eyed proofreading. Any errors are my own. For interest and encouragement I am very grateful to my parents and grandparents, Chris, Anne-Marie, James, Pete, Hutch, MDW and the families Hill and Ashbridge. The book would not have been completed with out the love and support of Michaela, to whom it is dedicated.

Material from Chapter 6 initially appeared as ' "Now – Here is My Secret": Ritual and Epiphany in Douglas Coupland's Fiction', *Literature and Theology*, 16.3 (2002), 326–8. I am grateful to Oxford University Press for permission to reprint this material in revised form.

1

Introduction: Coupland's contexts

I have always tried to speak with a voice that has no regional character –
a voice from nowhere . . . home to me . . . is a shared electronic dream of
cartoon memories, half-hour sitcoms and national tragedies . . . I used to
think mine was a Pacific Northwest accent, from where I grew up, but
then I realized my accent was simply the accent of nowhere – the accent
of a person who has no fixed home in their mind.[1] (*Life After God*, 1994)

Does Douglas Coupland's fiction 'speak' with 'a voice from nowhere'?
Is he a Canadian who strategically chooses to write with a US accent,
an involuntary American novelist who happens to hold a Canadian
passport or a writer whose narrative concerns transcend national
boundaries? The anonymous narrator of Coupland's short story, 'In
the Desert' (1994), a wanderer lost in the scorched American
wilderness, makes revealing connections between the simulated, late
twentieth-century 'electronic dream' of shared televisual memory
and the dubious coherence of his own life story. This insecurity about
the capricious, unstable nature of identity – including a sense of
ambivalence about national affiliations – isolates a broader set of issues
that are vital, not just for Coupland's many lonely or alienated
characters, but also to the aesthetic and ethical implications of his work.

This book – the first full-length study of Coupland's writing –
explores the prolific first decade and a half of his career, from
Generation X: Tales for an Accelerated Culture (1991) to *JPod* (2006),
a period in which he published ten novels and four significant
volumes of non-fiction. Since the publication of his debut novel,
Coupland has been exploring the textures and traumas of an era that,
superficially at least, appears hostile to conviction, community,
connection and continuity. Emerging in the last decade of the twentieth
century – amidst the absurd contradictions of instantaneous global

communication and acute poverty – Coupland's novels, short stories, essays and visual art have intervened in specifically contemporary debates regarding authenticity, artifice and art.

What place do conventional novels have in an era that has invested so heavily – literally and figuratively – in electronic media and the spectacular forms of film and television? A tacit anxiety about the legitimacy of the word and print culture informs Coupland's fiction. *Microserfs* (1995), the novelist's prescient exploration of the 1990s IT revolution, for example, wrestles with the possibility that its own form is anachronistic: 'I wonder if we oversentimentalize the power of books', reflects Daniel Underwood, both a child and architect of the digital age, and the novel's narrator.[2] This possibility is amplified in a question asked by Daniel's mother, fearful that her bibliophile-dependent profession may soon be outmoded: 'Do you think libraries are going to become obsolete?' (*MS*, p. 159).

It has become a critical commonplace simultaneously to credit those raised in the so-called Generation X epoch with a sophisticated visual literacy whilst lamenting an imagined loss of attention span, historical awareness, linguistic aptitude and sense of ethical responsibility. However, Tara Brabazon is surely right when she observes that 'those born between 1961 and 1981 have endured many (post) youth cultural labels from slackers to the chemical/blank generation and baby busters' without any careful cultural study of 'the literacies and popular culture that are the basis of – and for – this imagined and imagining collectivity'.[3] Coupland writes from this generational perspective and his work has focused primarily on people of the so-called postmodern epoch who, in Bran Nicol's terms, 'have never known reality unframed by mass media and are consequently unable to avoid relating everyday "real" experience to everyday fictional experience, especially that which has been screened'.[4] Where does this heavily mediated reality leave the possibility for originality or authenticity, for what Ralph Waldo Emerson once described as the desire for an 'original relation to the universe'?[5] What kind of literature is possible in an era saturated with instantly accessible, duplicated images?

In recent years, Coupland has returned to his training in the visual arts by creating conceptual, mixed media art for exhibitions including *Canada House* (2003) and *Lost and Gained in Translation* (2005); he has also written and performed a one-man play at the Royal Shakespeare Company and co-founded a film production company. Yet his creative work, marked by a strong visual sensibility, has displayed considerable faith in the potential of book culture. The novel, in its evolving, elastic form, has remained Coupland's principal mode of aesthetic experiment. Nicholas Blincoe is right, however, to emphasize that his fiction does 'not emerge from a literary tradition' but 'from contemporary culture itself'.[6]

This book is structured around thematically focused chapters that consider Coupland's engagement with narrative, consumer culture, space and religion. The conclusion uses *JPod*, Coupland's surreal tenth novel, to re-read aspects of his work and, in particular, his recurrent interest in visions of the future. This introduction locates Coupland's writing – both his novels and non-fiction – alongside parallel examples of music, film, television and cultural debate of the period. The chapter prioritizes his emergence in the 1990s in relation to the wider X generation phenomenon but also considers issues of reception and thematic and formal development. In most instances, the books have been grouped chronologically, although *Life After God* and *Girlfriend in a Coma* (1998) are discussed together primarily on the basis of a shared theme.

Is (Post)modern life rubbish? *Generation X: Tales for an Accelerated Culture* (1991) and *Shampoo Planet* (1992)

'We live small lives on the periphery; we are marginalized and there's a great deal in which we choose not to participate', confides Andy Palmer, the sole narrator of *Generation X*.[7] Coupland's debut novel performs the paradoxical task of rendering visible a body of people who primarily define themselves as imperceptible to the culture at large. To become an X person, in these 'tales for an accelerated culture', is also to be a member of a disunited generation that resists easy epithets. Andy has quietly stepped away from a life dominated by the perpetual fight for worldly success to live, instead, as a bartender, serving the prosperous in the highly artificial environment of Palm Springs, a wealthy resort on the edge of the Californian desert. In this strange space he connects with Dag and Claire, two similarly overeducated and dissatisfied twenty-somethings.

These desert sojourners are conscious that their experience of the 'new world' will always be second-hand – that their era is strewn with the cultural leftovers of countless previous epochs – but they look for meaning amidst the accretions of history. Andy's opening narrative, as

he anticipates sun rise over the San Andreas fault, in precise language
peculiarly reminiscent of Imagist poetry, juxtaposes natural splendour with a gross but comic picture. Andy is reluctantly removing
unpleasant gloop from his dogs' noses, suspecting that these animals
have been 'rummaging through the dumpsters out behind the
cosmetic surgery center again' (*GX*, p. 4). The novel's multiple images
of waste – a recurring motif in Coupland's fiction, and discussed in
more detail in Chapter 3 – anticipate *Underworld* (1998), Don DeLillo's
vast, visionary novel of American excess. 'Civilization did not rise and
flourish', states Detwiler, DeLillo's trash theorist, 'as men hammered
out hunting scenes on bronze gates . . . with garbage as a noisome
offshoot . . . garbage rose first, inciting people to build a civilization'.[8]
Similarly, Coupland's characters cope with an accelerated era – and a
capitalist culture that necessarily generates ever more waste – by
patiently constructing stories out of the 'garbage' pile on which their
world, literally and figuratively, precariously resides. The ritual of
'bedtime stories' shared by Andy, Dag and Claire – autobiographical,
amusing and apocalyptic tales – are a response to the junk culture that
they have inherited.

Ironically, Coupland's title has mutated into the most widely
recognized generational tag since the 1960s. A flood of newspaper
articles, fashion columns and films seized on Generation X as a
convenient label to define any youth culture activity that bordered,
however timidly, on the unconventional. The trend ignited debate
between ostensibly disparate interest groups: marketing gurus,
theologians and sociologists appropriated the tag and, with an array of
suspect motives, were keen to understand the aspirations and fears
of this emergent generation.[9] Angry and listless, apolitical and environmentally conscious, godless and spiritual are some of the contradictory
terms used as shorthand for a whole variety of sensibilities that seemed
to define sub-cultures not previously recognized or codified in the
popular media.[10] In a significant contribution to cultural debate, Neil
Howe and William Strauss explored the specifics of what they termed
the '13th Generation' and, later in the 1990s, James Annesley's *Blank
Fictions* (1998) suggested that a new literary identity was emerging in
relation to this culture.[11]

For some young writers and artists, Generation X signified an
empowering designation for a cohort who had grown up without any
substantial point of connection beyond their saturation in pop culture.
Douglas Rushkoff, editor of *The GenX Reader* (1994), for example,

asserted that using the label was not 'a cop out' but 'a declaration of independence'.[12] 'We were the first American generation in at least a century to lack a common cause,' reflects Tom Beaudoin, an American theologian who, like Rushkoff, has unashamedly accepted and deployed the Generation X moniker. For Beaudoin, the lack of a 'rallying point' such as the struggle for civil rights and protest against the intervention in Vietnam, campaigns with which 'baby boomers', the generation born shortly after the Second World War, had defined a collective identity, prevented his generation from discovering a substantial rationale for affiliation. Westerners who were born in the 1960s and 1970s had no shared political memories – or none that they were old enough to process meaningfully – and consequently this generation 'reached adulthood in the absence of a theme, and even with a theme of absence'.[13]

For John M. Ulrich, the different uses of the term, particularly since the 1960s, are linked 'with subcultural negationist practices and their often conflicted relationship to mainstream consumer culture'.[14] The basic plot and narrative sensibility of Coupland's *Generation X* echo these countercultural traditions. The novel's trinity of principal characters displays a visceral dislike of the grasping, aggressive career-driven worlds that they have abandoned but neither are they committed anti-capitalist agitators. Although Coupland does not directly address communism's demise, the collapse of this ideology provides the defining political context for the novel. The apparent victory of capitalism afforded by the former Soviet Union's embrace of market economics indicated that the world was now, as Zygmunt Bauman notes, 'without a collective utopia, without a conscious alternative to itself'.[15] Andy, Dag and Claire are living as 'last' men and women in the era that Francis Fukuyama, in an academic article and subsequent best-selling book, famously described, as the 'end of history'. For Fukuyama, this 'end' arrives with the collapse of 'monarchy, aristocracy, theocracy, fascism [and] communist totalitarianism' when 'there are no serious competitors left to liberal democracy': 'now, outside the Islamic world, there appears to be a general consensus that accepts liberal democracy's claims to be the most rational form of government'.[16]

The end of communism, in particular, represented for many, the death of a secular heaven. G. P. Lainsbury, in an excellent article, argues that, consciously or otherwise, Coupland's novel is a 'meditation on the end of history'.[17] The central characters' rejection of material acquisitiveness resonates with the dissident cultures that flourished in 1960s America but these characters have neither engaged in political protest nor embraced truly alternative lifestyles. They take a series of 'McJobs' ('low-pay, low-prestige, low-dignity, low-benefit') and their ambivalence towards capitalism does not encourage them to actively fight its influence (*GX*, p. 6). Coupland's novel emerges, in part at least, from an awareness of the disintegration of traditional politics: *Generation X* explores what Dag names as a crisis associated with 'a failure of class' (*GX*, p. 36). The storytellers, like the majority of Coupland's protagonists, are from distinctively middle-class, suburban backgrounds; their socio-economic milieu has been one of relative prosperity rather than unqualified financial privilege but they have never had to fear the spectre of poverty. Unlike their parents, however, they cannot effortlessly accommodate themselves to the expectations of everyday bourgeois life: their refusal to pursue traditional careers might be a sign of a rather desultory dissidence but it is also an indication that customary ways of reading class have become more complex. This dimension of the novel was, by Coupland's confession in his 1995 'eulogy' for Gen X in *Details* magazine, a response to Paul Fussell's *Class: A Guide through the American Status System* (1983), and specifically to a chapter entitled 'The X way out'. In this barbed survey of a phenomenon that is supposed to have been abandoned in the old, reactionary world of Europe, Fussell observed that a new category was needed to describe people who did not belong within any of the traditional class groupings:

> 'X' people are better conceived as belonging to a category than a class because you are not born an X person . . . you earn X-personhood by a strenuous effort of discovery in which curiosity and originality are indispensable. And in discovering that you can become an X person you find the only escape from class.[18]

Coupland's characters are fugitives from the story of middle-class aspiration, hoping to forge a new identity. The idea that this activity somehow negates class identity is, however, rather more problematic. A sceptical approach might suggest that Andy, Claire and Dag are tourists, visiting a world without pension schemes, healthcare benefits and stock options as a retreat from the less palatable elements of consumerist society but who always have the opportunity to return to this more secure financial world. Are Coupland's lyrical evocations of friendship, memory and the pursuit of meaning in a post-ideological era really nothing more than, in Jim Finnegan's terms, 'the privileged romanticisms of new bohemian aesthetes'?[19]

The public construction of an identity for a body of people who defied classification became one of the fiercest media debates in the 1990s. Sceptical critics, from both left and right, were swift to denounce this emergent (non)identity. P. J. O'Rourke, self-styled Republican Party Reptile and professional antagonist of liberal America issued his own, succinct 'memo to Generation X': 'Pull your pants up, turn your hat around, and get a job'.[20] One opinion piece in *Newsweek*, failing to notice Coupland's Canadian citizenship, accommodated *Generation X* to a 'long history of torpid American whining' that allegedly includes T. S. Eliot's *The Waste Land* (1922) and Hemingway's *The Sun Also Rises* (1926); where this appalled columnist could marshal some sympathy for early twentieth-century modernists who witnessed the visceral horrors of world war, he can find no similar justification for Coupland and his contemporaries: 'it's just the whine without the grievance . . . a world not ending but being made (Eliot again) with a whimper'.[21] A more apposite reference might have been the languid aesthetics of Walt Whitman, whose 'Song of Myself' (1855) celebrates the distinctly *un*-American urge to 'loafe and invite my soul', an unmistakable literary precedent for Coupland's posse of withdrawn, contemplative romantics.

Another columnist raged against what he defined as 'the ceaseless carping' of Gen X writers, who, in his dour view constituted 'a handful of spoiled, self-indulgent, overgrown adolescents'.[22] These irascible, rather pompous articles echo clashes between the so-called boomer generation and their unimpressed, younger counterparts in *Generation X*. The ill-tempered media debate is prefigured in an argument between Dag and his moneyed, ex-hippie boss who accuses his younger colleague and his entire generation of torpor and ingratitude; Dag, in turn, delivers an amusing but career-wrecking salvo against the wealth of the boomer generation (*GX*, pp. 25–6). A similar, quasi-oedipal conflict is used as a framing device in the credits sequence for *Reality Bites* (1994), Ben Stiller's directorial debut, in which Lelania Price (Winona Ryder), as college valedictorian, addresses her fellow graduates with a typical boomer-baiting piece of rhetoric. The oration ends with a moment of bathos as, losing her notes, the speaker is able only to answer her own portentous question ('How can we repair all the damage we inherited?') with an embarrassed, 'I don't know.' The apparently unintentional failure to propose any political solutions to replace the failed 'counterculture' of 1960s radicals slyly enacts the truism that 1990s youth culture, besides a vague sense of complaint, had nothing new to say.

Generational conflict about wealth, entitlement and the validity of cultural expression could hardly be seen as new trends in the 1990s and neither, in fact, was the use of Generation X as a term to describe youth culture. In the early 1950s, Robert Capa, an innovative photojournalist, presented a series of essay-portraits, published in magazines, of men and women turning twenty mid-way through the twentieth century; the project profiled young people from around the world and Capa used the term Generation X to indicate their ambiguous, unfixed identity. A decade later, Charles Hamblett and Jane Deverson re-deployed the epithet in a collection about British youth culture, *Generation X* (1964). The most nuanced 'genealogy' of 'Generation X' as a youth-culture tag is offered in Ulrich's superb introduction to *GenXegesis*.[23] Endeavours to attach a singular origin to the name are, however, bound to be frustrated, since it has been used to signify a variety of contradictory phenomena and perspectives. In Coupland's debut novel, for example, the emergence of a new, nameless generation is not a distinctively Western, let alone American, phenomenon. Andy uses the X label sparingly and unpredictably the term is introduced in the recollection of a time as a picture researcher for a Tokyo 'teenybopper' magazine, immediately before his unconversion from consumerist habits of mind. Invited to drink tea with the 'Americaphile' company director, Andy is exiled by his fellow workers, the '*shin jin rui*', a popular Japanese term for people in their twenties, meaning 'new human beings': 'We have the same group over here . . . but it doesn't have a name – an *X* generation – purposefully hiding itself' (*GX*, pp. 62–3).

Coupland's identification of a generation 'purposefully hiding itself' as it searched, in a distracted, leisurely fashion, for an identity of its own was swiftly associated with other subcultural narratives to produce a potent generational mythology. 'The twentysomething generation is [a] myth' or 'an imaginary resolution of real contradictions', argued Alexander Star in a 1993 piece for *New Republic*: 'Many young people do like grunge rock, gourmet coffee, and green politics, at least for the moment . . . But these characteristics don't cohere into a shared identity.'[24]

Various contemporary texts have since been consecrated (or cursed) with the Gen X label although, as Star suggests, the emerging sanitized legend unhelpfully erases the real differences between so-called 'alternative' artists. However, there are useful points of continuity and difference between Coupland's work and his peers. Richard Linklater, one of the most inventive US filmmakers to emerge in the 1990s, directs movies that raise similar formal and thematic questions to Coupland's fiction. Linklater's Whitmanesque debut *Slacker* (shot in 1989 but released in 1991) – the same year that *Generation X* was published – offered a consciously disjointed set of overlapping narratives amidst a languorous assortment of bedsit conspiracy theorists, anarchists, sloppy thieves, part-time musicians and unconvincing anti-artists in a single day in the college town of Austin, Texas. In an introduction to his screenplay, the director counters the conventional claim that his generation 'had nothing to say' with an assertion of faith in the novel ways in which his peers speak:

> It was a multitude of voices coexisting . . . that . . . couldn't easily be classified. Each individual had to find it in their own way and in the only place society had left for this discovery – the margins . . . This seems the place where the actual buzz of life goes on, where the conspiracies, schizophrenia, melancholy, and exuberance all battle it out, daily.[25]

This celebration of a gossipy, stimulating and enchanted space outside of the mainstream connects the universe of *Slacker* with that constructed in *Generation X*. The liberty embodied in these boundary worlds might only, in reality, be available via acts of the imagination in which banalities of routine, work and economic restrictions are transfigured by a skewed worldview. Linklater's focus on self-conscious (but half-hearted) nonconformists, whose mode of dissidence is insufficiently heroic or spectacular ever to warrant a place in Hollywood movies, certainly parallels the concerns of Coupland's debut, as do the experiments with fragmented or half-finished narrative. The intimate tales that Andy and his associates share are similar to the mini-stories that structure the disorderly form of *Slacker*, occupying a border between trivia and consequence. Where the use of sustained first-person narration in *Generation X* allows empathic identification with the Romantic, questing Andy Palmer, *Slacker* resists any kind of emotional attachment with its relentless movement away from any single character. Linklater's film offers a far colder, near-Brechtian approach to its sequence of broken stories and fleetingly witnessed characters. Coupland has since publicly identified himself with the film by writing a foreword to Linklater's screenplay. In this short essay, Coupland defends the concept of '*un*employment – opting out of the employment paradigm altogether' and offers a critique of the career ladder worthy of one of his characters.[26]

A declared affection for eccentric 'dreamers . . . characters out of key
. . . drifting, slightly twisted, still willing to listen' is also indicative of
the affinities between Coupland's fiction and aspects of the 1990s
Washington State grunge music scene.[27] The coincidence of the
author's geographical association with the Pacific Northwest certainly
strengthened these connections. *Nevermind*, Nirvana's second album,
was released in September 1991, six months after the publication of
Generation X. Its themes of generational discontent, disillusion and
disaffection, reaching their most intense (and commercially successful)
on 'Smells Like Teen Spirit' – issues vital to the novel – were probably
new only to those who had neither heard a punk record nor read Allen
Ginsberg's 'Howl' (1955). In Kurt Cobain's lyrics and the band's sound,
the synthesis of melancholy and black humour was fresh and, like
Coupland's novel, marketable. The album's now iconic cover image of
a baby boy, immersed in clear blue water, being tempted by the hooked
snare of a dollar bill also resonates with *Generation X*'s underlying
theme of the corrupting nature of consumer capitalism. However, one
point of significant disparity between Coupland and Cobain is their
approach to culture produced in a capitalist era: where the latter's lyrics
tended to emphasize a despairing antipathy for commerce in all its
insidious forms, Coupland's fiction, including *Generation X*, is more
equivocal and, indeed, attracted to certain modes of mass-produced
motifs and images.

The most widely acknowledged inspiration for the innovative print
style adopted in *Generation X* is its author's affinity with the aesthetics
of Pop Art. Coupland has expressed his enthusiasm for the sensibilities
of this movement, particularly for the concepts pioneered by Andy
Warhol, whom he quotes in an autobiographical piece on James
Rosenquist's seminal collage, *F-111* (1965): 'Warhol . . . said that once
you saw the world as Pop, you could never look at it the same way ever
again. Absolutely true.'[28] Viewing the 'world as Pop' signifies, in part,
a capacity for celebrating what certain aesthetes might deem clichéd or
commercial. Painters like Lichtenstein, Richard Hamilton, Warhol and
Rosenquist, who emerged in the 1950s and 1960s, were inspired by
their experience of mass culture: issues of consumerism and popular
culture, previously disdained by the artistic establishment as irrelevant
to any visual enterprise, became their creative focus. These artists
incorporated everyday consumer goods, such as images cut and pasted
from glossy magazine advertising copy, in collage and painterly
replication, and often stood on a barely visible line between the 'ironic

and sincere'.[29] Coupland, similarly ambivalent about the delights and disenchantments of life in an era when consumerist values have become normative, also deploys mundane, too familiar motifs in an aesthetic context. The first piece of narrative in *Generation X*, for example, is a Lichtenstein-like cartoon of a young woman, with perfect hair and a vast cup of coffee, dispensing a cynical piece of relationship wisdom. *Generation X* displays a heightened sense of textuality and an awareness of its status as material object. The distinctive typography and hectic use of paratextual material – including a witty postmodern glossary and acerbic cartoons – has no real precedent in contemporary fiction and is a signal of Coupland's ongoing relationship with the avant-garde in the visual arts. For Lainsbury the 'appropriation of techniques from other media' including the 'infoblip sidebars' are indicative of an enthusiasm for 'technological innovation'.[30] Formally, then, *Generation X* suggests that Coupland is engaged in a modernist quest for the new, even in an epoch that no longer believes in originality.

Novels, particularly in their paperback editions, are Pop Art artefacts: they are mass-produced, democratic, commercial and potentially subversive. The early printing of *Generation X*, with its wide format and generous margins, resembles a catalogue for a Pop Art retrospective rather than a work of literary fiction. The slogans that disrupt the main text ('Nostalgia Is A Weapon', for example, *GX*, p. 175) consciously echo Jenny Holzer's text-based public art. Holzer's defamiliarizing slogans have appeared in various civic, commercial, religious and other shared public spaces since the 1970s; her words, enigmatic and direct, have been printed on paper, transformed into LED signs and carved into marble. Massive advertising billboards bear statements such as 'Abuse Of Power Comes As No Surprise' and 'Money Creates Taste'. These particular aphorisms, later collected in her *Truisms* (1977–79) collection, initially materialized on street posters in Manhattan and subsequently on clothes, cash receipts and in electronic form. In Holzer's words, this compilation of 'numberless one-liners' was written from 'multiple points of view'; they present a perplexing fusion of intimacy and distance, playing contradictory political messages off against one another.[31] Holzer's work thrives on the collision of statement and spaces that might be mutually hostile: for example, the plea 'Protect Me From What I Want', from the *Survival* series (1983–85), appeared in electronic form above the uncompromisingly commercial arenas of New York's Times Square and Caesars Palace, Las Vegas.[32] The destabilizing impact that these slogans have on the places in which they are located prefigures Coupland's use of the apparently random epithets in the margins of *Generation X*: just as Holzer's work attempts a redefinition of public space, so do the slogans in Coupland's novel, with their Imagist compression of meaning, produce an alternative shape for the contemporary novel. One sequence in Holzer's *Truisms*, uncomfortably addressed directly to the reader/spectator – including, for example, the statement 'You are guileless in your dreams' –unmistakably foreshadows a device that Coupland uses in chapter titles across a number of his texts.[33] The Irish rock band, U2, deployed a strikingly similar use of text in their 1992 Zoo TV stadium tour, in which a riot of confusing messages flashed across vast television screens, including one distinctly Holzer-like phrase: 'Everything You Know is Wrong'.

Re-viewing the frenzy of debate that crystallized around the publication of his debut novel, Coupland later claimed that 'marketers and journalists never understood that X is a term that defines not a chronological age but a way of looking at the world'.[34] This 'eulogy' for Generation X is evidence, for some commentators, of Coupland's self-importance but, more importantly, it is a reminder to those who sought to appropriate the slippery moniker that no one group or author could own something so hybrid. Perhaps as a sign of uncontrolled social acceleration, Coupland's debut novel is all too conscious that the fortuitous ascendancy of gentle, introspective Gen X souls will necessarily be brief. In the chapter 'Why Am I Poor?', Andy receives a phone call from Tyler, his younger brother, part of the next, self-conscious generation of fresh-faced Americans who, without apparent irony, style themselves 'Global Teens' (*GX*, p. 120). Tyler wants to rent one of the empty houses that neighbours Andy's bungalow for an impeccably behaved New Year's sojourn with his improbably named posse; in figurative terms, this vacation in his brother's makeshift, sunlit sanctuary is a sign that Andy's cultural centrality, the moment in which he might define an aspect of the Zeitgeist, will soon end.

Tyler is only half a decade younger than Andy but embodies a shift in worldview as fundamental as that between the so-called 'baby boomers' and 'busters'. Although he and his friends have inherited, if anything, more financial uncertainty than their older siblings, this young cohort, in Coupland's vision, are happy to exchange personal independence – Tyler and his friends tend to live in their family homes

– for the momentary consumer thrill of buying the coolest current merchandise. Where Andy, Dag and Claire have rejected traditional career paths and refuse to define their aspirations in terms of material success, the 'global teens' (sometimes referred to as Generation Y) are determined to succeed in the rapacious world of late capitalism. Instead of writing poetry in the desert, running a co-operative, fairly traded coffee shop or playing bass in a professionally fractious grunge trio, they aspire to 'work for IBM when their lives end at the age of twenty-five' (*GX*, p. 122).

Such a rapid change in generational identity portends a break in political sensibilities. X-ers like Andy are politically hesitant: their liberal and democratic instincts are unlikely to manifest in any loyal party political affiliations since they grew up in an era of political impotence – they were dimly aware that political protest did not end the Vietnam war – and by scandals exemplified by President Nixon's disastrous association with the Watergate affair. Tyler and his friends are similarly apolitical but they distinctively belong to the US culture created by Ronald Reagan's belligerent free-market economics (*GX*, p. 122). These embryonic middle managers and corporate strategists have been raised to act according to the 'ethics' of enlightened self-interest, a dream that has come to dominate in the absence of an alternative.

The most significant difference between Andy and his younger brother's generation is their contrasting pessimism and hope for the future (*GX*, p. 160). Tyler connects *Generation X* with its immediate – and much criticized – successor, *Shampoo Planet*. In some ways, Coupland's difficult second novel reads like a direct sequel to *Generation X*. The novel focuses on characters a decade younger than those in the Coupland's debut and, like Tyler Palmer, the narrator of *Shampoo Planet* (*SP*) is confident, unashamedly materialistic and obsessed with all things contemporary. In a cheeky piece of self-reference, Coupland even gives his second narrator the same first name, and many similar attributes as the 'original' Tyler. It is a strategy of repetition and simulation that the novelist has deployed throughout his work, with key motifs and narrative conceits self-consciously cut, pasted and reworked in an echo of the Pop Art aesthetic of creative repetition.

Tyler Johnson, whose 'memories begin with Ronald Reagan', is the child of hippie parents, and, as the novel begins, his still idealistic mother is going through a divorce from Tyler's vile, failed property-developing stepfather, Dan.[35] Tyler has reached a happier

accommodation with a culture of conspicuous consumption than Andy
Palmer, his figurative older brother, but his desire to be divested of the
past echoes the sentiments expressed in *Generation X*: 'Squalor is so
retro . . . Give me metal, protein capsules, and radium *any* day of the
week' (*SP*, p. 157). If Andy is scarred by the consumerist compulsions
of the 1980s, Tyler's defining disappointment is that he has apparently
missed out on the possibilities of excess. In one chapter, set in the
town's sole, rather meagre mall, Tyler mourns the 'postshopping world
of frozen escalators and nothing for sale' in which 'young people roam
bravely, trying to maintain the semiforgotten tingling feeling of plenty'
(*SP*, p. 141). Tyler's self-conscious obsession with shopping as a
worthwhile leisure pursuit foreshadows the subculture portrayed in
Kevin Smith's rather weak second film, *Mallrats* (1995). After the
potential subversion of *Generation X*, *Shampoo Planet* might appear
to retreat into a passive acceptance of consumerism. Yet Tyler – who
has a frequent intuition that he has arrived at 'the end of an epoch' –
gradually becomes aware that his desire for a glossy, speeded-up reality
has political implications (*SP*, p. 106). In the interstices of Tyler's
ostensibly irony-free, *Bildungsroman* journey to adulthood and
financial independence are a number of reminders of injustice and
sorrow: one of the novel's minor characters dies from a Aids-related
illness and, in a reminder of death on a global scale, a video of the first
Gulf War plays in a bar, just perceptible in Tyler's peripheral vision
(*SP*, p. 284). Tyler's encounter with the drug addicts at Lancaster's
Free Clinic, is another moment of social awakening (*SP*, p. 71). In an
echo of Irvine Welsh's *Trainspotting*, addiction is figured not as an
alternative to consumer capitalism but as its twin: Tyler is dimly aware
that he too is an addict but that his own cravings are for goods deemed
socially acceptable.

The novel's denouement is also tacitly political: Tyler's bloody, life-
threatening brawl with the repulsive Dan is not just a fight between
rival generations. This apparently materialistic narrator is defending
his gentle, bohemian mother against an aggressive individual who
seems to embody the greedy, value free and laissez-faire 1980s. The set
piece is one of the most violent episodes in Coupland's remarkably
serene early fiction – though this tranquillity is shattered in the high-
school murders narrated in *Hey Nostradamus!* (2003). If Tyler is the
novel's victor – pragmatic but not soulless, conscious that material
success will not answer all of his questions – he, like Andy Palmer
before him, recognizes that he is not indispensable to his world. In

fact, Tyler's belief that 'the most unmodern facet' of his identity – an 'inability to achieve computer nirvana like a true hacker' – anticipates a future focus of Coupland's fiction: the digital revolution of the mid-1990s (*SP*, p. 146).

'An odd little nook of time and space': *Microserfs* (1995) and *Polaroids from the Dead* (1996)

In 'Stalking the Billion Footed Beast' (1989), a conservative manifesto appealing for renewed literary realism, Tom Wolfe reflected on the emergence, in the 1960s, of a critical consensus that not only was 'the realistic novel . . . no longer possible', but that American experience 'no longer deserved the term *real*. American life was chaotic, fragmented, random, discontinuous; in a word absurd.'[36] The logical aesthetic answer to this malaise, Wolfe proposed, was a return to the journalistic, documentary approach to fiction championed in the nineteenth century by Balzac, Zola, Dickens and Thackeray. Wolfe's prediction that the future of fiction 'would be in a highly detailed realism based on reporting . . . a realism that would portray the individual in intimate and inextricable relation to the society around him' is partially fulfilled in Coupland's fourth and fifth books.[37]

   Microserfs (1995), like Wolfe's *Bonfire of the Vanities* (1989), originally serialized in *Rolling Stone*, stemmed from a collaboration with a magazine. *Polaroids from the Dead* (1996), a collection of occasional essays for newspapers and magazines, intimate 'postcards', travel writing and short stories, is, in Coupland's own words, an attempt to explore 'the world that existed in the early 1990s, back when the decade was young and had yet to locate its own texture . . . People seemed unsure that the 1990s were even going to be *capable* of generating their own mood' (*PD*, p. 1). The collection begins with an evocation of nostalgia, 1990s style, for the dream of unity imagined by 1960s radicals, the last American countercultural moment characterized by optimism: a cycle of overlapping short stories, set at the Grateful Dead's December 1991 Californian festival, explore the sensation – 'an essence of purity' – of experiencing a moment that has long since passed (*PD*, p. 62). An underlying theme of the collection is the continuing human impulse to preserve experience, personal and shared, in narrative form despite the prevalence of destructive commercial forces that are determined to re-wire this capacity for remembrance. *Microserfs* is similarly concerned with the impact of new technologies on the shape and integrity of private recollection. Both texts, with their unsettling movement between fact and fiction, represent Coupland's negotiation with the peculiar contours of postmodern life and his evolving experiments in narrative.

From 1993 to 1994, in collaboration with *Wired*, Coupland immersed himself in the world of the tech revolution that was underway at Microsoft's Redmond campus in Washington State and amongst the countless new start-up companies of the Silicon Valley in California. The writer documented the experiences and aspirations of young programmers, who, in words of Coupland's narrator, Daniel Underwood, represent the 'first Microsoft generation – the first group of people who have never known a world without an MS-DOS environment' (*MS*, p. 16). Where *Generation X* narrated the lives of romantics who refuse to participate in the commercial-professional fields for which they once trained and *Shampoo Planet* delineated the aspirations of a young American desperate to gain access to that same world, *Microserfs* focuses on a group of twenty – and thirty-somethings who are defined primarily by their enthusiasm and aptitude for work. Dan, a 26-year-old 'bug checker' working for Microsoft, records his experience as a relatively lowly member of the global economy's new social order.

Fittingly for a novel of the so-called 'tech revolution', *Microserfs* embraces narrative and structural experiment in a way not anticipated by the nineteenth-century bias of Wolfe's proposal: Dan's narrative is presented in a traditional epistolary form but with the conceit that the novel itself is a PowerBook. 'Language is such a technology,' reflects Dan (*MS*, p. 174). The entries of this electronic journal are interspersed with pages of code (some of which have been translated by very patient critics), slogans and Dan's own experiments with different voices, including a programme that transforms his idiom into the style used by 'Minnesotan Funkmeister, Prince' (*MS*, p. 18).[38] The novel is saturated with precise period detail – including many specific pop cultural references to *Star Trek: The Next Generation*, *The Simpsons*, and bands from the Pacific Northwest rock scene – in a way that opens up this technophile narrative to the ravages of time. Many of the essays and short stories in *Polaroids from the Dead* are similarly time-specific and precisely dated: 'The German Reporter' begins on 27 May 1994, for example, and the 'Brentwood Notebook', the most experimental piece in the collection is dated 4 August 1994. Coupland has reflected on this aesthetic interest in temporality and 'time-expiry' in literature:

Microserfs . . . [is] loaded with pop references, consumer culture
references – all of which are out of date now. But it seems to work even
better because of that. Starting with Evelyn Waugh right up to the present,
the books that I like . . . are where you can almost tell the week it was
written because of what's going on in the news.[39]

Dan's narrative, set specifically during the period between
September 1993 and January 1995, allows Coupland to participate in
an ironic critique of his own, rather unexpected, literary legacy and,
particularly, in the already ossified terminology associated with Gen X.
In one rather self-conscious moment, Michael, the novel's own
aspirant avatar of Bill Gates, seethes about 'media-hype generation'
and the obviously redundant notion that 'we're all "*slackers*" . . . [W]ho
thinks up these things?' (*MS*, p. 242). The short answer is, of course,
fashionable novelists and commentators like Coupland. However, this
self-reflexive (and, perhaps, self-mocking) allusion is also indicative of
the novelist's scepticism about the validity of generational categories
per se; these names, to appropriate one of his favourite maxims, will
'time-expire' rapidly and rarely demonstrate the complexity of human
experience: 'we really *do* inhabit an odd little nook of time and space'
but 'it's where *I* live – it's where I *am*' (*MS*, p. 63).

Jefferson Faye suggests that *Microserfs*' principal hypothesis 'is that
countries are fundamentalist even if their citizens aren't, and the once-
obvious line separating spirituality and commerce has blurred'.[40]
'Beware of the corporate invasion of private memory', reflects Dan
(*MS*, p. 177). A key concern of *Microserfs* is the legislated theft of
individuality and personal identity by insidiously powerful corporations
and big brand names such as Microsoft. Yet, at the level of traditional
politics, particularly regarding the influence of free-market economics
on virtually every aspect of human identity, *Microserfs* is hesitant to
commit itself to an uncompromisingly anti-capitalist viewpoint. I
certainly cannot concur with Daniel Grassian's view that the narrative
has 'Marxist intentions'.[41] Indeed, Rob Latham's reluctant observation
that Coupland's fertile representation of the 'mingled promise and
horror of Silicon Valley' cannot be read as the result of 'a truly
dialectical conception' is more accurate.[42] Todd and Dusty's brief and
comic dalliance with a spectrum of Marxist philosophies is mocked
not just by their colleagues, but implicitly by the narrative logic of the
novel itself. Michael's declaration, after another frenzied ideological
clash, that 'this . . . is the end of politics' seems to constitute a hope
beyond the irritating specifics of office infighting; in fact, it might

reflect a certain political quietism in the novel. Dusty's unexpected pregnancy is used to represent the end of politics – she even tells her friends that she can feel 'ideology . . . leaving [her] body' (*MS*, p. 282). Rick Perlstein's testy review of *Microserfs* in *The Nation* condemns the novel's political blindness: Coupland's apparent celebration of the more progressive elements of new technologies permits his crowd of bright young programmers 'to ignore the true Microserfs – the Valley's 100,000 manufacturing workers, predominantly women, predominantly nonwhite, predominantly nonunionized, many of them doing piece work out of their homes, and some working in what can only be called sweatshops'.[43]

Microserfs, in spite of its ostensible focus on the remote, chilly field of new technologies, is the most sensuous and embodied of Coupland's novels. After the decision to pursue a start-up business in California, the narrator angrily reflects on the 'cramped, love-starved, sensationless existence' that seems to be one of the tacit deprivations of working for a successful corporation (*MS*, p. 90). Despite the friendly 'campus' atmosphere and free beverages, Dan and his friends recognize that Microsoft – like any big tech business – treats its rolling body of young coders primarily as incorporeal intellects; ignorance of the body has become an obligatory sacrifice in the pursuit of efficient, marketable code. 'Why are we all so hopeless with our bodies?' asks Dan of himself and his housemates: the restoration of physical sensitivity is a vital counterpoint to the broader narrative of unchecked cultural and economic change stimulated by artificial, disembodied intelligence (*MS*, p. 76)

If the novel is a distinctively 1990s rites of passage narrative, it is also an understated exploration of what it means to possess a body, to be incarnate as well as cerebral. A number of the characters undergo bodily reawakenings during the narrative: Dan gains a new awareness of the correlation between mind and body through Karla's shiatsu massages 'as a means of thawing memory frozen inside the *body*' (*MS*, p. 67); Karla, in her turn, confronts a long-running struggle with anorexia and Bug Barbecue ('the World's Most Bitter Man') is able to articulate his own long repressed sexuality (*MS*, p. 12). Susan, the wildly articulate co-founder of the new business, embarks on a similar process of self-fashioning (or 'self-reconstruction') that culminates in establishing her mischievous Chyx collective. This neo-feminist online community is another of Coupland's very contemporary references, to the self-styled riot grrl collectives that emerged in the USA and Britain in the early 1990s. These groups – usually founded around a punk rock band such as Bikini Kill, Huggy Bear or Sleater-Kinney – took a DIY-feminist approach to contemporary culture and challenged the chauvinist notions associated with a supposedly liberal music scene. However, Susan's willingness to use mainstream television to further her cause – appearing on CNN and becoming a cult star – are playfully at odds with some of the more politically severe elements of a phenomenon that frequently disdained co-operation with conservative and commercial media.[44]

Bug and Susan's respective reclamations of repressed corporeality are linked to the novel's marked interest in what Todd and Dusty rather earnestly refer to as the 'New Human Body': these dedicated body-builders (whose pursuit of physical perfection is quite unlike the stereotypes associated with 'geek' subculture) want to become 'post-human' and, before their short-lived ideological conversions, this intrepid couple displays a belief in the infinite malleability of the body that unconsciously reiterates ancient, supernatural ideas regarding the possibility of metamorphosis (*MS*, pp. 240–1). In fact, *Microserfs'* emphasis on a recuperation of sensation and physical intimacy is arguably the novel's most audaciously political element. '[B]odies are political, too' Dusty informs her mildly interested colleagues (*MS*, p. 255).

One significant moment, peripheral to the central plot, is indicative of Coupland's willingness to advance a progressive politics of the body: a surprising healing embrace that Dan offers to Ethan, his body, ravaged with the scars of excised tumours, 'a matrix of bandages, dried blood and micro-pore tape' (*MS*, p. 168). Ethan, Interiority's acquisitive CEO and one of the least sympathetic characters in Coupland's fiction who, as Dan observes, has no sense of the link between wealth and ethics, becomes vulnerable before his younger colleague. When Dan delicately holds Ethan's body, the older, more cynical, man emits 'the moan of someone who has found something valuable that they had thought was lost forever' (*MS*, p. 169). The 'lost' Ethan returns to a space of shared hope in what Bauman, after Emmanuel Levinas, might call a moment of 'being-for-the-Other, going towards the Other through the twisted and rocky gorge of affection'.[45] The hug is fraught with homosocial and economic tension but, like the fleeting kiss that Dag gives Andy before his arrest in *Generation X*, this impulsive gesture constitutes an instant of openness and generosity rather than sexual manipulation; the disturbing Other becomes the cared-for and caring neighbour. Later in the narrative, Dan states that the company is not primarily driven by professional ambitions but by a desire to keep the group 'together' (*MS*, p. 199). Is this an authentic objective or a sentimental ideal that ignores the financial realities of their capitalist enterprise?

Like Coupland's first novel, *Microserfs* displays signs of what Dan sceptically names 'proactive humanism'; it privileges loyalty and friendship above more abstract affiliations to political causes. The prominence of a surrogate extended family, one that is also inclusive enough to incorporate Dan's parents and Abe's ghostly, e-mail-only presence, anticipates new forms of family unit that became a basic theme of 1990s pop culture and fiction: the sentimental, long-running sit-com *Friends* (1994–2004) for example, was structured around a non-standard 'family' grouping. The imagined, surrogate family becomes a kind of secure, sacred space amidst the anxieties of the post-industrial world. Significantly, for all their interest in the specific textures of the moment, both *Microserfs* and *Polaroids from the Dead* end with visionary, epiphanic moments that signify Coupland's evolving engagement with spiritual language, foreshadowing an escalating interest in the poetics of revelation.

'It's the end of the world as we know it (and I feel fine)': *Life After God* (1994) and *Girlfriend in a Coma* (1998)

Should we be surprised – or even disturbed – that religious themes have become such an insistent presence in Coupland's fiction? 'Perhaps the best way of encapsulating the gist of an epoch,' suggests Slavoj Žižek, 'is to focus not on the explicit features that define its social and ideological edifices but on the disavowed ghosts that haunt it'.[46] In *Life After God* – a melancholy, fragmented novel constructed around thematically connected short stories – and the dystopian romance, *Girlfriend in a Coma*, the novelist concentrates on the search for spiritual meaning in an era that ostensibly no longer needs God. Faith is one of the 'disavowed ghosts' that now haunts the liberal West: fears of the return of long-repressed pious histories have been given shape by the rise of a variety of fundamentalisms. The middle-class milieu of Coupland's fiction is, however, more often associated with the hollow victory of humanism and the apparent arrival of a secular heaven on earth than it is with religious conviction. In an era of prosperity, the threats and promises of organized belief frequently become either redundant or little more than folk memories. Indeed, in *Girlfriend in a Coma*, Richard Doorland's mother reflects, with unconscious prescience, that their peaceful North Vancouver suburb was 'like the land that God forgot'.[47] Similarly, in the final story of *Life After God*, the narrator reflects that the comforts of his own middle-class childhood – 'a life lived in paradise' – made the debate of 'transcendental ideas pointless' (*LAG*, p. 273). Yet, in both texts, Coupland's central characters reject the idea of a middle-class earthly Eden in favour of a less comfortable, potentially unrewarding quest for spiritual challenge and renewal.

Life After God intensifies the most melancholic undercurrents from *Generation X* and *Shampoo Planet*: its sequence of distinct but interconnected narratives, focus on alternative experiences of isolation, loneliness and depression. This unhappiness is, surprisingly, the foundation of the novel's psalm-like religious dynamic. 'I think I am a broken person', confesses Scout, the narrator of the final story – '1,000 Years (Life After God)' – and his antipathy for the 'compromises' that he has made in life is symptomatic of Coupland's ambivalence about life at the *fin de siècle* (*LAG*, p. 309). If those individuals labelled Gen X-ers were frequently associated with a particular brand of sardonic humour – audible in the compulsive self-deprecation and sarcasm of Dag in *Generation X* and Chandler in *Friends* – this febrile wit, christened 'Knee-Jerk Irony' by Coupland, was, according to much popular wisdom, camouflage for a sense of emotional numbness (*GX*, p. 174). Martine Delvaux has carefully identified the curious and insinuating language of diagnosis that came to dominate public discussion of 'the Generation X *syndrome*' in the 1990s: to be part of this age bracket was simultaneously to inherit a set of labels associated with psychopathology, as if commentators unconsciously assumed that a peculiar therapeutic astrology was the most legitimate mode of interpreting cultural difference.[48]

Is Coupland's third, full-length work of fiction – primarily narrated by lost or dejected characters – guilty of flirting with what Kirk Curnutt has named 'misery chic'?[49] The emphasis that *Life After God*, published in the same year as Elizabeth Wurtzel's melancholy memoir *Prozac Nation: Young and Depressed in America*, places on grief and loss (what one character calls the 'unique sorrow of being human') might, superficially, seem to contribute to this austere vision of generational despair (*LAG*, p. 80). The book received some stern criticism: Kim France, in an otherwise sympathetic piece, wrote that '[a]t times *Life After God* reads like 70s feel-good best-seller *Jonathan Livingston Seagull*, or any number of L. Ron Hubbard books' and castigated Coupland for 'the self-important sound of the title'.[50] The use of antidepressants, in the final story, as a kind of 'cosmetic surgery of the brain' that makes Scout 'more efficient' and 'nicer' but no longer himself suggest a dystopian worldview (*LAG*, p. 276). Yet these stories also validate the pursuit of meaning amidst the sadness, a belief that the world contains the possibility of a 'finer, simpler state of being which we may strive to attain' (*LAG*, p. 81).

In contrast to this sensation of incipient faith, a dominant motif in media debate about the phenomenon of 1990s youth culture was that of self-destructive nihilism. The clearest example of this, Delvaux rightly suggests, is the way in which the suicide of Kurt Cobain in 1994 became 'the emblem of a generational *malaise*'.[51] Cobain's iconic status – and outspoken aversion to his reputation as prophet for a hopeless generation – made his premature, violent and self-inflicted death a tempting image for the media to use as an instructive symbol of an era.[52] The crudeness of this epoch-making, mass-media iconography ignores the sadness brought about by the loss of one very famous, very lonely person to addiction and depression; it sacrifices individual identity for an image that is somehow easier to remember and, therefore, more saleable. However, the death of Kurt Cobain, rightly or wrongly, did constitute a media event that allowed fans to express fears about the possibilities of emotional connection, community and even spirituality in their own times.

Nick Hornby's second novel, *About a Boy* (1998) – the title a rewriting of a song title from Nirvana's first album, *Bleach* (1989) – concludes with a disparate group of people, including the emotionally repressed narrator, converging in a record shop on the day of Cobain's death. The event constitutes a moment of epiphany, in which an apparently secular process becomes sacred:

> He was not a man given to mystical moments . . . but he was very worried he was having one now . . . Will couldn't recall ever having been caught up in this sort of messy, sprawling, chaotic web before; it was almost as if he had been given a glimpse of what it was like to be human.[53]

Using the suicide of a well-known singer-songwriter as a narrative spur and point of human connection might seem opportunistic, but Hornby's novel reflects the way in which the sad end of Kurt Cobain's life resonated in pop culture as something quite unlike the many rock casualties whose deaths are viewed as the predictable cost of a decadent lifestyle. Coupland, perhaps unsurprisingly, wrote his own epitaph for Cobain – a piece notable for its lack of Gen X smartness or ironic sensibility. The 'Letter to Kurt Cobain' is a lyrical souvenir of a specific moment that the singer seemed to embody ('this child of *here*, of newness') and an unashamedly emotive piece dedicated to one lost individual. Coupland's elegy for his unhappy contemporary uses a religious idiom ('I figure you're in heaven, too') that is developed in his third full-length work of fiction (*PD*, pp. 98–9).[54]

Life After God could be the title of an atheist treatise but the novel prioritizes the fragile hope that faith might be possible in an ostensibly post-religious age. A muted, inchoate spirituality informs Coupland's early work but a candid search for the transcendent coalesces in the various melancholy journeys of the lonely, abandoned or guilt-ridden figures whose stories fuse together in *Life After God*. These narrators are rarely 'religious' in the sense of belonging to a particular faith community but their stories – particularly 'In the Desert' and '1000 Years (Life After God)' – turn on surprising confessions of a need to believe in God (*LAG*, pp. 210, 359).

The condensed, apocalyptic vignettes of 'The Wrong Sun' – a series of fragmented descriptions of nuclear disaster followed by uncanny, ghostly voices describing heaven – clearly anticipates Coupland's fifth novel, *Girlfriend in a Coma*. This eccentric and allusive millennial fable, co-narrated by the ghost of a teenage Vancouver football hero, echoes the oral 'bedtime' stories told by the trinity of friends in *Generation X* and is particularly reminiscent of those 'end-of-the world' fantasies favoured by Dag but, whereas those brief tales tended to emphasize the cold war imminence of nuclear catastrophe, *Girlfriend in a Coma* represents an unforeseen and illogical apocalypse. Karen McNeil's awakening from a seventeen-year coma is followed by a mysterious plague-sleep to which the entire world succumbs, with the exception of Karen's daughter and her small, disillusioned band of former high-school friends. The novel shares aspects of the millennial imagery explored in *Last Night* (1999), Don McKellar's muted (and Canadian) response to the apocalyptic mood of the late 1990s. This tone was exploited more luridly by mainstream 'Judgment Day' movies such as *Deep Impact* (1998) and *Armageddon* (1998). Unlike these blockbusters, however, which traded divine wrath for the secular threat of civilization-destroying asteroids, Coupland's fifth novel displayed a surprising interest in apocalypse as a theological idea. The novel's complex exploration of religious language is discussed in detail in Chapters 2 and 5 but, in terms of 1990s culture, *Girlfriend in a Coma* gave shape to an unrelenting but unfocused desire for the sublime in supposedly scientific societies. Jenny Turner has pointed out the novel's affinities with Paul Thomas Anderson's film, *Magnolia* (1999).[55] Both narratives are littered with what one of Coupland's characters names the uncanny phenomena of 'profound omens and endless coincidence' that, in the absence of religion, are read without 'guidebooks to help' discern 'a higher meaning' (*GIAC*, p. 99).

Chuck Palahniuk's vicious *Fight Club* (1996) might also be read alongside the stumbling search for salvation enacted in *Girlfriend in a Coma*. The cultic, subterranean spaces of Palahniuk's novel – vividly realized in David Fincher's 1999 film adaptation – represent a brutal spiritual surrogate for a post-religious generation. Whereas Coupland's awkward seekers recover a sense of the divine through their ability to question and to celebrate ordinary human connection, Palahniuk's troupe of outcasts discover a desolate, masochistic mode of godless spirituality. Tyler Durden, the narrator's charismatic, shadowy double, encourages his emasculated disciples to recover identity through acts of cathartic violence. 'We are God's middle children,' intones the narrator, 'with no special place in history and no special attention . . . Which is worse, hell or nothing?'[56] This odd, Nietzsche-lite sermon echoes a similar – if less stark – moment of recognition in *Generation X*: 'when you're middle class, you have to live with the fact that history will ignore you' (*GX*, p. 171). Andy makes this statement after another frustrating, emotionally repressed family reunion. Unhappy domestic life – identified by Palahniuk as the principal sign of grief stricken modernity – is the major theme of Coupland's first two novels of the twenty-first century.

Imitation of Life: *Miss Wyoming* (2000) and *All Families Are Psychotic* (2001)

'Feeble and forlorn and floundering and foolish and frustrating and functional and sad, sad.' Paul Hood, one of the gauche adolescent protagonists of Rick Moody's *The Ice Storm* (1994), offers an alliterative and damning assessment of Nixon-era 'family values'.[57] The traditional, nuclear family might have become a site of insidious political pressures, its significance disputed by left and right, but it still forms the dramatic centre of much contemporary North American literature. Coupland's fiction has explored the odd dynamics of family or surrogate families since *Generation X* – including the sprawling, inclusive Underwood home in *Microserfs* and the chaotic crew of survivors in *Girlfriend in a Coma* – but an interest in the domestic world intensifies in *Miss Wyoming* and *All Families are Psychotic*. These novels mark a shift away from a focus on characters in their twenties and early thirties and announce a temporary change in narrative technique. Whereas Coupland's first five novels rely on introspective, first-person storytellers, these Pop Art-style fictions of domestic dysfunction deploy omniscient narrators and cinematic flashback structures.

Miss Wyoming, the successor to two primarily Vancouver-set novels, is Coupland's most geographically chaotic – and populous – narrative to date. Criss-crossing the USA, the novel explores the bizarre and banal craving for fame that appears to govern modern aspirations. Susan Colgate, forced to participate in humiliating beauty pageants as a child, briefly a nationwide pin-up as the 'good sister' on an idealistic TV-sitcom, *Meet the Blooms*, is given the opportunity to reinvent her despised, cliché-ridden identity following a plane crash in which she is assumed to have died. Jenny Turner has observed that the novel shares *Girlfriend in a Coma*'s interest 'in coincidence and catastrophe, deus ex machina and chance absurdity'.[58] However, in *Miss Wyoming* fevered parental expectation, psychological abuse and the delusions of Hollywood replace the unusual metaphysics of its predecessor. In his earlier novels, Coupland's contemplative narrators evoke complex interior lives. By contrast, *Miss Wyoming* – as its low-level celebrity title suggests – deals with people whose life consists of elaborate, status-bound role-play games.

Los Angeles – the city in which Tyler Johnson of *Shampoo Planet* failed to realize his ambitions – frames the novel's emphasis on simulated reality. Even the novel's most sympathetic characters are implicit in perpetuating the manipulative aspects of the entertainment industry: Susan, habituated to exploitation, does little to abandon a life she knows to be counterfeit until faced with her own 'death'. Many of the other, highly eccentric characters who populate the narrative – including Susan's ferociously ambitious mother-from-hell, Marilyn – superficially resemble stereotypical figures from bad daytime TV. Susan's adventures are an attempt to recover a mythic 'blank slate quality' as an alternative to the predetermined set of selves that family and fame had imposed on her.[59]

Andrew Clark describes *Miss Wyoming* as an 'absurdist parable' and suggests that the novel represents a shift from Coupland's earlier 'cold modernism', comparing it, instead, with the lyrical modernity of F. Scott Fitzgerald.[60] The novel certainly shares Fitzgerald's fascination with the consequences of excess and moneyed make-believe but it also plays with anti-establishment ideas popularized by writers from the Beat movement. Susan's journey of self-reinvention is paralleled by the story of John Johnson – 'sleazebag' producer of blockbuster movies – who has begun his own Jack Kerouac-style quest for a more authentic existence. John's loss of faith in the ethos of greed leads him, like the characters in Coupland's first narrative, into a frustrating search amid the desert wastes of America and, ultimately, into a more optimistic, generous encounter with other similarly confused individuals.

All Families are Psychotic replicates *Miss Wyoming*'s concentration on the everyday unhappiness of modern domestic life. The novel constitutes a further departure for Coupland in its narrative emphasis on Janet Drummond, mother of the titular dysfunctional tribe, who, rare among his central characters to date, was born in the first half of the twentieth century. In Moody's novel, one ill-fated character, vulnerable and alone in the snow, yearns 'for the consolations of some imagined and perfect family'.[61] The Drummond family constitutes a kind of inverted image of that illusory group. The scattered, half-Canadian Drummonds – whose 1970s backstory in suburban Vancouver is relayed in flashback chapters – have reconvened in Orlando, Florida for the debut space flight of their one successful member, Sarah. In this motif of space exploration – also alluded to in *Generation X*'s tale of Buck the Astronaut – Coupland revives associations of an earlier, more confident American age, when technology was happily viewed as the pathway to a golden future. Yet Sarah's body, damaged in the womb by Thalidomide, is a reminder of the rather less palatable counter-narrative of science as a potentially dystopian force. The novel's unconventional cast list includes a billionaire pharmaceuticals heir with twin Anglophile and gangster proclivities, a wayward charmer who would like to become a super-hero with the power to make people see God and a depressive, failed revolutionary whose partner refuses to include vowels in her name for political reasons.

Coupland's picaresque narrative with its frantic, twisting plot – including a bungled diner robbery, the attempt to smuggle a letter allegedly stolen from the late Princess of Wales' coffin and multiple stories of infidelity – echoes the pastiche *noir* of films by Quentin Tarantino or the Coen Brothers as much as it does contemporary literary fiction. The backdrops of the novel frequently seem like consciously artificial film scenery rather than mimetic representation: one character even observes that the '*landscape is from an amusement park*'.[62] A brief, rather sinister excursion into Disney World is another reminder that the narrative is located in an imagined, heightened reality; the incidents that take place in a variety of diners, prison cells, motel rooms and automobile interiors are reminiscent of the synthetic landscape that punctuates the scenes of contemporary American film and television.

The saga of a disintegrating family, led by a generous mother and self-centred father, as a lens through which the major political issues of Aids, national identity, poverty and freedom might be explored, has clear similiarities with Jonathan Franzen's *The Corrections* (2001). In a parallel world, an enthralling bar-room chat (or fight) might have occurred between Franzen's charming Chip Lambert and his peer and spiritual cousin, Wade Drummond. Yet the luminous, cartoon-like ambience, arbitrating between dark farce and big issues, suggests that Coupland's seventh novel has still more in common with the fictional world of twenty-first century America's most celebrated family: in many ways, *All Families are Psychotic* reads like a homage to *The Simpsons*.[63] Like Matt Groening's epoch-defining household, the Drummonds move between bouts of homicidal behaviour – Ted Drummond shoots his eldest son – and sweet moments of rapprochement. Coupland's engagement with the surreal or the utterly improbable is also resonant of the animated world in which Homer Simpson gleefully gambols. Is this an appropriate idiom to address the devastating implications of Aids and related human suffering? The novel's use of miracle is discussed in more detail in Chapter 5 in relation to the broader theme of Coupland's complex approach to religious ideas. For all its anti-conservative satire, Groening's cartoon is sentimental about the redemptive possibilities of family life and this, too, is a facet shared by *All Families are Psychotic*. The novel's final chapter features a televised image of the idiosyncratic – and, in some instances, badly injured – Drummond clan reunited for the launch of Sarah's first NASA mission. Via television – inflected by the illusion of simultaneous intimacy and distance – the fragile family, briefly united, looks like a modern miracle. Group identity, whether familial or national, is represented as a transient phenomenon in Coupland's writing. This Polaroid-style image of the unruly, half-American, half-Canadian family – Vancouverites in unhappy exile – parallels the writer's own turn towards the fragile and fissiparous subject of national identity.

'Young Country': *City of Glass* (2000), *Souvenir of Canada* (2002) and *Souvenir of Canada 2* (2004)

How significant is Coupland's recurrent self-identification as Canadian? The novelist's book jackets usually remind readers that he was born 'on a Canadian NATO base' in the former West Germany and now lives and works in Vancouver. Grassian's suggestion that, symptomatic of 'postcolonial homogenization', Coupland's 'fiction, even when it is based in Canada, appears almost indistinguishable from American fiction' is misjudged.[64] There may once have been a case, as Alan Bilton suggests, given the thematic and spatial focus of Coupland's early writing, for regarding him as a 'canonical American writer' who happens to have Canadian citizenship.[65] The Pacific Northwest has provided the geographical framework for his fiction: to date, most of the novels are set primarily on the North American west coast, between California to the south and his native British Columbia to the north, with occasional detours into Portland and Washington State. Even the Florida setting of *All Families are Psychotic* is interspersed with frequent flashback sequences that take place in Vancouver, home city of the Drummond family. Although Coupland's characters often undertake journeys away from the West, these expeditions are equally often disastrous or disappointing. In *Souvenir of Canada*, Coupland made explicit a strand of his thinking regarding nation that had been present, but muted, in his fiction:

> sometime in the 1990s, Canada rapidly became *different* from the United States. Not superior and not worse, but undeniably *different* . . . Oddly, Canada's process of differentiation is occurring just when it theoretically ought *not* be happening: our country is being hosed over by free trade agreements, it's being inundated by American media from every conceivable outlet, and it's committing cultural suicide as the government totally disengages from the arts.[66]

Souvenir of Canada is part of sequence of non-fiction books, including *City of Glass*, a pictorial homage to Vancouver, that suggest a subtle shift in Coupland's public persona. They are a passionate, rather than aggressively patriotic, evocation of home in which Coupland renegotiates his perceived status as a 'half-American' writer. In the introduction to the book – which includes images and a series of alphabetized entries – the writer is clear that he is writing specifically for his fellow Canadians. The synthesis of photographs and commentary might, he concedes be disorientating for American readers: 'I wanted to create images understandable only to Canadians.' Using still-life photographs, based around distinctively Canadian objects, the author reflects that his project is to confront readers with 'our nation's shared memories' (*SOC*, p. 3).

In *All Families are Psychotic*, Janet Drummond speculates that her suitor from New Haven is specifically attracted by her national identity: 'Americans think Canada is sort of glamorous. Mysterious' (*AFAP*, p. 50). The non-fiction, illustrated, coffee-table style of *Souvenir of Canada* allows the author to explore this avowed fascination with the mystery and glamour of his own country. Significantly, Coupland's writing is never militantly nationalistic and, indeed, he has happily displayed affinities with crucial aspects of American cultural consciousness. However, in the first decade of the twenty-first century the question of the novelist's national identity has become simultaneously clearer and more ambiguous. In Jefferson Faye's timely, combative review essay of Coupland's first six books, 'Canada in a Coma' (2001), the critic focuses on the specifically Canadian nature of Coupland's intervention in debates regarding US cultural imperialism. Faye's article explores the paradox of a writer who has produced 'quintessentially south-of-the-border novels' that are simultaneously written from a non-US citizen's perspective. More bold still is the claim that '[t]aken as a single text, the last chapter of which is *Girlfriend in a Coma*' – a body of work that begins with *Generation X* and includes the *Polaroids from the Dead* anthology – 'Coupland's chronicle of America's cultural expansionism . . . becomes an adept vision of the consumer hell that is being imposed upon Canada.'[67] Certainly, his novels consciously represent the processes by which exported American culture, in its most insidiously commercial forms, either erase or reconfigure identity.

In *Souvenir of Canada,* Coupland observes that 'Canada's fourth-largest city is Los Angeles. More Canadians live there than in Ottawa or Calgary or Edmonton or Winnipeg or Quebec City' (*SOC*, p. 63). The US state provides the milieu for *Generation X* – principally Palm Springs – and Los Angeles is Tyler Johnson's home in Part Three of *Shampoo Planet*. In *Microserfs*, Daniel Underwood returns to his parents' home, near Palo Alto, with his surrogate family of Microsoft staffers. *Polaroids from the Dead* includes a number of essays and short stories centred in California and many of the events in *Miss Wyoming* take place in LA. With the exception of this novel of Hollywood – a kind of farewell to Los Angeles – most of Coupland's fiction since *Life After God* has been set at least partly in Vancouver.

Just as 'Canada stopped being Nowhere some years ago' so should Coupland's identity as a de facto US novelist have been revised (*SOC*, p. 27). His work performs an elaborate narrative of engagement with what it means to belong to a country and to a moment in history. There is a strong emphasis in both the novels and the non-fiction on the youth of Canada as a nation and the contrasting signs of ancient geology that mark the country's vast wilderness. In an essay on Lions Gate Bridge – included in both *Polaroids from the Dead* and *City of Glass* – Coupland uses the shimmering, delicately lit architectural expanse to celebrate Vancouver's youth, its 'greatest blessing' is that 'we live in the youngest city on Earth, a city almost entirely of, and *only* of, the twentieth century'; Coupland's home is 'not so much . . . a city' as 'a dream of a city'.[68] In the collection's final essay, on YVR, Vancouver's airport, he reflects, with a fusion of sentiment and science, that Vancouver is 'a fractal city – a city of no repeats. It's unique, and it's my home' (*COG*, p. 151). Images of Vancouver are discussed in every chapter of this book, though specific focus is given to the writer's evocation of the connection between the city's suburbs and the estranging proximity of wilderness in Chapter 4.

In a sense, Coupland's salute to Canada, and to Vancouver in particular, is a political statement against 'the trend toward homogenization and pasteurized global taste' (*COG*, p. 151). Yet, there is also an echo of transcendentalist appreciation of the wilderness and the 'covenant' between the land and its people. The final image of *Souvenir of Canada* is of Coupland's own father as a young man in the 'unmapped wilds of Labrador' confronting the hazards of the untamed landscape. The message, reflecting this writer of the accelerated era, lost in familial memory, is 'that we *are* the land, and the land *is* us – we are inseparable . . . this knowledge binds us together in a covenant that is as sacred and precious as any . . . since the creation of the world'

(*SOC*, p. 142). Coupland's sense of the sacred is not merely sentimental. The landscape always contains the possibility of violence:
mankind can pollute the earth, and nature itself is not always benign.
If Canada is a place of potential – and Vancouver, specifically, a space
of inventiveness and modernity – it is also haunted by souvenirs of
death and ruin (*SOC*, p. 142).

'Darkness in this world': *Hey Nostradamus!* (2003) and *Eleanor Rigby* (2004)

Mortality, indiscriminate violence and the legacies of grief are recurrent
themes in Coupland's writing but his fiction since the terrorist attacks
of 9/11 and the subsequent 'war on terror' has been conspicuously
sombre. *Hey Nostradamus!* constructed around four, introspective
first-person narratives, is ostensibly a fictional response to a different
form of futile violence in America. Like Gus Van Sant's dreamlike film
Elephant (2003) and D. B. C. Pierre's *Vernon God Little* (2003), the
novel fictionalizes North American high school massacres, of which
the shootings in Columbine remain the most notorious. However,
Coupland focuses less on the specifics of senseless slaughter – the
peculiar motivations of the teenage gunmen are not analysed, for
example – than on the fragile capacity of human beings for emotional
recovery and forgiveness. The novel also returns to the theological
terrain mapped in the fable-like *Girlfriend in a Coma*, with which it
shares a suburban Vancouver setting; it explores difficult questions of
theodicy and divine justice, the hope of mercy and the meaning of
human suffering. An adolescent ghost narrates the novel's opening
section, in another echo of *Girlfriend in a Coma*: Cheryl Anway,
a recent convert to Christianity, evokes the circumstances of her
shooting, alongside many other innocents, in the quotidian setting of
the school cafeteria. Cheryl – like the narrator of Alice Sebold's *The
Lovely Bones* (2002), speaking from an unnameable midpoint between
heaven and earth – reflects that she never became old enough to lose
her 'sense of wonder about the world . . . a glorious place . . . filled with
so many unexpected moments'.[69] Yet she is also painfully aware of
humanity's 'capacity . . . to commit all possible sins' and ends her story
with the sorrowful reflection that 'there will always be darkness in this
world' (*HN*, pp. 3, 42).

Cheryl's sepulchral tale is itself haunted: her story is interspersed
with the 'prayers and curses' of the living (*HN*, p. 9). Some voices

pray that the souls of the dead will be healed whilst others rail against God in the absence of 'any meaning or evidence of divine logic' in the 'bloodshed' (*HN*, p. 14). These disembodied voices – and particularly Cheryl's poignant descriptions of her short life – parallel *School Spirit* (2003), Coupland's collaboration with Pierre Huyghe, in which pages from multiple high school yearbooks are interrupted by the voice of Kelly Harding, a student who died on her sixteenth birthday, 14 April 1984.[70]

Hey Nostradamus! confronts the violent contingency of the world with characters who still wish to believe that some order, logic or grace shapes reality. Yet it does not pacify a sense of anger at injustice or avoid the devastating consequences of bloodshed. The second section of the novel, narrated by Jason 11 years after the murders, is constructed as a letter to his 'nephews', whom he later reveals are his children. Jason's life – and faith – have been ruined by Cheryl's murder. He, like the riotously irreverent narrator of *Vernon God Little*, was an early scapegoat for the killing spree. Despite never being charged, local people continue to suspect Jason's involvement in the shootings. Similarly, his self-righteous father, Reg, condemns the fact that he prevented further deaths by killing one of the gunmen.

The intertwined themes of religion, violence and the elusive search for Eden in the 'New World' of the Americas are emphasized in Jason's angry reflections on Nostradamus's 'prophecies': '*Did you predict that once we found the Promised Land we'd all start offing each other?*' (*HN*, p. 91). Implicit in Jason's angry rejection of superstition is the suggestion that in the early twenty-first century, ideas of progress, innate humane decency and the prospects of a benign future are undermined by the mundane reality of gratuitous murder.

Jason's unexplained disappearance, described by Heather in the novel's third section, develops a vital but low-key motif that has run through most of Coupland's fiction: the trope of the dead or missing family member or friend. These figures preoccupy the narrators of *Microserfs* (Dan's late younger brother, Jed), *Life After God* (Laurie, the absent sister in 'Patty Hearst'), *Girlfriend in a Coma* (Jared, Karen and Linus) and the narrative of *Miss Wyoming* (both John and Susan abscond), for example. The end of *Hey Nostradamus!*, in which the penitent Reg wanders in the British Columbian wilds, expecting the 'miracle' of his son's return, uncannily prefigures the beginning of *Eleanor Rigby* (*HN*, p. 244). The novel opens with a reflection on the 'miracles of modern medicine' and is followed by a description of the return of the narrator's estranged son.[71]

Eleanor Rigby, the first of Coupland's novels to be narrated solely by a female voice, returns to the themes of anomie and crushing isolation developed in *Life After God* but also seems to be anticipated by a specific moment in *Miss Wyoming*. During John Johnson's flight across America as a born again drifter, without possessions or identity, he has numerous encounters with lonely women who he describes as 'the secret nation of Eleanor Rigbys who existed just under the threshold of perception' (*MW*, p. 167). In fact, this label for lonely women coined by Lennon and McCartney is alluded to in one of Abe's e-mails in *Microserfs*: the hierarchy at Microsoft, he suggests, is dominated by married couples: 'Elearnor Rigbies need not apply' (*MS*, p. 272 (sic)). This 'secret nation' and the theme of social invisibility is the principal theme of Coupland's ninth novel. Liz Dunn believes that she has no real identity: 'like that one Scrabble tile that has no letter on it . . . a Styrofoam puff used in packaging . . . a napkin at McDonald's . . . invisible tape' (*ER*, p. 171).

Liz, middle-class and in early middle age, lives in friendless solitude, without belief or hope for the future. Her unappealing life echoes a sentiment expressed by Jasmine – Tyler Johnson's mother – in *Shampoo Planet*: 'loneliness is the most universal sensation on the planet . . . loneliness *will* pass. You *will* survive and you *will* be a better human for it' (*SP*, p. 130). For Liz, loneliness is accompanied by a sensation of 'time sickness' in which the sensation of exclusion wrecks 'both the present and the future' (*ER*, p. 12).

The novel, however, is not an exercise in postmodern solipsism. Liz's isolation is shattered by the reappearance of her son, Jeremy Buck, whom she gave up for adoption at birth. This reconnection with a child after twenty years – a son whose birth itself seemed miraculous in her unloved, high-school years – precipitates a shift in Liz's perception of the world. Jeremy is a mischievous mystic (the nature of his visions are discussed in more detail in Chapter 5) but one whose life is too short. The revelation that he is suffering from MS and dies before the end of the novel might transform Coupland's narrative into the plot of one of the sentimental movies Liz watches during her '*verklempt*-o-thon' (*ER*, p. 12). However, Coupland transfigures sentiment into something still stranger: via a series of coincidences – and modern technology – Liz encounters Jeremy's mysterious, Austrian father, Klaus. This odd, life-embracing and obsessive-compulsive figure has been arrested on the streets of Vienna – the city, we are reminded where the subconscious was '*discovered*' rather than '*invented*' (*ER*, p. 204). This dapper prophet's offence has been one of religious harassment: in an act of (subconscious?) self-parody, Klaus speaks like one of the born again protagonists of *Girlfriend in a Coma* after their 'Great Experience' (*GIAC*, p. 3). The novel's conclusion, in an upbeat rewriting of *Hey Nostradamus!* anticipates death and birth, ending and new beginning, everyday suffering and miracles, themes that have been crucial to Coupland's fiction since *Generation X*.

Notes

1 Douglas Coupland, *Life After God* (London: Simon & Schuster, 1994), pp. 173–4. All subsequent references will be given parenthetically as *LAG*, followed by page reference.
2 Douglas Coupland, *Microserfs* (London: Harper, 2004), p. 141. All subsequent references will be given parenthetically as *MS*, followed by page reference.
3 Tara Brabazon, *From Revolution to Revelation: Generation X, Popular Memory and Cultural Studies* (Aldershot: Ashgate, 2005), p. 2.
4 Bran Nicol, 'Introduction: What We Talk About When Talk About Postmodernism', in *Postmodernism and the Contemporary Novel: A Reader*, ed. by Bran Nicol (Edinburgh: Edinburgh University Press, 2002), pp. 1–19 (p. 4).
5 R. W. Emerson, *Nature* (1836) in *The Complete Prose Works of Ralph Waldo Emerson* (London: Ward, Lock, 1898), p. 310.
6 Nicholas Blincoe, 'A Modern Master' (Review of *All Families Are Psychotic*), *New Statesman* (10 September 2001), 52–3 (53).
7 Douglas Coupland, *Generation X: Tales for an Accelerated Culture* (London: Abacus, 1992), p. 14. All subsequent references will be given parenthetically as *GX*, followed by page reference.
8 Don DeLillo, *Underworld* (London: Picador, 1999), p. 237.
9 Non-literary titles that have used the Generation X epithet include: Karen Ritchie, *Marketing to Generation X* (New York: Lexington, 1995); Richard Flory and Donald Miller (eds), *GenX Religion* (New York: Routledge, 2000); Stephen C. Craig and Stephen Earl Bennett, *After the Boom: The Politics of Generation X* (Lanham: Rowman & Littlefield, 1997); Gordon Lynch, *After Religion: 'Generation X' and the Search for Meaning* (London: Darton, Longman and Todd, 2002).
10 See, for example, Harvey Cox's list in his foreword to Tom Beaudoin, *Virtual Faith: The Irreverent Spiritual Quest of Generation X* (San Francisco: Jossey-Bass, 2000), p. ix.

11 Neil Howe and William Strauss, *13th Generation* (New York: Vintage, 1993); James Annesley, *Blank Fictions: Consumerism, Culture and the Contemporary American Novel* (London: Pluto Press, 1998).

12 Douglas Rushkoff, 'Us, by Us', in *The GenX Reader*, ed. by Douglas Rushkoff (New York: Ballantine, 1994), pp. 3–8 (p. 3).

13 Beaudoin, p. 10.

14 John M. Ulrich, 'Introduction: Generation X: A (Sub)Cultural Genealogy', in *GenXegesis: Essays on Alternative Youth Culture*, ed. by John M. Ulrich and Andrea L. Harris (Madison: University of Wisconsin Press, 2003), pp. 3–37 (p. 3).

15 Zygmunt Bauman, *Intimations of Postmodernity* (London: Routledge, 1992), p. xxv.

16 Francis Fukuyama, *The End of History and the Last Man* (London: Penguin, 1992), p. 211.

17 G. P. Lainsbury, '*Generation X* and the End of History', *Essays on Canadian Writing*, 58 (1996), 229–40 (p. 232).

18 Paul Fussell, *Class: A Guide through the American Status System* (New York: Summit, 1983), p. 179.

19 Jim Finnegan, 'Theoretical Tailspins: Reading "Alternative" Performance in *Spin* Magazine', in Ulrich and Harris (2000), pp. 121–61 (pp. 127–8).

20 P. J. O'Rourke, *All the Trouble in the World: The Lighter Side of Famine, Pestilence, Destruction and Death* (London: Picador, 1995), p. 17.

21 Michael Elliot, 'Global Whining: We're No. 1', *Newsweek*, 123.23 (6 June 1994), 69.

22 David Martin, 'The Whiny Generation', originally printed as the 'My Turn' column in *Newsweek*, (1 November 1993). Reprinted in *The GenX Reader*, edited by Douglas Rushkoff (New York: Ballantine Books, 1994), pp. 235–7 (p. 235).

23 Ulrich, pp. 3–37 (p. 3).

24 Alexander Star, 'The Twentysomething Myth', *New Republic*, 208.1–2 (4 January 1993), 22–5 (25).

25 Richard Linklater, *Slacker* (London: St Martin's Press, 1992), p. 4.

26 Douglas Coupland, 'Foreword', in Linklater, pp. 1–2 (p. 2).

27 Ibid., p. 2.

28 Douglas Coupland, *Polaroids from the Dead* (London: Flamingo, 1997), p. 122. All subsequent references will be given parenthetically as *PD*, followed by page reference.

29 See David McCarthy's discussion of Richard Hamilton in *Pop Art* (London: Tate Gallery, 2000), p. 6.

30 Lainsbury, p. 230.

31 David Joselit, Joan Simon and Renata Saleci, *Jenny Holzer* (London: Phaidon, 1998), p. 26.

32 Diane Waldman, *Jenny Holzer* (New York: Guggenheim, 1997), p. 84. See also the cover photograph.

33 Waldman, p. 44.
34 Douglas Coupland, 'Eulogy: Generation X'd', *Details* (June 1995), 72.
35 Douglas Coupland, *Shampoo Planet* (London: Simon & Schuster, 1993), p. 20.
36 Tom Wolfe, *The Bonfire of the Vanities* (London: Picador, 1990), p. xiv.
37 Ibid., p. xvii.
38 For analysis of the pages of code see Graham Thompson, ' "Frank Lloyd Oop": *Microserfs*, Modern Migration, and the Architecture of the Nineties', *Canadian Review of American Studies*, 31 (2001), 119–35.
39 Sheryl Garratt, 'Why is Douglas Coupland Fascinated by Garbage?', *Word*, 8 (October 2003), 24–5 (24).
40 Jefferson Faye, 'Canada in a Coma', *The American Review of Canadian Studies*, 31.3 (2001), 501–10 (505).
41 Daniel Grassian, *Hybrid Fictions: American Literature and Generation X* (Jefferson: McFarland, 2003), p. 134.
42 Rob Latham, *Consuming Youth: Vampires, Cyborgs, and the Culture of Consumption* (Chicago: University of Chicago Press, 2002), p. 173.
43 Rick Perlstein, 'Reality Bytes Cybergeek', *The Nation* (26 June 1995), 934–5 (935).
44 For a detailed discussion of riot grrl politics see the previously cited essays by Nehring, Finnegan and Curnutt, all in *GenXegesis*.
45 Zygmunt Bauman, *Life in Fragments: Essays in Postmodern Morality* (Oxford: Blackwell, 1995), p. 69.
46 Slavoj Žižek, *The Fragile Absolute – or, Why is the Christian Legacy Worth Fighting For?* (London and New York: Verso, 2000), p. 3.
47 Douglas Coupland, *Girlfriend in a Coma* (London: Flamingo, 1998), p. 39. All subsequent references will be given parenthetically as *GIAC*, followed by page reference.
48 Martine Delvaux, 'The Exit of a Generation: The "Whatever" Philosophy', *Midwest Quarterly: A Journal of Contemporary Thought*, 40.2 (1999), 171–86, (pp. 173–5). On mental illness and Generation X see also Catherine J. Creswell, ' "Touch Me I'm Sick: Contagion as Critique in Punk and Performance Art', in Ulrich and Harris, pp. 79–102.
49 Kirk Curnutt, 'Generating Xs: Identity Politics, Consumer Culture, and the Making of a Generation', in Ulrich and Harris, pp. 162–83 (p. 175).
50 Kim France, Interview with Douglas Coupland, *Elle Magazine* (September 1993). Reprinted in Rushkoff, pp. 11–16 (p. 11).
51 Delvaux, p. 75.
52 See Creswell's discussion of this issue, particularly p. 80.
53 Nick Hornby, *About a Boy* (London: Victor Gollancz, 1998), p. 272.
54 The 'Letter to Kurt Cobain' was originally published in the *Washington Post* and reprinted in *Polaroids from the Dead*.
55 Jenny Turner, 'Top of the World', *London Review of Books*, 22.12 (22 June 2000) www.lrb.co.uk/v22/n12/turn03_.html (10 November 2005).

56 Chuck Palahniuk, *Fight Club* (London: Vintage, 1997), p. 141.
57 Rick Moody, *The Ice Storm* (London: Abacus, 1998), p. 274.
58 Turner, www.lrb.co.uk/v22/n12/turn03_.html (10 November 2005).
59 Douglas Coupland, *Miss Wyoming* (London: Flamingo, 2000), p. 73. All subsequent references will be given parenthetically as *MW*, followed by page reference.
60 Andrew Clark, 'Finding true love in LA', *Macleans* (17 January 2000), www.macleans.ca/shared/print.jsp?content=29187 (10 November 2005).
61 Moody, p. 214.
62 Douglas Coupland, *All Families are Psychotic* (London: Flamingo, 2001), p. 171. All subsequent references will be given parenthetically as *AFAP*, followed by page reference.
63 Coupland has declared his long-time admiration for the show in a foreword to Chris Turner's *Planet Simpson: How a Cartoon Masterpiece Documented an Era and Defined a Generation* (London: Ebury Press, 2005), pp. vi–vii.
64 Grassian, p. 182.
65 Alan Bilton, *An Introduction to Contemporary American Fiction* (Edinburgh: Edinburgh University Press, 2002), p. 220.
66 Douglas Coupland, *Souvenir of Canada* (Vancouver: Douglas & McIntyre, 2002), p. 114.
67 Faye, p. 503.
68 Douglas Coupland, *City of Glass: Douglas Coupland's Vancouver* (Vancouver: Douglas & McIntyre, 2000), p. 118. All subsequent references will be given parenthetically as *COG*, followed by page reference.
69 *Hey Nostradamus!* (London: Flamingo, 2003), p. 10. All subsequent references will be given as *HN*, followed by page reference.
70 Douglas Coupland with Pierre Huyghe, *School Spirit* (Paris: Editions Dis Voir, 2003), p. 1.
71 Douglas Coupland, *Eleanor Rigby* (London: Fourth Estate, 2004), p. 1. All subsequent references will be given parenthetically as *ER*, followed by page reference.

2

'Denarration' or getting a life: Coupland and narrative

It has been said that as animals, one factor that sets us apart from all other animals is that our lives need to be stories, narratives, and that when our stories vanish, that is when we feel lost, dangerous, out of control and susceptible to the forces of randomness. It is the process whereby one loses one's life story: 'denarration'.

Denarration is the technical way of saying, 'not having a life'.[1]
(*Polaroids from the Dead*, 1996)

How might a novelist represent contemporary, globalized reality if that world and its citizens have become plotless? The phenomenon of 'denarration' described in Coupland's 'Brentwood Notebook' (1994) – a collage-report of a single day in this blandly affluent LA suburb, a putative 'secular nirvana' – thematizes the author's ongoing concern with the failure of old stories to adequately explain, or render meaningful, the complexities of living in a new era (*PD*, p. 148). This embryonic trend named by a writer from Canada's west coast, much of whose early work focuses on the odd textures of 1990s Californian experience, echoes observations made twenty years earlier by the French polymath Michel de Certeau who identified a 'Revolution of the Believable' at play in capitalist societies in which the systems of 'credibility', necessary for any society to operate, were dissolving:

Dogmas, knowledges, programs, and philosophies are losing their credibility; they are shadowless bodies that neither the hand nor the mind can grasp, but whose evanescence irritates or deceives the gesture that continues to seek them; they merely leave us, tenaciously, with the illusion of the desire to 'hold them.'[2]

The apparent disintegration of erroneous, coercive social narratives – stories that condemn individuals to lives of economic and imaginative servitude – might reasonably have given hope to anti-capitalist thinkers in the 1970s. Yet, as the authority of coherent public convictions liquefied, the illusive language of the market, fuelled by consumer dreams, filled the narrative gap with a seductive *virtual* story and gave birth to the epoch of globalized capitalism narrated by Douglas Coupland. If Coupland *qua* novelist necessarily has a professional interest in narrative, his work – including the non-fiction and visual art collections – also distinctively prioritizes explicit engagement with alternative forms of narration. His work seeks, creatively and perhaps obsessively, to define new idioms that might represent and recover the strangeness of contemporary life. Exemplary in this regard is the 'Brentwood Notebook' which has an experimental structure – incorporating statistics on infrastructure, photographs, scraps from magazines, restaurant menus, lists of resident celebrities and lyrical reflection on time and space – that incarnates a period sensibility of political/spiritual ambivalence and, more significantly, aspects of its author's boundary-crossing narrative technique.

The absence of narrative purpose in contemporary culture is attributed directly (and rather simplistically) in the 'Brentwood Notebook' to 'the deluge of electronic and information media into our lives' causing the 'stencils within which we trace our lives to vanish' (*PD*, p. 180). The fact that during the 1980s it became 'possible to be alive yet have no religion, no family connections, no ideology, no sense of class location, no politics and no sense of history' has transformed, perhaps irreversibly, notions of citizenship and collective memory (*PD*, p. 180). The idea that identity has been converted into such a fluid property might once have promised to deliver the 1960s dream of liberating diversity, but this too has a cost. As Terry Eagleton (among others) has observed, in the absence of other absolutes, the 'norm is now money', a 'promiscuous' social system that 'has absolutely no principles or identity of its own' and is therefore incapable of establishing any kind of contentment, consensus or social stability.[3]

In the Notebook's 'catalogue of the new temptations', Coupland lists the seductive alternatives afforded by contemporary life including 'information overload', 'willful ignorance of history', 'belief that spectacle is reality' and 'vicarious living through celebrities' (*PD*, p. 156). If these postmodern transgressions seemed vaguely shocking in 1994, they are now part of the common currency of cultural debate, so familiar as to have become bland and shapeless. In such an era the delicate line between fact and fantasy disappears, the imagination is penetrated and rewired by an ever more pervasive mass media. For novelists who attempt to engage with a world immersed in electronic data, the prospect of fictionalizing an already heavily mediated reality demands a sensibility that can live with, and even thrive on, a world in which absurdity reigns.

In *Generation X* (1991), Coupland coined dual neologisms to define a new sensibility of media-saturated disorientation: 'Historical Underdosing' and 'Historical Overdosing'. The former describes life in an age without major event and its twin, unsurprisingly, refers to a period of excessive change. Both, however, share identical 'symptoms' including 'addiction to newspapers, magazines, and TV news broadcasts'.[4] This pathologizing lexis – media saturation as symptom of some greater malaise – indicates an ethical concern regarding the consequences of capitulating to a fantasy life funded by a market of commercial narratives. One of the specifics of life in an era of advanced capitalism is an overwhelming sensation of controlled unreality or a gnawing suspicion that any scrap of authenticity has been eradicated. Coupland is faced with a double bind: representing an era and a mode of life that are simultaneously utterly fictional – based on a series of illusions and possessed, in particular, with the fantasy of celebrity – and somehow story-less.

Coupland's writing is animated by an anxiety that, for Western culture, any prospect of living within a liberating communal story has been all but eradicated. The sensation of 'personal storylessness' that Coupland defines as a characteristic of mid-1990s life suffuses the narrator-figures in a number of the novels (*PD*, p. 180). Andy Palmer in *Generation X* and his figurative younger brother, Tyler Johnson in *Shampoo Planet* (1992), have very different approaches to US consumer culture but are connected by a shared sense that older generations have squandered any sense of narrative rationale; Andy and Tyler have no imaginative inheritance but have been bequeathed, instead, a chronic sense of disorientation. Personal contentment, or its lack, is correlated directly to a nascent awareness that narrative purpose, if it ever existed, has somehow been misplaced. Indeed, a repeated motif of the novels is storytelling as a means to asserting identity. For example, Liz Dunn, the lonely narrator of *Eleanor Rigby* (2004), reflecting on her isolation and sense of ennui, echoes the sentiments of the 'Brentwood Notebook': '[l]ike anybody, I wanted to find out if my life was ever going to make sense, or maybe even feel like a story'.[5] Her narrative becomes an examination into the possibility of storytelling itself.

Coupland's fiction confronts the consequences of the apparent evaporation of a believable narrative from everyday Western life. Is that loss genuinely something to be mourned or does it represent a liberating opportunity? Can the old narrative be recuperated or a new one constructed? One of the major challenges for our era is not that there are no longer any instructive moral stories but that so many of them exist in apparently irresolvable conflict; an anxiety of choice is inevitable. 'Our society has become a recited society,' claimed de Certeau, 'it is defined by *stories* (*récits*, the fables constituted by our advertising and informational media), by *citations* of stories, and by the interminable *recitations* of stories.'[6] The multiplicity of competing narratives in a mass media age – many of them commercial – weakens the idea that any single story can provide a meaningful pattern for life.

This chapter addresses Coupland's formal and thematic approach to narrative: it traces the relationship between what de Certeau names the 'interminable *recitations*' of those now prevalent commercial stories and the necessity, in Coupland's fiction, of the storytelling act. A crucial concern is the novelist's ongoing interest in the representation of time. Coupland's persistent literary exploration of temporality and its relationship with human identity resonates with H. Porter Abbot's claim, informed by the ground-breaking work of Paul Ricoeur, that '*narrative is the principal way in which our species organizes its understanding of time*'.[7] His focus on linear, clock time and the experience of *kairos* – time shaped by a sense of meaningful future – connects his writing with the modernist desire to preserve the moment.[8] Is the experience of time, transformed by the twentieth-century obsession with speed, damaged by the advent of what Paul Virilio has named 'a new atrophy of the instant'?[9]

The first section explores the recurrent trope of Coupland's protagonists finding momentary emancipation or healing via acts of narration; these dazed figures actively seek a more compelling version of both private and public history. Does narrative become redemptive or might it merely disguise unresolved problems of representation, evading political engagements? Is the confidential, secret-sharing voice of the first-person narrator still viable in the contemporary novel? The second section turns to one of the most intractable problems encountered by narrators of late modern life: how can we rely on private memory in a throw-away, consumerist age that seems positively to demand amnesia? Section three examines the novelist's self-conscious experiments with alternative narrative genres as a response to this amnesiac age and, in particular, the role that dreams and visions play in his redefinition of realism. The final section focuses on the phenomenon of 'Legislated Nostalgia' – the idea that societies now generate memories in lieu of authentic history – and considers Coupland's response to this commodified past (*GX*, p. 47).

'Closer to getting a life': interiority and the story-telling ethos

In *Generation X*, Claire Baxter makes a somewhat desperate entreaty for her life and the lives of her friends to become more story-like (*GX*, p. 10). Claire and her fellow exiles are active, if compromised, opponents of impersonal market forces that cheat people into forfeiting identity and purpose. Her impulsive friend, the improbably named Dagmar Bellinghausen, an articulate and largely peaceable individual who is also given to arbitrary acts of casual vandalism, seems highly 'susceptible to the forces of randomness' explored in 'The Brentwood Notebook'. In one such moment of 'randomness', Dag, without clear motivation, drags a rock across the hood and windshield of an expensive car bearing a smug 'baby boomer' slogan ('We're spending our children's inheritance', *GX*, p. 5). The residue of a confidently storied culture is visible only in unsatisfying 'blips and chunks and snippets' such as that emblazoned on the defaced Cutlass Supreme, an anachronistic symbol of material success and autonomy. In this act of random, perhaps jealous defacement, Dag enacts Zygmunt Bauman's claim that the postmodern worldview, at its most caustic, 'is a state of mind marked above all by its all-deriding, all-eroding, all-dissolving *destructiveness*'.

Groundless postmodern philosophy reliant on a tactic of demolition suggests that as 'a critique' it faces extinction simply 'because it has destroyed everything it used to be critical about; with it, off went the very urgency of being critical. There is nothing left to be opposed to.'[10] The characters in Coupland's first novel wish to discover a mode of being that is more complex and compelling than the facile refuge of yet more indifferent, unfocused and lacklustre opposition to everybody, every idea and everything. James Annesley suggests that this trinity, with their 'lack of ambition' and 'quest for subtle, sensuous and existential pleasures' subtly connect the novel with the writing of 'nineteenth-century *fin de siècle*'. Their desire to flee from 'the alienating materialism of the modern world' and the attempt 'to withdraw from it and find a space untouched by its seemingly degraded influence', Annesley claims, are more resonant of decadence than of Bret Easton Ellis's work.[11] This argument is valuable as it locates *Generation X* in an ambiguous storytelling tradition born out of ennui but with the power – as in Oscar Wilde's *The Picture of Dorian Gray* (1891) – to transfigure cultural boredom into a powerful critique of contemporary obsessions and, perhaps more problematically, to seek a more sacred understanding of complex human behaviour. One implicit difficulty that dominates Coupland's always ethically engaged but rarely didactic fictions, is the question of how, in the absence of externally determined moral or political absolutes, an individual might choose to exercise his or her freedom in a way that is generous and liberating for others.

The fall of communist states in the years immediately before the novel's publication – and the attendant idea that ideology itself was defunct – resulted in what Zygmunt Bauman names the '*privatization of dissent*'.[12] Similarly, Dag's occasional acts of consumer sabotage are, at best, comically ineffective because they do not belong to a bigger narrative of social action. Dag's own unsure rationale resonates with a broader theme of 'storylessness': 'I don't know . . . whether I'm just upset that the world has gotten too big – way beyond our capacity to tell stories about it' (*GX*, pp. 5–6).

This allusion to the end of faith in grand narratives, stories that can explain and justify, is not, however, mere sophistry, a way of defending recreational sabotage. Neither is Jean-François Lyotard's celebrated definition of the 'postmodern condition' simply capitulated to in Coupland's fiction.[13] His characters, *pace* Lyotard, mourn the lack of a defining story or mythology and the narrator states that this absence is what inspired him and his friends to take refuge in the desert: 'this is why the three of us left our lives behind and came to the desert – to tell stories and to make our own lives worthwhile tales in the process' (*GX*, p. 10). Dag's frustration also echoes John Hawkes' famously iconoclastic statement, made in a 1965 interview, on his novelistic practice: 'I began to write fiction on the assumption that the true enemies of the novel were plot, character, setting and theme, and having once abandoned these familiar ways of thinking about fiction, totality of vision or structure were really all that remained.'[14]

The group of oral storytellers in *Generation X* are attempting to revive 'plot, character, setting and theme' in a context that appears hostile to these traditions. Coupland's fractured sequence of narratives, his novel constructed from multiple *petits récits*, is a late twentieth-century response to avant-garde narrative techniques at work in American fiction since the 1960s. If Hawkes and other advocates of metafiction viewed narrative itself with a suspicion bordering on contempt, the act of sharing stories holds a redemptive promise for Coupland's displaced searchers. Rituals of narration are the central drama of *Generation X*, and Alcoholics Anonymous is cited by Andy as the inspiration for this practice: as a confessional, storytelling community it is the nearest that he has come to a group that continues to revere the significance and sanctity of narrative. This self-help style storytelling – that has strong similarities with religion – is also explored in Chuck Palahniuk's *Fight Club* (1996). As Michael Edwards has argued, narrative is crucial in the construction of religious identity and sense of purpose for individuals and communities: 'Story offers an otherness, of unity and purposive sequence. It also offers, in particular, beginnings and ends . . . The specific of story is that it appeals to the desire for a new beginning.'[15]

Andy, Dag and Claire have no formal religion but their emotional investment in storytelling and attempts to constitute life according to the lessons discovered in each other's tales take on a sacred aura. The only rules for these 'bedtime stories' are vetoes on interruption and criticism ('just like in AA') (*GX*, p. 16). Some of the narratives are explicitly biographical, others mythic, but all are told with the hope of engendering a refreshed perspective on a cynical world. One of Andy's stories – the Jorge Luis Borges-like tale of Edward, an alcoholic recluse trapped in 'his own private world', a sophisticated book-filled cube – is a secret withheld even from his fellow storytellers and shared only with the reader (*GX*, p. 55). The tale ends with the collapse of Edward's enchanted sanctuary and his forced exile into the turbulent world of the city, where (naturally) he becomes a jazz pianist and map-maker for those, like himself, who are lost. This private parable seems simultaneously to reject the idea that literature is a valid alternative to lived experience – the beautiful library becomes a prison – and to acknowledge that all existence, even so-called 'real' life, is heavily fictionalized. The city that Edward staggers through is a postmodern paradise – or purgatory – in the shape of a 'shimmering, endless New York', both cartoon-like and tangibly real (*GX*, p. 57).

The 'denarrated' sensibility experienced by Andy and his alter ego also inflects Daniel's electronic journal in *Microserfs* (1995). In fact, this narrator's conversational, period-specific language is peppered with many references to being 'deficient in the having-a-life department' – a version of the distinctively 1990s casual insult that briefly enjoyed ubiquitous popularity – 'Get a life!' In *Microserfs*, this familiar slur takes on a darker resonance concerning the loss of a vividly experienced emotional existence.[16] One of Dan's former co-workers and room-mates from the secure but infantilizing Microsoft 'campus' at Redmond, Washington, reflects that it is possible that 'thinking you're supposed to "have a life" is a stupid way of buying into an untenable 1950s narrative of what life *supposed* to be'. People with 'no life', he suggests, not particularly convincingly, might be 'on the new frontier of human sentience and perceptions' (*MS*, p. 187).

The name given to the group's start-up company, coined by Daniel after a competitive brain-storming exercise, is Interiority. The brand conflates the narrator's search for personal identity via the act of writing his electronic journal ('to try to see the patterns in my life') with the novel's broader critique of a culture that increasingly negates the possibility of maintaining a unique interior life (*MS*, p. 4). Karla, Dan's girlfriend and perhaps the most fiercely articulate character in any of Coupland's novels, is more sanguine than her peers regarding the loss of 'traditional identity-donating structures' from post-industrial culture. In the absence of religious belief, political ideology, inherited morality or the limits of familial responsibilities, she recognizes that individuals are faced with the vertiginous fact of their own freedom: 'You're on your own here. It's a big task, but just *look* at the flood of ideas that emerges from the plastic!' (*MS*, p. 236). The theme of denarration – viewed less enthusiastically than Karla's optimistic embrace of self-determination might suggest – is also a connecting thread between the melancholic secret sharers who narrate the short stories in *Life After God* (1994). Each character is searching for a way to escape from the apparent randomness of late twentieth-century life without succumbing to loneliness, depression or chemically controlled indifference. In the final story of the collection, '1,000 Years (Life After God)', the narrator, Scout, briefly finds a point of connection with a bigger story when he spontaneously decides to travel to Washington DC to witness the inauguration of the US President: 'I was beginning to feel like a person inside a story for the first time in years. I almost didn't want to sleep that night, not wanting that feeling to vanish.'[17]

Daniel Grassian has argued that the implicit approval of 'the restorative power of narrative which has been lost in disjointed postmodern culture' separates Coupland's fiction from a mode of contemporary writing that disdains any notion of metanarrative. Grassian's claim that, unlike the traditions of 'academic, American postmodern writing', Coupland's work somehow validates 'literature as personal meaning-maker as well as psychological bulwark' is provocative if debatable.[18] Indeed, official literary culture plays a marginalized role in the lives of his characters. TV shows, bad movies and computer games are frequently cited but the novels feature comparatively few allusions to fiction or poetry. Similarly, in a review of *All Families are Psychotic*, Nicholas Blincoe wryly observed that since Coupland's work bears few if any of those 'signs of anxious sparring with his literary predecessors', earnestly searched for by readers in the manner of Harold Bloom, 'his work evades one of the most favoured tools of contemporary scholarship'.[19] Although Coupland is an actively allusive writer whose work features countless references to music, film, painting and current affairs, his fiction rarely makes explicit citation of other literary works. However, the German poet Rainer Maria Rilke (1875–1926), whose spiritually restless work anticipates aspects of Coupland's lyrical fiction, is quoted in both *Generation X* and *Polaroids from the Dead*. The 'Brentwood Notebook', an evocation of a world without memory, is surprisingly prefaced with a quotation from the modernist writer on the imagined and retrospective nature of origins (*PD*, p. 145). In *Generation X*, Andy Palmer offsets the recollection of a sordid incident that took place during his time in Japan – when a powerful executive reveals that his most treasured possession is a unique pornographic image of one of Brentwood's former residents, Marilyn Monroe – by citing Rilke. The narrator contrasts Mr Takamichi's belief that his obscene photograph constituted a moment of intimacy or frozen time, made sacred in an image, with the poet's emphasis on personal integrity. This odd memory triangulates alternative national perspectives: youthful American ennui collides with Japanese enthusiasm for US pop culture that, in turn, is subverted by European literature in a moment of destabilizing social conflict. The fact that Andy becomes disillusioned with his own storyless, image-dominated existence in Japan rather than the USA, suggests that he needed to be literally removed from his own country in order to see its strange and disturbing reflection in the gaze of other cultures.

Despite this brief romantic allusion to Rilke, the language that Andy, Dag, Claire and their contemporaries are able to rely on to narrate their experience primarily derives not from literature but from television. In ironic moments of what Coupland calls 'Tele-parablizing' – finding meaning in the events of one's own life by paralleling them with the clichéd plots of TV – his characters are aware that the idea of a unique, interior identity has been compromised (*GX*, p. 138). The ascension of societies structured around liberal economic principles – free-market democracies – is dependent upon what Francis Fukuyama playfully describes as the 'ultimate victory of the VCR'.[20] That Fukuyama's phrasing now seems sweetly antiquated is appropriate: in an accelerated culture, technology swiftly becomes obsolete, and this forms the basis of a desire culture. New consumer-based technologies – such as video players in the 1980s – hold seductive authority that supposedly draws societies towards capitalism. The central characters in *Generation X*, in their attempt to evade the negative emotional effects of a market-based economy, are no longer TV junkies, but were raised in a world dependent on the illusions fostered by the medium. For Coupland, narrative begins in the act of wrestling with life in a world saturated with artifice and superficial spectacle. Indeed, Alan Bilton suggests that uncertainty regarding the synthetic, simulated contours of contemporary experience embodies the defining dilemma of Coupland's project:

> How should an artist, in whatever medium, respond to the barrage of signs, images, messages and codes which makes up our daily, mediated environment? Repudiate it utterly as a deadening of the senses, a falsification of experience, something banal, maddening, even corrupt? But if one simply closes one's eyes, then does art run the risk of irrelevancy, obsolescence, and denial?[21]

Coupland's fiction explores the ways in which individuals accommodate themselves to the realities of life amongst this 'barrage of signs' or what de Certeau has named 'the forest of narrativities'.[22] Coupland has acknowledged that the frequent allusions to pop culture in the early novels – sometimes witty, sometimes mournful – are, in part, a 'common bank of experience' and a short cut to communication 'with relative ease to someone who grew up thousands of miles away'.[23] This apparent collapse of national identities into a single currency of shared memories engenders both optimistic associations and doubt in his work. Brian McHale has suggested that one problem for the fiction writer in the postmodern era is that 'everything in our culture tends to deny reality and promote unreality, in the interests of maintaining high levels of consumption' and, consequently, 'official reality' is no longer the most potent, bullying metanarrative with which citizens, and novelists, are compelled to contend. In the place of an authorized sense of history-as-plot emerges 'official *unreality*', including the bombardment of advertising images that saturate our everyday experience and, according to one conservative perspective, 'postmodernist fiction, instead of resisting this coercive unreality, acquiesces in it, or even *celebrates* it'.[24] As a writer who is concerned with life amidst the artifice – and one who thrives on what Douglas Rushkoff has named the Gen X capacity to 'derive meaning from the random juxtaposition of TV commercials, candy wrappers, childhood memories, and breakfast treats' – Coupland is vulnerable to such accusations of compliance to 'this coercive unreality'.[25] Although both *Generation X* and *Shampoo Planet* are shot through with misgivings about the encroaching influence of the commercial world on individuality and community, later novels, including *Life After God* and *Girlfriend in a Coma* (1998) are more emphatic regarding the potentially destructive delusions of capitulating to a virtual life: sedated by drugs, illegal or otherwise, the characters in these fables encounter a punitive version of contemporary reality, a counterfeit dream-life – structured around confused memories – from which they must awake.

Remembering 'What you chose to forget': memory and narrative

'We're human; we're amnesia machines' remarks Dan in *Microserfs* (*MS*, p. 101). If, as the novel suggests, humanity might recover a sense of teleology, of purposeful story, via carefully used new technology, can that machinery ever compensate for a manifest defect in its creator? Memory loss, anguished cultural commentators frequently observe, is a curse of the over-stimulated, neglectful postmodern imagination.[26] 'The culture of consumer society is mostly about forgetting, not learning', observes Zygmunt Bauman, and Coupland's fiction is informed by similar anxieties regarding the impending collapse of private, unmediated memory.[27] 'I think I am losing my memory' confesses the writer, in one of a series of 'postcard' essays included in *Polaroids from the Dead* (*PD*, p. 107). Indeed, anxieties regarding a contemporary propensity for the accidental or deliberate erasure of important shared memories are overtly foreshadowed in the titles of a number of the collection's short stories. 'Our Capacity For Amnesia Is Terrifying', 'Technology Will Spare Us the Tedium of Repeating History' and 'You Can't Remember What You Chose to Forget' all express, with imagistic intensity, an urgent sense of cultural bereavement.

The narrator of the latter story reflects that, after the blank space of early childhood, 'memories overpower all else in your life, forever making the present moment seem sad and unable to compete with a glorious past that now has a life of its own' (*PD*, p. 47). Indeed, the experiences that we can recall are, if anything, of greater concern to Coupland than what we 'chose to forget'. Reflecting on the delicate distinction between private and public remembrance, this writer of the 'accelerated' era acknowledges that his imaginative life has not escaped the power of advertising. After seeing a TV commercial for the first time in twenty years, Coupland realizes, with a certain degree of alarm, that he has almost perfect recall of a document that is both utterly trivial and strangely enthralling:

> Like many people my age, I was exposed to extreme amounts of well-produced, high-quality information and entertainment from birth onward . . . I guess my head is stuffed with an almost-endless series of corporation-sponsored consumer tableaux of various lengths. These 'other' commercialized memories are all in my head, somewhere. (*PD*, p. 112)

Coupland's disquiet about the consequences of media saturation is connected to the broader issue of 'denarration': if personal memories are displaced or rewritten by, say, accumulated and distorting memories of fizzy beverage adverts, sci-fi serials and comedy double acts consumed in childhood, how much of 'me' is left? One of the writer's slogans in a Jenny Holzer-like piece, 'Agree/Disagree: 55 State-ments About the Culture' (1995), provides a compressed version of this problem: 'Personal memory and corporate memory are so blurred together that individualism has become a shaky concept.'[28] The apparently limitless reach of marketable images – whether designed to sell a product or as part of the disposable but intoxicating aesthetics of TV – destabilizes the whole notion of a privately determined, tran-scendent identity. Elsewhere Coupland has described television and film as the 'twentieth-century dream apparatus' that 'manufacture[d] and reinforce[d] the American mythic canon'.[29] Whatever the psychic or spiritual damage inflicted by life in an age of simulated selves and phoney memories, Western culture, paradoxically, continues to privilege a supposedly authentic 'real' world. As Coupland observes, 'we're not supposed to consider the commercialized memories in our head as real' but instead are expected to assume that 'real life consists in time spent away from TVs, magazines and theaters' (*PD*, p. 112).

If a theoretical hierarchy of memories is desirable and a genuine, unmediated interior life exists, is that reality compromised by the many simulated versions that surround us? The pace and proliferation of new technologies mean that, before long, in Coupland's view, the world will 'be entirely populated by people who have only known a world with TVs and computers'; and identity, once communication technology becomes normative, will necessarily change (*PD*, p. 112). This statement problematically overlooks the fact that access to this world of advanced information technology remains limited to those who live in economically privileged countries. Coupland tries to exorcise the influence of the transient – to stop certain images assuming the precious status of memory. Technologies that emerged from the modernist project of progress, designed to preserve or freeze time, also have the special effect of altering our relationship with time and memory. Coupland's fiction regularly returns to this concept. In '1,000 Years (Life After God)', for example, Scout and Kristy reflect on the apparent acceleration of history: Scout suggests that a consequence of the technophile *Zeitgeist* – the increasing dependency on communication technology including answerphones and video recorders – is the collapse of time (*LAG*, p. 334). *Microserfs* is similarly interested in the changing perception of linear time in the era of advanced capitalism: the frequent allusions to Fukuyama's 'end of history' thesis are coupled with a sense that the modern form of labour these programmers are governed by irrevocably accelerates standard chronology (*MS*, p. 23).

In Coupland's fourth novel, Dan and Karla, budding architects of the electronic revolution, remain optimistic about the consequences of their own endeavours, but are troubled by other aspects of the mass media. Ironically, these are two individuals whose expertise with information technology facilitates the new, virtual colonial power of simulated, consumer dreams. As Rob Latham comments, the 'systematic commodification of experience has been facilitated if not hastened

by cybernetic tools'.[30] Similarly, Ethan, Dan and Karla's materialistic
but philosophical company director is conscious that his industry has
produced a temporal revolution: 'we have increased the information
density of our culture to the point where our perception of time has
become all screwy' *MS*, pp. 163–4). This morally ambiguous prophet
of the digital age tells colleagues that his whole life is now dedicated to
rendering the experience of time more palpable and sustained (*MS*,
p. 165). Even Todd, during his phase of political radicalism, claims that
the post-industrial economy is based on the 'redistribution of *time*'
rather than money (*MS*, p. 279). Despite the epochal impact of the
digital revolution – its challenges to identity and the possibilities that
it presents for the preservation as well as the erasure of the past –
information technology is not the first cultural intervention to alter
temporality. The novel itself is a form of technology that assists and
transforms the experience of time and shared memory.

In a highly self-reflexive passage in 'Patty Hearst', for example, a
short story that features Coupland's trope of a lost family member, the
grieving narrator reflects on the ways in which narrative sequence has
come to dominate his imagination. He is caught between the standard
conviction that life is constituted of a linear sequence of cause and
effect and the alternative possibility that this 'storyboard' approach is
simply a 'bookkeeping device we're stuck with as humans to try to make
sense of our iffy situation here on Earth' (*LAG*, p. 217). His brother,
Brent, responds to these anxieties by emphasizing that the experience
of 'linear time' is a distinguishing characteristic of the human 'animal':
'agonizingly endless clock time' is our 'curse', he claims, as is the
burden of remembering this sequence and pattern of experiences
(*LAG*, p. 223).

The idea of the human 'animal' with its idiosyncratic need to locate
itself in time is frequently, perhaps obsessively, returned to in the
novels: in *Microserfs*, for example, Karla tells Dan in their first conversation that a 'new, supra-animal identity' is gradually emerging from
humanity's desire to rid itself of animalistic origins; this, she suggests,
is defined by the belief in a future – and in the concept of generations
– that other animals appear not to need (*MS*, pp. 17–18). Brent's
sermonic speech on the human compulsion to live within narrative
explicitly parallels the description of 'denarration' in the 'Brentwood
Notebook', and even stresses that the absence of a specific story causes
individuals to 'feel lost somehow' (*LAG*, p. 223). Although there is
no evidence that Coupland is responding directly to philosophical

analyses of time, these recurrent debates in his fiction echo Paul Ricoeur's highly influential *Time and Narrative* (1984–85). Ricoeur asserts that *'time becomes human to the extent that it is articulated through a narrative mode, and narrative attains its full meaning when it becomes a condition of temporal existence'*.[31] A number of Coupland's characters – not all of them narrators – are aware that their experience of narrative time is under pressure, and this frequently precipitates a sensation of disorientation and melancholy that Liz Dunn, the narrator of *Eleanor Rigby*, describes as 'time sickness'. This idiosyncratic pathology appears to 'wreck' time past, present and future in a miasma of loneliness and narrative disconnection (*ER*, p. 12).

'We lose our days – and our ability to retrieve them – and yet there are some days that should never be lost,' reflects Coupland in *Polaroids from the Dead* (*PD*, p. 86). This essay, 'The German Reporter', blends fiction and reality, memory and possibility, as the writer confronts the fear that even the most valuable memories can be misplaced. In *Microserfs*, Dan observes that lack of time has become a persistent topic of polite conversation: 'How can time just . . . *disappear*?' (*MS*, p. 146). The young programmer's uneasy observation is echoed in Coupland's next novel, *Girlfriend in a Coma*. When Karen McNeil – whose sense of linear chronology has effectively been erased – awakes from her seventeen-year coma she notices a difference in the perception of passing time: 'Nobody *has* time anymore. What's the deal?'[32] This postmodern Sleeping Beauty has missed an entire decade and, fulfilling Brent's fantasy of forgetting in 'Patty Hearst', she has no memories of the 1980s, a decade in which her friends' lives were marked by moral failure. Karen's defamiliarizing, 1970s perspective allows Coupland to re-examine a world in which time has been restructured by countless labour-saving devices and a mechanized desire for efficiency. The major conceit of the novel is that Karen's missing seventeen years anticipate the global collapse of time itself: human history comes to an abrupt end and chronology appears to evaporate. This apocalyptic novel – energized by borrowings from science fiction and the language of Christian eschatology – tacitly calls for deceleration: if a benign future is to be imagined, humanity must recognize that time is not an element simply to be defeated.

All Families Are Psychotic, though not charged with the same end-of-the-world urgency, is similarly concerned with the ravages of time. *'When time is used up, does it go to some kind of place like a junkyard?'* speculates Wade Drummond, invoking Coupland's parallel interests in time and trash: '*Does time evaporate and turn into rain and start all over again?*'[33] In an echo of T. S. Eliot's *Four Quartets* (1935–42), this unlikely mystic yearns for the redemption of time. Wade, and Janet (mother of the 'psychotic' Drummond family), connected by their fractious domestic past and a shared terminal illness, are painfully aware of passing time. Janet, conscious that precious and unpleasant memories are indiscriminately 'erased in little bits', describes a moment of temporal confusion during a visit to London (*AFAP*, p. 121). In order to check the time, she looks at the watches in a shop window, assuming that these timepieces will be 'collectively precise to the second'. However, the individual watches show a different time and Janet briefly experiences the sensation of having 'passed into the other side of the mirror where there was no time at all' (*AFAP*, p. 122). Although the fleeting evasion of clock time is as illusory as Lewis Carroll's Looking Glass world, the moment of transcendence is illustrative of the ways in which narrative can reconfigure the experience of history. *All Families are Psychotic* – one of only two Coupland novels to date to use an omniscient narrator rather than the lyric voice of the first person – is structured around a pattern of flashbacks. This movement between time past – the embarrassments and schisms of 1970s suburban life – and the murky comedy of time present, mimics the desire for the recuperation of lost time. Storytelling might be a quixotic process but as a genre the novel can give meaningful shape to what Ian McEwan has memorably named 'the vandalising erasures of time'.[34]

In writing for an 'accelerated' epoch, however, Coupland has to contend with what Agnes Heller describes as a 'culture of the *absolute present*.'[35] In fact, Michael Brockington observes that the urgency of Coupland's early fiction, written in a televisual present tense, 'flirts with the fashion vortex of absolute now'.[36] The novelist's propensity for deploying the specifics of everyday life – TV shows, adverts, consumer products – renders his fiction all the more perishable but it also reflects what Virilio describes as 'a new atrophy of the instant' brought about by the emphasis on speed.[37] Literary fiction competes with the power of electronic images in the twenty-first century. The rise of the novel helped to mythologize the independent, evolving human self. However, an economy that relies on a ceaseless flow of images – on television, on billboards, on the Internet and, more insidiously, in the movement of these images in the subconscious of every consumer – inevitably transforms that 'self' into yet another product. In *Girlfriend in a Coma*, for example, one character regrets her wasted years, spent as a supermodel – a period when she incarnated desire culture, because it has diminished rather than intensified her sense of individuality: 'There's only a small fraction of "me" left. I used to think there was an infinite supply of "me."' (*GIAC*, pp. 72–3). Linus, the novel's most philosophical character, admonishes the hyper-ironic Hamilton for incessantly talking 'in little TV bits', his habit apparently a symptom of irredeemable insincerity (*GIAC*, p. 82). In '1,000 Years' (*Life After God*), Todd, one of the narrator's childhood friends, asks: 'What is *you*, Scout? What is the *you* of *you*? What is the link? Where do *you* begin and end? This *you* thing – is it an invisible silk woven from your memories? Is it a spirit? Is it electric? What exactly *is* it?' (*LAG*, pp. 304–5).

The 'tales' in *Generation X* are partly shaped by the narrator's troubled awareness that his access to the past, both in the form of private memory and what he calls 'genuine capital *H* history', has gradually been compromised (*GX*, p. 175). Andy's entertaining description of a professionally taken family photograph, shot in the late 1970s on 'possibly the most unhip day of [his] life', illuminates similar concerns. This dated photograph, in which the Palmer family look '*perfect*', tells a story that is bound to its historical moment (*GX*, p. 153). It still exists, hanging in a rarely used room, mocking the depredations of time and compromise. One critic, focusing on this embarrassed recollection, has argued that the novel's use of 'stylized memories' invites its readers 'to decode the memory by specifying the style of its components'. The 'message of the family portrait is a certain patriotic optimism about the future', argues Caren Irr, and according to this logic, the reader, like Andy, needs to situate that buoyancy 'in the "corn-fed" and thoroughly shampooed moment of the late 1970s'.[38] The photograph constitutes a simulated past, it is neither a lie, nor is it quite the truth, but its optimism, for Andy, seems to encode a different way of looking at time. These reflections are situated in the context of his family's unspoken present-day resolution to abandon the great expectations that the photograph seems to represent.

However, the emotionally strained Christmas family visit that prompted this particular memory concludes with an attempt at a different kind of 1970s historical connection. Andy and his younger brother break their journey to the airport with a visit to a Vietnam memorial. Tyler has no real point of emotional connection with a conflict during which he was born but of which he has no memories.

Indeed, for Tyler's generation, the Vietnam War, fictionalized in so many Hollywood treatments – what de Certeau calls *'recitations* of stories' – is likely to have taken on the status of cinematic myth rather than retrievable historical crisis.[39] For Andy, however, these 'ugly times' were, he suspects, his sole opportunity to witness, even if in dully remembered televisual fragments, real 'history': 'before history was turned into a press release, a marketing strategy, and a cynical campaign tool'. The 'Garden of Solace', the first memento mori in Coupland's writing, allows the narrator, 'in the bizarre absence of all time cues', to connect 'to a past of some importance', however insubstantial the link (*GX*, p. 175). Andy and his creator might, sceptically, be accused of seeking to make a vicarious connection with a national catastrophe that was not, in any meaningful way, their own. Despite these reservations, the episode is, most specifically, a reminder that the search for personal meaning cannot escape the force of broader political and economic changes, even if the age of 'capital *H* history' has passed.

Yet the muted call for a recovery of history (or History) is always ambivalent in *Generation X*. For example, Andy notes that his journey to the heightened unreality of Palm Springs was prompted by his desire 'to erase all traces of history from [his] past' (*GX*, p. 41). Each character has a conversion story that describes how they came to resent the limits of their lives and reject them for something at once more risky yet strangely more secure. Dag's crisis narrative concludes with a contradictory entreaty for the simultaneous erasure and creation of a personal story: 'I needed a clean slate with no one to read it . . . My life had become a series of scary incidents that simply weren't stringing together to make for an interesting book' (*GX*, p. 36). Dag's problem is not exclusive to his generation and, indeed, the wider context of Coupland's fiction emphasizes a humanist idea that the search for a coherent life story is a core element of our identity as a species. In *All Families are Psychotic*, for example, Janet Drummond, born shortly before the Second World War and clearly neither a baby boomer nor a Gen X slacker, is frustrated 'because she was unable to remember and reexperience her life as a continuous movie-like event' (*AFAP*, p.12). This craving echoes the disappointed awareness of Tyler Johnson in *Shampoo Planet* that, as he grows older, 'the act of imagining . . . life as a rock video becomes harder'.[40]

Film displaces literature as the medium that these figures construe as the most vivid form through which life might be perceived. This

visual sensibility is more surprising in Janet than Tyler, who has never
known a world without multi-channel television. Significantly, the
character craves a cinematic simulation of the past rather than memory
itself. However, in lieu of the 'movie-like event', Janet can find only
fragments of 'punctuation here and there' to constitute her identity.
She finds it impossible to connect the small child that she was during
the 1940s with her present identity as a middle-aged woman, attending
her daughter's first space mission at the turn of the twenty-first century:
'there seemed to be no divine logic behind the assemblage. Or any flow.
All those bits were merely . . . bits' (*AFAP*, p. 12).

The playful, metafictional resonance of Dag's declaration and Janet's
frustration raises questions regarding the relationship between
Coupland's fractured series of narratives, his characters and their
readers. Dag paradoxically both resists being 'read' and laments the
lack of narrative unity from his existence. There is a tension between
his craving for purity and a distinct nostalgia for a vivid personal
history, a conflict paralleled in Donna Tartt's *The Secret History* (1992).
Richard Papen, Tartt's unhappy narrator, confesses early in his bloody
narrative – the 'only story that [he] will ever be able to tell' – that he
has regularly fictionalized the details of his childhood in a sunlit
Californian suburb: 'My years there created for me an expendable past,
disposable as a plastic cup . . . I was able to fabricate a new and far more
satisfying history . . . a colourful past, easily accessible to strangers.'[41]
The concept of an 'expendable past' that might be discarded and
exchanged for an alternative history is both disturbing and seductive.
Yet the elasticity of one individual life story is not unique to
the malleable, consumerist identities available in the postmodern
moment: Puritan settlers of the so-called New World, after all, were
committed to the belief that the self would become a new creation in
the experience of true conversion. Dag's desire for a 'clean slate' echoes
the Puritan desire for regeneration; even Tartt's narrator, complicit in
murder and ruined by concealed guilt, is aware that his worldview has
been shaped by a repressed 'Puritan streak'.[42]

Postmodern Puritanism emerges in unexpected ways in Coupland's
approach to narrative. Tyler Johnson – the least visibly puritanical of
Coupland's narrators – tells Stephanie, the young French woman he
is trying to impress, that in the USA 'you're allowed to redo history –
erase your tapes and start over again'. Indeed, he figures this deliberate
deletion of the past as distinctively American: when Stephanie and
her fellow Parisian, Monique, visit Lancaster, Washington State, they

quickly acquire more detailed knowledge of its history than Tyler and his family. This 'modern freedom' is a displaced, and less ethically demanding, trope of America's religious origins (*SP*, p. 170). As if to amplify these echoes of the nation's founding piety, one of Tyler's friends claims that the only real 'tragedy' that might be caused by contemporary America's floundering grasp on history would be Hollywood's failure to simulate the past accurately enough: 'like Pilgrims on the Mayflower eating kiwi fruits or burritos' (*SP*, p. 170). These mischievous reflections on the gradual replacement of history by the hyperreal substitutions of film and television are reminiscent of Jean Baudrillard's theory of the 'disappearance of the real', particularly in his *Simulacra and Simulation* (1981; trans. 1994). We might say, after Baudrillard, that this putative, anachronistically propped Mayflower 'masks the *absence* of a profound reality'.[43] A simulated Puritanism also has an impact, consciously or otherwise, on the formal pattern of Coupland's work. The first-person mode deployed in the majority of his novels echoes the tradition of spiritual autobiography. The confessional style that gives structure to postmodern parables like *Life After God* and *Hey Nostradamus!* (2003) is particularly resonant of this genre. Even Tyler's story, described by Jefferson Faye as 'an ersatz coming-of-age novel', despite its ostensible simplicity, plays with the literary-religious idea of the awakening conscience.[44] This brash, entrepreneurial narrator is not punished for pursuing consumer dreams but his moral sensitivity is stirred: 'I guess I broke something valuable. Or traded it away' (*SP*, p. 296).

Similarly, Dag's unconscious performance of a seventeenth-century spirituality that stresses the necessity of a second, spiritual birth foreshadows the delirious plot of *Miss Wyoming* (2000). In Coupland's sixth novel, two minor celebrities attempt to shed the weird and destructive narrative conferred by their synthetic stardom. John Johnson wishes to erase his overscripted, clichéd existence: 'He would be – *nobody* – he would have nothing: no money, no name, no history, no future, no hungers.'[45] Paradoxically, only as a narrative '*nobody*' can he acquire a significant story; in symbolic death, he might, like a penitent Puritan, be reborn without the taint of history. Coupland's narrative seems to validate John Johnson's and Susan Colgate's parallel quests to shed the ephemeral, vampiric identities conferred on them by a now widely-longed-for kind of fame that is seductive but spurious. The semi-conscious, artificial vision that facilitates John's (temporary) rebirth as an *On the Road*-style drifter is connected with Susan's apparent demise in the crash of Flight 802 from New York to Los Angeles. As a former beauty pageant queen, child star, a (gay) rock musician's wife and 'low-grade celebrity', Susan is oddly buoyant as she anticipates death: 'She felt a surprising relief that the plastic strand of failed identities she'd been beading together across her life was coming to an end' (*MW*, p. 16).

The self as something both artificial and plural contradicts essentialized American ideals of uniqueness and separation – both in terms of the individual and the nation state – but such performative roles might also constitute the reality for the majority of people. In another echo of Baudrillard, after rising, physically unscathed and psychically reborn from the plane crash, Susan reflects that the 'events on TV seemed more real to her than did her actual experience' (*MW*, p. 19).

The plot plays with contemporary perceptions of remembrance and identity. Late in the narrative, Susan is compelled to feign memory loss in order to explain her absence and reluctant return to mainstream culture; her private life turned, once more, into a tawdry tabloid story. 'Amnesia's bullshit', is John Johnson's blunt assessment of Susan's supposed condition. In fact, he suggests that total memory loss is something less real than 'bullshit': it is 'only a movie device' (*MW*, p. 250).

One of the minor characters in *Miss Wyoming*, Randy Montarelli, a lonely man who expends bitterness and sexual frustration by generating preposterous celebrity gossip on the Internet, embraces his opportunity to 'rewrite himself' as a consequence of this 'movie device' (*MW*, p. 232). This chance emerges when he becomes an accidental rescuer for Susan – the woman whose image he had once worshipped – in a moment of crisis. When the former child star attempts both to lose her status as soiled celebrity and to assert a quietly authentic identity, her devotee is invited to integrate his own disappointing past into Susan's evolving story. Randy, part of a highly self-reflexive generation, suffers from a painful awareness of the depressing 'narrative arc' of his existence as a result of drenching himself in too many surrogate stories (*MW*, p. 276). The dramatic transformation of Randy's lonely life, when an ostensibly resurrected Susan Colgate appears at his door and promptly gives birth in an apparent 'Bethlehemical miracle', is a slyly self-conscious narrative conceit (*MW*, p. 232). This improbable event, trading off Gospel accounts of the Nativity, resembles nothing so much as one of the many outrageous plot twists of the daytime TV soap hell from which Susan is trying to escape. Yet this highly conventional, even clichéd, moment of dramatic resolution allows Randy's own 'narrative arc' (in which he is perpetually one of life's minor characters), to feel more substantial and real.

Nicholas Blincoe acknowledges that Coupland's fiction necessarily includes 'a certain dancing with cliché'. His argument that characters in a number of the novels 'are forced to engage with soap-style plots, but are not themselves soap characters' is a useful way of framing the novelist's use of narrative contrivance.[46] Questions regarding the fragile relationship between irony and sincerity in Coupland's writing have, unsurprisingly, dominated aspects of his critical reception. One critic, keen to demystify Coupland's status as progenitor of the whole Generation X phenomenon, has castigated the writer for his 'characteristically camp, ironic phrasing'.[47]

Despite the free-wheeling irony of many of his characters – including Dag in *Generation X*, Hamilton in *Girlfriend in a Coma* and even Florian, the cartoon villain of *All Families are Psychotic*, for example – the narratives themselves display a considerable anxiety about the implications of embracing an ironic worldview. Mark Forshaw has identified the 'deep level of dissatisfaction not just with "knee-jerk" irony but also with the still accumulating and apparently ineluctable inheritance of ironic postmodernism' that informs Coupland's work.[48] Coupland's most perceptive protagonists frequently recognize the absurd pattern of their own experience as an uncanny echo of a simulated story: for example, in *All Families are Psychotic*, Wade notes that the farcical erotic mischief in which his family has become embroiled has 'devolved' their life 'into a low-budget 1970s sex comedy' (*AFAP*, p. 216). Similarly, in *Miss Wyoming*, Susan and John, like Dan and his fellow 'Microserfs', Andy and the 'accelerated culture' storytellers, want to cast off the sense of inhabiting quoted or appropriated lives – to escape an existence that plays out like an exhausted pastiche of reality.

'Linear thinking is out': Coupland, narrative and the logic of dreams

Coupland deploys alternative narrative strategies to represent, and to defy, the oppressive order of life, time and memory in a forcefully simulated society. A number of the novels re-enact the dream-like, coincidence-laden, and highly illusory world of contemporary

American life. *Miss Wyoming* and *All Families Are Psychotic* play with
the improbable, but the implausibility of their plots is of the order of
'real life disaster'; a narrative that is read, consumed and forgotten
every day in gossip magazines and tabloids. In the latter novel, Janet
Drummond has started to embrace the belief that no real order exists
in the universe and that her suffering is simply the result of 'chaos'
or 'a cosmic Lotto draw' (*AFAP*, p. 121). The narrative, however, is
prefaced with one of Jenny Holzer's slogans: 'IN A DREAM YOU SAW A
WAY TO SURVIVE AND YOU WERE FULL OF JOY.' Janet's existential
despair – or the capitulation to chaos and contingency – is confronted
by an alternative narrative logic that implies the possibility of connection and purpose. One of the marked ways in which Coupland
departs from the conventions of traditional, mimetic realism is in a
recurrent exploration of the blurred line between dreams and reality.
Blincoe rightly compares Coupland's daydream sensibility with the
out-of-kilter dream-logic of the Japanese novelist, Haruki Murakami.[49]
In *All Families are Psychotic*, for example, Wade's ability to distinguish
between reality and simulation is tested by the near omnipresence of
television: in his stressed psychological state he experiences 'the nightly
evening news' not merely as a sequence of narrative images but as 'a
recurring fever dream' (*AFAP*, p. 92).

Coupland's exploration of the interstices between the banalities of
everyday experience and the anomalous logic of dreams connects his
fiction with the evolving mode of magic realism. This slippery term
has been deployed to describe a variety of different literary forms,
frequently deriving from non-anglophone literatures. Isabel Allende,
the Chilean novelist, claims that the traditions of this narrative mode
allocate 'a place in literature to the invisible forces that have such a
powerful place in life . . . dreams, myth, legend, passion, obsession,
superstition, religion, the overwhelming power of nature and the
supernatural'. These forms of enchantment, she suggests, are taken for
granted in most world literatures and have only been 'excluded' from
Western writing in the later half of the twentieth century by 'white male
authors who decided that whatever cannot be controlled doesn't exist'.[50]

Late twentieth-and early twenty-first century narrative, however, has
witnessed a revival of interest in dreams, altered states of perception
and the power of the supernatural. This turn to paranormal and mystic
phenomena is not limited to genre fiction: spectral figures, moments
of miraculous healing and the collision of alternative worlds are at
play in a variety of significant forms of contemporary narrative. The

claustrophobic and indeterminate films of David Lynch, the paranoid worlds of Thomas Pynchon and Don DeLillo and the fiction of Toni Morrison all feature encounters with the ineffable or the unexplained. Brian McHale describes this shift towards the impossible and the magical as part of the 'ontological' dominant of postmodernism: 'What is a world? What kinds of world are there, how are they constituted, and how do they differ? What happens when different kinds of world are placed in confrontation, or when boundaries between worlds are violated?'[51] The 'boundaries between worlds' are frequently violated in Coupland's fiction.

In *Microserfs*, Michael, Dan and Karla's colleague, an aspirant Bill Gates doppelgänger, explains that he is happily losing his ability to distinguish between his waking and 'dream life' (*MS*, p. 128). Dreams, for this single-minded programmer and entrepreneur, become another resource that can be exploited to improve productivity. Similarly, his maverick financial partner, Ethan, claims that '[l]inear thinking is out' (*MS*, p. 165). In a number of Coupland's other novels, however, the disintegration of difference between these two different modes of consciousness is less an economic resource than a vital narrative and aesthetic device. Coupland plays with uncanny repetitions and ambiguous, dreamlike experiences in a number of his novels. In *Eleanor Rigby*, for example, Liz Dunn's first meeting with her estranged son – whom she has not encountered since she gave birth to him in her teens – as he lies unconscious in a hospital bed, is an echo of a traumatic childhood event. At the age of 12, Liz discovered a brutally murdered body by a railway line (*ER*, p. 22). This encounter with the mutilated corpse of a man – clothed in a skirt, lumberjack shirt and make-up – anticipates Liz's initial encounter with Jeremy's unconscious form in the Lions Gate Hospital. The police had found Jeremy, like the murdered transvestite, wearing make-up and lingerie. The echo is both disturbing and comic: Jeremy seems, unconsciously, to be representing his mother's experience; he is not dead, and even the lingerie is a gothic costume rather than a genuinely transgressive statement. For Liz, the reunion with Jeremy 'felt like the fulfillment of a prophecy' (*ER*, p. 31).

These events repeat a motif from Coupland's most uncanny novel, *Girlfriend in a Coma*: most explicitly, Jeremy's near-death experience and unconscious state recalls Karen McNeil's comatose body. Another moment in *Girlfriend in a Coma* uncannily anticipates the plot of *Eleanor Rigby*: as Richard walks around the train tracks near Eagle

Harbour, Vancouver, he imagines 'the possible pulp-fiction thrill' of finding a dead body in the undergrowth (*GIAC*, p. 57). This moment of fictional self-consciousness – the episode in both novels echoes Stephen King's rites-of-passage short story 'The Body' – foreshadows the novel's marked turn to a distinctively postmodern uncanny, a sense of the supernatural that is all too familiar from previous narratives.

The final two-thirds of *Girlfriend in a Coma* might be read as a vision, a lucid dream in which Richard reimagines the world's contingency together with the failures and suffering of his friends as figurative of a larger, more benevolent reality. This end-of-the-world narrative (the theological implications of which are discussed in more detail in Chapter 5) reads rather like a particularly uncanny instance of one of Dag's apocalyptic 'bedtime stories' and echoes that character's account of his breakdown in his mid-twenties when he 'lost the ability to take anything literally': 'All events became omens' (*GX*, p. 36).

Coupland's continuing interest in the delicate distinction between dream-life and reality, represented by an idiom saturated with apocalyptic urgency, are developed in *Life After God*. This element of *Girlfriend in a Coma*, in particular, is anticipated by two specific stories. In 'Patty Hearst', the narrator's brother suggests that, since he already attempts to decipher his dreams, a viable alternative might be to 'interpret . . . everyday life as though *it* were a dream, instead' (*LAG*, p. 258). This counter-intuitive mode of analysis appears to transfigure banal events into signs of grace and consequence. The idea is echoed, still more idiosyncratically, in '1,000 Years (Life After God)', when a friend from the narrator's youth, an unexpected convert to a radical form of Christianity, informs him that during the imminent apocalypse there 'will be great destruction; structures like sky-scrapers and multinational corporations will crumble. Your dream life and your real life will fuse' (*LAG*, p. 298). Dana's vivid and violent description of the coming 'end-times' reads like a prophecy of the novel that was to become *Girlfriend in a Coma*. The latter novel does not need to be rationalized as a dream vision, in the style of William Morris's utopian *News from Nowhere* (1891), to succeed. Indeed, whatever the source of Richard's story, the alternative, visionary landscape made possible in *Girlfriend in a Coma* is a strategy to ask questions about current human behaviour and beliefs. The narrative has little nostalgia for the imagined innocence of the 1970s – the world, it suggests, was equally marked by corruption and greed – and, in the place of longing for an illusory, golden past, the novel suggests that a humane, even miraculous, future might be imagined.

An audacious daydream rationale even informs the documentary mode of *Microserfs*. A vital, if muted, element of the novel is the narrator's struggle to find an idiom through which to write his cultural moment, to represent its specific textures, sensations and mood. Dan, a child of the information age, is fascinated by the aesthetics of surrealism. This Modernist movement, pioneered by André Breton (1896–1966), was energized by Freudian psychoanalysis and a specific emphasis on the wildly irrational and creative forces of the unconscious mind. Such a manifesto ostensibly seems utterly at odds with the journalistic empiricism of *Microserfs* and the banal commercialism – the '*endless*, boring, mad scramble for loot' – of the world that it narrates (*MS*, p. 117). Surprisingly, however, the novel subtly deploys a surrealist narrative strategy to destabilize that confident logic. Susan's claim that much contemporary culture – specifically image-led TV and magazines – provides a depthless mimicry of surrealism without the unifying force of an underlying, albeit fragmented, unconscious mind is tested by Dan in the creation of a 'subconscious' file on his PowerBook (*MS*, pp. 44–5). In this file he stores random phrases, words and ideas; pages littered with these odd (and occasionally revealing) idioms appear, apparently haphazardly, interrupting the realist dynamic of Dan's private narrative. These pages provide a visual echo of the novelist's experiments with hypertext in *Generation X*. Most significantly, however, they are a reminder of the delicate relationship between artifice and spontaneity, cultural hegemony and narrative independence in Coupland's fiction. The pages of 'subconscious' data are structured around an estranging collision of brand names (CNN, Calvin Klein, Microsoft); pop cultural fragments (Han Solo, Ziggy Stardust, Creamsicles) and idiosyncratic, gnomic shards of philosophy ('Cross the uncrossable', *MS*, p. 361). In one sense, *Microserfs* is the first quietly *sur*realist novel to represent an era of hyperreality: the imitation of consciousness promised by new generations of artificial intelligence is dependent on harnessing the unknown, potentially subversive energies of the unconscious mind.

Significantly, Dan and his colleagues, though wary of the manipulative presence of the mass media in their lives, do not view information technology itself as a threat to human identity. Indeed, in a fervent defence of their profession, Karla insists that computer design is both utopian and pragmatic. Furthermore, she claims that carefully calculated code will facilitate the human narrative and prevent it from 'going nonlinear' (*MS*, p. 61). According to this argument, the geek will not only inherit the earth but might save it too. Karla's rhetoric explicitly deploys visionary language: 'We're all of us the fabricators of the human dream's next REM cycle' (*MS*, p. 61). An ambivalent technophilia is at play within the novel. Dan's PowerBook becomes a potent prosthetic that allows him both to tell a story specific to his era and to come to terms with aspects of his still embryonic identity. *Microserfs* emphasizes the more liberating narrative potential of carefully designed software, but in *Life After God* and *Girlfriend in a Coma* reliance on commercial technology is figured as a potentially destructive addiction. Karla's optimism might, in the light of these other narratives, be construed as a naive evasion of the economic and psychological consequences of new technology. Who will benefit from this dream and who will be abandoned or punished by its 'next REM cycle'?

'Legislated nostalgia': commodified time

Despite Coupland's resistance to what McHale calls 'coercive unreality', his novels are also prepared to have fun with aspects of the sit-com seductiveness and artifice of late twentieth- and early twenty-first century life.[52] In *Shampoo Planet*, for example, the ultra-modern sensibility of Tyler Johnson is represented in his kitsch appreciation of the minutiae of pop culture. Tyler is prepared to believe in the therapeutic properties of consumption in the absence of other credible narratives. However, this faith is always bordered by a certain ironic playfulness; his belief is genuine but provisional. The 'Telethon-ese' that Tyler and his girlfriend, Anna-Louise, use to express affection, characterized by the overbearing fake sincerity of TV charity appeals, is symptomatic of a simulated inner life. Coupland's witty and openly acquisitive narrator is intuitively aware that his world is drenched with a counterfeit reality, and this sensation is heightened during moments of intimacy with Anna-Louise and in his brief encounters with a scarred but sublime North American landscape (*SP*, pp. 82–3). The Tyler of *Generation X* – on whom Coupland self-consciously based the narrator of his second novel – tells his older brother that he would abandon his highly conventional, materialist aspirations immediately if he were presented with a 'plausible alternative' (*GX*, p. 173).

Yet *Shampoo Planet* does not promote an 'alternative' authentic version of reality as somehow superior to the chemically enhanced world in which Tyler and his generation must struggle to succeed. The narrator's disappointing reunion with Neil, his biological father, at a decaying hippie commune is followed by extraordinary relief as he drives back into the ordinary, polluted landscape of modern California. Neil's embittered rebuke to his son – 'Young people have no memories. You're unable to mourn the past' – is more than a moment of generational conflict (*SP*, p. 213). The accusation also encodes a schism in the North American mind-set regarding the value of history. This bruising encounter produces no longing for a more wholesome, bohemian past and, indeed, compels Tyler to seek contentment in a technological future: 'Next stop: a pilgrimage to Apple headquarters' (*SP*, p. 216). Coupland would later make his own figurative 'pilgrimage' to the Silicon Valley in *Microserfs*. This first fictional visit, as a young American, born in British Columbia, flees his father's commune, suggests that Coupland's own narrative priorities are more invested in visions of a possible future – however mechanized – than in the utopian dreams of a misplaced counter-culture. It also articulates an incipient apprehension about the future of memory in North American culture.

What compels people in a wealthy contemporary culture to seek solace in a revived, simulated past? 'When the real is no longer what it was', claims Jean Baudrillard, 'nostalgia assumes its full meaning'.[53] Daisy Johnson, unlike her resolutely modern brother, is homesick for a past that she never knew: she and her boyfriend are obsessed with the 1960s, and attempt to recreate the look and sensibility pioneered by her hippie parents and their generation. Tyler describes these virtual time-travellers as 'the McDead': 'The sixties are like a theme park to them. They wear the costume, buy their ticket, and they have the experience' (*SP*, p. 24). Tyler's neologism, a fusion of one of the world's most famous brands and the name of one of the leading rock bands of the counter-culture (The Grateful Dead) typifies Coupland's irreverent approach to American longing for a mythic dissenting past. Indeed, in his non-fiction prose, Coupland is much more explicit in his appraisal of commodified, and sanitized, history.

One of the essays in *Souvenir of Canada*, 'Canada™', reflects on shifts in the nation's consciousness regarding the status of its past: in the last two decades of the twentieth century, Canada's history, he suggests, mutated from 'something taught in schools to becoming something that was processed and sold back to us as a product' (*SOC*, p. 7). Elements of the country's national iconography – or available stereotypes – had previously been marketed to tourists; by the end of the century, he notes, Disney 'was given the franchise to license all RCMP spinoff merchandise' (*SOC*, p. 7):

> We have to watch out, because our reservoir of myths is far smaller and far more fragile than those of some other nations. Once the supplies dry up, they dry up. What happens then is that you start recycling myths, which turn into clichés; and before you know it, history has turned into nothing more than clip art. (*SOC*, p. 7)

This unequivocal emphasis on the value of a 'usable past' – a past that must not be sold off to the most persuasive bidder – renders explicit an approach to nostalgia, and its dangers, that has been at play in Coupland's work since his debut novel. What kind of past is worth recovering? These ideas parallel Fredric Jameson's influential work on the 'nostalgia mode' at work in late twentieth-century consumer cultures. He cites, in particular, George Lucas's evocation of early 1960s youth culture, *American Graffiti* (1973), and more surprisingly, the director's original *Star Wars* trilogy, set long ago in a 'galaxy far, far away' (1977–83). Jameson argues that the latter, apparently futuristic films, with their explicit borrowings from the visual style and storytelling pattern of 1930s movie serials, play on a desire to return to an innocent and optimistic past both for middle-aged spectators and for generations who were born decades later.[54]

Coupland's similar – if less openly materialist – engagement with the subtle seductions of the manufactured past is established in *Generation X*. One of the novel's gnomic slogans claims that 'Nostalgia is a Weapon' (*GX*, p. 175). This ambiguous declaration suggests that nostalgia might be deployed for different political purposes, either to reinforce or to subvert prevailing beliefs. Although these political implications are not pursued in the novel, Coupland emphasizes the stealthy influence of this wistful, nostalgic mood on everyday life. Even the storytelling rituals, born out of resistance to the pressures of consumerist life, bring about a certain longing for a mythic version of reality. In his description of a perfect memory, Andy recalls that he felt 'homesick for the event while it was happening' (*GX*, p. 108). This is the experience of 'Ultra Short Term Nostalgia' or 'Homesickness for the extremely recent past' (*GX*, p. 109).

Daisy, a born-again hippie (who has a distinctly non-bohemian enthusiasm for personal hygiene), might be guilty of what *Generation*

X names 'Now Denial' – a belief that previous or future eras must offer a more significant way of life than the present – and is certainly a victim of 'Legislated Nostalgia', its twin condition (*GX*, p. 47).

This rather sinister neologism denotes the processes at work in popular culture that generate sacred auras around selected moments in history: the past becomes a plastic entity and people are compelled 'to have memories they do not actually possess' (*GX*, p. 47). The concept is developed in the titular short story sequence that begins *Polaroids from the Dead*: set at a series of Grateful Dead concerts held in California, during December 1991, these nostalgia-focused tales explore the slippery connection between memory, narrative belonging and commerce. 'History is cool,' comments one young character, praising a piece of retro-fashion in the opening story, 'The 1960s Are Disneyland' (*PD*, p. 9). This title is only semi-satirical, as are the stories themselves: the sanitized version of the 1960s offered by rejuvenated bohemians, briefly escaping their now all too ordinary lives, might be infantile and fake, but it also offers a point of communal connection largely absent from a contemporary culture that is figured as both isolating and too coldly conformist. The stories are informed by Coupland's ambivalence about this selective, playful resuscitation of the 1960s: there is an ironic awareness that reviving the past is a conservative move that contradicts the spirit of those politicized times; yet, the concerts are also marked by joy. The concluding, mystically inflected story, 'How Clear is Your Vision Of Heaven?' implies a renewed belief in the power of an oral storytelling culture to recover a sense of connection with the past and future.

The phenomenon of 'Legislated Nostalgia' is explored in more detail in *Microserfs*. One of the apparently arbitrary phrases collected in the 'subconscious' file of Dan's PowerBook proclaims that '[t]his is the end of the Age of Authenticity'. Dan and Karla, alarmed by the collision of commerce and memory on television, discuss the ways in which their generation, whose earliest memories might well be of TV, are now subject to not so subtle manipulation by advertisers who have somehow taken possession of their cultural history. Dan observes that television frequently presents 'all of these "moments"' that 'are sponsored by corporations . . . "*This nostalgia flashback was brought to you by the proud makers of Kraft's family of fine foods*"' (*MS*, p. 131). Karla's warning that in the future, time will be replaced by brand names ('They'll just get right to the point and call three o'clock, "Pepsi"') seems prescient, funny and chilling. Dan is similarly concerned that the 'structure of time' has been damaged by the gradual integration of the 'corporate realm' with private memory (*MS*, p. 131). In this depressing vision, time past, present and future becomes another commodity.

By contrast, Michael's optimistic belief that various technologies of memory – including 'books and databases' – have displaced the mess of 'history' is utopian in the extreme (*MS*, p. 253). That Michael's Fukuyama-like thesis is not directly (or convincingly) challenged in the narrative does not necessarily indicate the novelist's tacit endorsement. Coupland's fiction is rarely polemical. However, its patient evocation of the ideas and practices that perpetuate the concept of virtual memory is presented in the narrative context of lives that are muddled, sensual and compellingly vulnerable. Michael is able to theorize (or ventriloquize) an end to history, but his own life – and those of his colleagues – seems to undermine this remote, chilly concept. The romantic or erotic plots that are fulfilled in the novel's final section – as one by one, the previously inhibited, quasi-ascetic programmers are awakened to basic, human desires – suggests that the electronic past and 'Legislated Nostalgia' is less compelling than the ongoing mess of lived experience. The debilitating stroke that Dan's mother suffers is a reminder that history cannot simply be contained or turned into a fetish. For Dan – as for Michael, Bug, Susan, Karla, Todd and Dusty – the virtual world that their company is dedicated to create is displaced by a need to connect with the rude realism of human history.

If the Western world (as well as the West Coast of America) is now a 'laboratory of denarration', Coupland's fiction becomes an equally experimental arena to test the possibility of re-narration (*PD*, p. 180). One of Dan's 'subconscious' slogans states that it is no longer possible to '*create the feeling of an era . . . of time being particular to one spot in time*' (*MS*, p. 75). The lyric voices of confused, 'time sick' narrators like Liz Dunn in *Eleanor Rigby*, naively optimistic diarists such as Daniel Underwood and *Generation X*'s hopeful pioneer, Andy Palmer, embody the attempt to recover this sense of '*time being particular to one spot in time*'. Coupland's negotiation with the traditions of realism – including the documentary modes of *Microserfs*, the hallucinatory fable of modern celebrity in *Miss Wyoming* and the miraculous visions of *Girlfriend in a Coma* – are works in progress or provisional representations of a strange, skewed reality. Contemporary narrative always risks collusion with artificial, commercial stories. Indeed,

Coupland's hesitant representation of consumer culture is the subject of Chapter 3. Yet, for this novelist of the 'accelerated' era, the storytelling act can challenge the insidious processes of 'Legislated Nostalgia' and the grim prospect of trademarked time.

Notes

1 Douglas Coupland, *Polaroids from the Dead* (London: Flamingo, 1997), p. 179. All subsequent references will be given parenthetically as *PD*, followed by page reference.
2 Michel de Certeau, *Culture in the Plural*, translated from the French, *La Culture au Pluriel* (1974) by Tom Conley (Minneapolis: University of Minnesota Press, 1997), pp. 5–6.
3 Terry Eagleton, *After Theory* (London: Penguin, 2004), pp. 16–17.
4 Douglas Coupland, *Generation X: Tales for an Accelerated Culture* (London: Abacus, 1992), p. 9. All subsequent references will be given parenthetically as *GX*, followed by page reference.
5 Douglas Coupland, *Eleanor Rigby* (London: Fourth Estate, 2004), p. 3. All subsequent references will be given parenthetically as *ER*, followed by page reference.
6 Michel de Certeau, *The Practice of Everyday Life*, translated by Steven Rendall (Berkeley: University of California Press, 1984), p. 186. See Graham Ward's valuable exploration of these ideas in *Theology and Contemporary Critical Theory*, second edn (Houndmills: Macmillan, 2000), p. 149 ff and his introduction to the *Certeau Reader*, ed. Graham Ward (Oxford: Blackwell, 2000), pp. 1–14.
7 H. Porter Abbott, *The Cambridge Introduction to Narrative* (Cambridge: Cambridge University Press, 2002), p. 3.
8 For the key discussion of the distinction between *chronos* and *kairos* see Frank Kermode's *The Sense of an Ending: Studies in the Theory of Fiction* (Oxford: Oxford University Press, 1967).
9 Paul Virilio, *The Aesthetics of Disappearance*, translated by Philip Beitchman (New York: Semiotext(e), 1991), p. 105.
10 Zygmunt Bauman, *Intimations of Postmodernity* (London: Routledge, 1992), pp. vii–viii.
11 James Annesley, *Blank Fictions: Consumerism, Culture and the Contemporary American Novel* (London: Pluto Press, 1998), p. 118.
12 Bauman, p. 181.
13 'Most people have lost nostalgia for the lost narrative. It in no way follows that they are reduced to barbarity.' Jean-François Lyotard, *The Postmodern Condition: A Report on Knowledge*, translated by Geoff Bennington and Brian Massumi (Manchester University Press, 1984), p. 17. See also Bauman, p. 38.

14 Quoted by Malcolm Bradbury in *The Modern American Novel* (Oxford: Oxford University Press, 1992), p. 196.

15 Michael Edwards, *Towards a Christian Poetics* (London: Macmillan, 1984), p. 73.

16 Douglas Coupland, *Microserfs* (London: Harper, 2004), p. 4. All subsequent references will be given parenthetically as *MS*, followed by page reference.

17 Douglas Coupland, *Life After God* (London: Simon & Schuster, 1994), p. 321. All subsequent references will be given parenthetically as *LAG*, followed by page reference.

18 Daniel Grassian, *Hybrid Fictions: American Literature and Generation X* (Jefferson: McFarland, 2003), p. 91.

19 Nicholas Blincoe, 'A Modern Master' (Review of *All Families Are Psychotic*), *The New Statesman* (10 September 2001), 52–3.

20 Francis Fukuyama, *The End of History and the Last Man* (London: Penguin, 1992), p. 108.

21 Alan Bilton, *An Introduction to Contemporary American Fiction* (Edinburgh: Edinburgh University Press, 2002), p. 223.

22 Certeau, p. 186.

23 Douglas Coupland, interview with Kim France, *Elle* magazine (September 1993). Reprinted in *The GenX Reader*, ed. by Douglas Rushkoff (New York: Ballantine, 1994), pp. 11–16 (p. 13).

24 Brian McHale, *Postmodernist Fiction* (London: Methuen, 1987), p. 219.

25 Douglas Rushkoff, 'Introduction: Us, by Us', in *The GenX Reader*, ed. by Douglas Rushkoff (New York: Ballantine, 1994), pp. 3–8 (p. 6).

26 See, for example, Terry Eagleton's 'The Politics of Amnesia', chapter 1 of *Life After Theory*.

27 Zygmunt Bauman, *Globalization: The Human Consequences* (Cambridge: Polity, 1998), p. 81.

28 Douglas Coupland, 'Agree/Disagree: 55 Statements About the Culture', *New Republic* (21 August 1995), 213.8/9, 10.

29 Douglas Coupland, *Souvenir of Canada* (Vancouver: Douglas & McIntyre, 2002), p. 131. All subsequent references will be given parenthetically as *SOC*, followed by page reference.

30 Rob Latham, *Consuming Youth: Vampires, Cyborgs, and the Culture of Consumption* (Chicago: University of Chicago Press, 2002), p. 170.

31 Paul Ricoeur, *Time and Narrative*, translated by Kathleen McLaughlin and David Pellauer (Chicago and London: Chicago University Press, 1984), p. 52. Italics are in the original text.

32 Douglas Coupland, *Girlfriend in a Coma* (London: Flamingo, 1998), p. 154. All subsequent references will be given parenthetically as *GIAC*, followed by page reference.

33 Douglas Coupland, *All Families are Psychotic* (London: Flamingo, 2001), p. 71. All subsequent references will be given parenthetically as *AFAP*, followed by page reference.

34 Ian McEwan, *The Child in Time* (London: Vintage, 1992), p. 48.

35 Agnes Heller, 'Where are we at home?', *Thesis Eleven*, 41 (1995). Cited in Zygmunt Bauman, *Globalization: The Human Consequences* (Cambridge: Polity, 1998), p. 90.

36 Michael Brockington, 'Five Short Years: Half a Decade of Douglas Coupland' www.sfu.ca/~brocking/writing/couplong.html (7 October 2005).

37 Virilio, p. 105.

38 Caren Irr, 'From Nation to Generation: The Economics of North American Culture, 1930s–1990s', *Canadian Review of American Studies*, 27.1 (1997), 135–44 (137–8).

39 Certeau (1984), p. 186.

40 Douglas Coupland, *Shampoo Planet* (London: Simon & Schuster, 1993), p. 176. All subsequent references will be given parenthetically as *SP*, followed by page reference.

41 Donna Tartt, *The Secret History* (London: Penguin, 1992), p. 5.

42 Ibid., p. 9.

43 Jean Baudrillard, *Simulacra and Simulation*, translated by Sheila Faria Glaser (Ann Arbor: University of Michigan Press, 1994), p. 6.

44 Jefferson Faye, 'Canada in a Coma', *The American Review of Canadian Studies*, 31.3 (2001), 501–10 (504).

45 Douglas Coupland, *Miss Wyoming* (London: Flamingo, 2000), p. 48. All subsequent references will be given parenthetically as *MW*, followed by page reference.

46 Blincoe, p. 53.

47 Jim Finnegan, 'Theoretical Tailspins: Reading "Alternative" Performance in *Spin* Magazine', in *GenXegesis: Essays on Alternative Youth Culture*, ed. by John M. Ulrich and Andrea L. Harris (Madison: University of Wisconsin Press, 2003), pp. 121–61 (p. 128). Finnegan's 'ideological' critique of Coupland emphasizes the novelist's apparent inability to locate his own work in an historical, counter-cultural tradition.

48 Mark Forshaw, 'Douglas Coupland: In and Out of "Ironic Hell"', *Critical Survey*, 12.3 (2000), 39–58 (39). 'Knee-Jerk Irony', included in Coupland's marginalia, is defined as 'The tendency to make flippant ironic comments as a reflexive matter of course in everyday conversation' (*GX*, p. 174).

49 Blincoe, p. 53.

50 Peter Lewis, 'Making Magic', *The Independent* (3 April 1993), 24–6 (26). Quoted in Linden Peach, *Toni Morrison* (Houndmills: Macmillan, 1995), p. 12.

51 McHale, p. 10.
52 Ibid., p. 219.
53 Baudrillard, p. 6.
54 Fredric Jameson, *The Cultural Turn: Selected Writings on the Post-modern, 1983–98* (London: Verso, 1998), pp. 7–10.

3

'I am not a target market': Coupland, consumption and junk culture

> Let me describe the real estate that remains one year after the world ended
> . . . Theater screens fray and unravel like overworn shirts. Endless cars
> and trucks and minivans sit on road shoulders harboring cargoes of rotted
> skeletons behind the wheel. Homes across the world collapse and fall
> inward on themselves; pianos, couches and microwaves tumble through
> floors . . . Most foods and medicines have time-expired . . . Cathedrals
> fall as readily as banks; car assembly lines as readily as supermarkets.[1]
> (*Girlfriend in a Coma*, 1998)

Douglas Coupland is captivated by rubbish, its possible uses and its
plural connotations. Motifs of household garbage, environmental
pollution and technological junk are everywhere in his fiction and
visual art – the substance of his work is frequently constructed from
broken things, forgotten concepts, obsolete inventions and the many
'time-expired', disposable items that we routinely ditch. In his 'Canada
House' exhibition (2003; 2004–5), for example, a number of sculptures
incorporate salvaged odds and ends – discarded tin cans, plastic bottles,
food packaging, shreds of clothing, broken buoys and the assorted,
shop-worn treasures of the tenacious beachcomber – all of which are
redeployed to form new aesthetic objects.[2] Similarly, images of wrecked
technology, disintegrating architecture and dead 'real estate' give shape
to a dream of civilization's end in *Girlfriend in a Coma*. The dystopian
vision of decay and corrosion shared by Jared, the novel's ghostly
co-narrator, imparts a recurrent anxiety about the transience of culture.
Cathedrals with their spires reaching toward eternity, the most visible
souvenirs of a theologically oriented era, are just as ephemeral as the
consciously fleeting pleasures of celluloid or shopping.

Yet this prophetic story of societal decay also exemplifies James B.
Twitchell's claim that 'Garbage has become mythic' in the Western

imagination: rubbish is somehow both repellent and sacred; it reveals hidden stories about our relationship to the material and the transcendent, to space and time.[3] Remnants of this fictional disintegrated society, carefully itemized by Jared like holy relics, are simultaneously signifiers of contemporary materialism and poignant reminders of humanity's capacity to make things and stories, to define itself as a species via creativity. The sepulchral narrator, who died at the end of the 1970s before he or his friends could truly lose their sense of youthful innocence, is sombre, impish and nostalgic. The pictures of a ruined, silent future – a possible outcome of the speeded-up, permanent present tense of today – act as negative photographic shots of our contemporary world dominated by incessant movement, unthinking consumption and the constant generation of refuse.

This chapter explores Coupland's ambiguous representation of consumption with particular reference to his evolving, and idiosyncratic, fascination with rubbish; waste is a vital and ethically complex category in his fictional aesthetic. Indeed, the novelist's work resonates with the founding concept of Don DeLillo's *Underworld* (1998), that 'waste is the secret history, the underhistory' of civilization.[4] If the turn to rampant consumerism is a given for novelists of the contemporary West – 'There's a truth that you won't get to if you ignore consumption,' claims Coupland – so too must fiction come to terms with the consequential proliferation of waste.[5] In her polemical account of the 'Hidden Life of Garbage', Heather Rogers presents a horrifying description of the 'phantasmagoric rush of spent, used and broken riches' that 'flows through our homes, offices and cars, and from there is burned, dumped at sea, or more often buried under a civilized veil of dirt and grass seed'.[6] Similar visions of detritus and environmental chaos haunt Coupland's narration of the most superficially pristine cultures. Indeed, the bold title of one of the short stories in *Polaroids from the Dead* (1996) – 'You Are Afraid of the Smell of Shit' – symbolizes the distinctively modern desire to sanitize, or erase, all reminders of excess or decadence from civilization's surface.

Chapter 2 examined the writer's engagement with commodified time and the manipulative, consumer-led phenomenon of 'Legislated Nostalgia'.[7] This chapter focuses on Coupland's interpretation of the practices and unconscious habits of mind that surround contemporary commercial activity. Andy Palmer, Coupland's first narrator, reflects that he and his friends were once afflicted by 'compulsions that made us confuse shopping with creativity' (*GX*, p. 14). Yet, we might ask, does Coupland's fiction suffer from the same affliction? Can a body of writing that resolutely focuses on the delights and dissatisfactions of consumer culture be anything other than complicit in its continuing influence? Jefferson Faye's claim that Coupland's first four novels illuminate 'the singular angst resulting from the inescapable sensory dominance of "American commercial culture"' evades the issue of these novels' simultaneous appreciation of the benefits of living within such a culture.[8]

Coupland's work displays a genuine ambivalence about consumerism and the pursuit of wealth in the Western imagination. '[O]ne can just as easily imagine him attending an anti-capitalist rally as shopping in a designer goods store,' notes Alan Bilton.[9] From one perspective, *Generation X* (1991), *Microserfs* (1995) and *Girlfriend in a Coma* read like postmodern jeremiads against the excesses of the age, prompted by loathing for a mindless and corrupt commodity culture. Yet the novels cannot conceal a distinct sense of thrill at some of the novelties and enticements that such a way of life might generate; the narratives also seem to endorse a tactile appreciation for made things. Coupland's work certainly displays revulsion for what he names the 'grey, soulless mist falling over the world, turning everything into either a sweatshop or a generic cultureless discount highway mall'.[10] The narratives, however, are energized by a sense that Western culture – despite its corruptions – is not an entirely bankrupt civilization. Indeed, most of Coupland's novels demonstrate a keen awareness and moral ambivalence regarding what one character describes as 'the excitement and glamour and seduction of progress' (*GIAC*, p. 280). Uncertainty generates morally and aesthetically complex fiction rather than foreclosed anti-capitalist manifestos.

This chapter is organized around three distinct phases in the cycle of consumption. The first section focuses on Coupland's evocation of consumer culture. It engages with contemporary theories and histories of Western consumption in relation to key motifs in Coupland's writing. The argument traces the writer's multiple – and sometimes contradictory – images of expenditure and the processes of desire that define consumption.

Postmodern popular wisdom seems to assume, rather hazily, that consumerism – vaguely considered to be a bad thing – is a very recent social phenomenon that commenced some time between Ronald Reagan's first photo call in the Oval Office at the dawn of the 1980s, and the publication of Naomi Klein's anti-corporate report, *No Logo*, in 2000. Yet the claim that we live in 'a consumer society' must, as Zygmunt Bauman observes, be 'more than the trivial observation that all members of that society consume' because 'all human beings, and, moreover, all living creatures, have been "consuming" since time immemorial'.[11] Examining the linguistic origins and social connotations of the term 'consumption', one group of commentators notes that 'paradoxically . . . "consumption" means both "destroying" (using up) and "creating" (making full use of)' and can 'be thought of as a "form of creative destruction"'. Despite this fundamental ambivalence, these critics conclude that 'consumption probably remains semantically closer to consumerism than it does to (mere) subsistence; tied to abundance and affluence rather than to dearth and scarcity'.[12] Does Coupland offer a clear moral or economic critique of Western greed and commodity fetishism? Are novels such as *Shampoo Planet* (1992) and *Microserfs*, replete with their characters' habitual allusions to brand names coupled with keen financial ambition, guilty of political quietism?

The second and third sections explore the *afterlife* of objects: the first of these focuses on Coupland's narratives of disposal. The quotidian activity of dumping unwanted material dominates his novels: objects, people, identities and ideas are routinely thrown away, and this section explores these intricate images of abandoned things. Yet gradual decomposition in a burgeoning landfill is rarely the ultimate destination for rubbish in Coupland's writing. The final section considers the trope of recycling – of rubbish reborn – in which abandoned, broken and exhausted objects are transfigured into something new and powerful.

'Shopping is not creating': the consumer experience

In *Generation X*, Dag offers a memorably repugnant personification of contemporary culture as a consumer insouciantly gorging on its own faeces. 'Marketing,' he states is 'about feeding the poop back to diners fast enough to make them think they're still getting real food.' This modern form of alchemy is, in his words, 'not creation, really, but theft, and *no one* ever feels good about stealing' (*GX*, p. 33). The dubious science of sales depends on the maintenance of an invisible cycle, the implications of which most consumers, he suspects, are happily oblivious. Consumption, excretion and reconsumption are disguised by the fraud of advertising as something pure, new and original. Yet bodily waste, synthetically effaced from everyday transactions, is an inescapable element of popular culture. The parasitic relationship between creativity and 'theft' identified in Dag's rites-of-passage tale embodies an ethical distaste for excess and exploitation, both visceral and rationalized, that informs Coupland's work as a whole. However, the story of Dag's unconversion from the 'taint that marketing' had bestowed on him encodes the novel's underlying ambivalence regarding the consumer economy (*GX*, p. 33).

Narrating his gradual but resolute rejection of a life determined by greed, Dag remembers that as an affluent young executive he positively loved the 'thrill of power to think that most manufacturers of lifestyle accessories in the Western world considered me their most desirable target market' (*GX*, p. 22). *Generation X* does not simply pretend that consumption is the preserve of faceless corporations: Dag, by his own admission, was happily hoodwinked. His superficially exhilarated sensation of personal empowerment sponsored by the iridescent promises of advertising resonates with David Lyon's argument that in an advanced capitalist culture: 'identities are constructed through consuming. Forget the idea that who we are is given by God or achieved through hard work in a calling or a career; we shape our malleable image by what we buy – our clothing, our kitchens, and our cars tell the story of who we are (becoming).'[13]

Dag's refusal to collude any longer with this imperative, however, does not derive solely from pure political motives. The vicious argument between this twenty-something and his once idealistic boss – a man whose pony-tail is a reminder of his countercultural past but who has evidently long since lost the liberal values that he held in the 1960s – is characterized by Dag's witty and astute socio-economic analysis but it is also shaped by more selfish interests. The younger man is primarily angry that his own generation has not benefited from the accident of history – the 'genetic lottery' – that apparently gifted the so-called 'baby boomer', post-Second World War age group so much wealth (*GX*, p. 26).

'I am Not a Target Market' is the defensive title of the chapter in which Dag narrates his unconversion. Paradoxically, however, this symptom of generational antipathy for slick advertising inspired a paradigm shift within the marketing industry. In *Marketing to Generation X* (1995) – a title without a hint of irony – Karen Ritchie implores her colleagues to re-evaluate the potential of this generation of 'cautious consumers, cost-conscious shoppers, and skeptical audiences for advertising'.[14] '[M]arketers,' she suggests, 'have under-estimated the importance of Generation X as consumers'; as a demo-graphic, this unknown group 'dislike *hype*' rather than 'advertising'.[15] Is Coupland's debut novel simply a generational complaint aimed at an industry that fails to respect the intelligence of people born after 1960?

The post-corporate identity that Dag takes on – as a long-haired 'Basement' person who wears ethnic dress, eats lentils and discusses Latin American literature – should represent a complete reversal of desire culture (*GX*, p. 33). Yet this literally subcultural world is no less codified, and no more authentic, than the corporate sphere that he has fled: both fields derive their character from patterns of consumption – Dag merely substitutes the ostentatious symbols of career success for superficial signifiers of recreational dissidence. Coupland's narrative anticipates Ritchie's thesis but suggests that advertising, in whatever guise, is a coercive and conformist phenomenon. Yet his fiction frequently tests the boundaries between commercial viability and rebellion. 'At what point along the road to commercial success does a countercultural statement lose its integrity, its ability to generate real resistance to dominant culture?' asks Leslie Haynsworth. Citing the promisingly seditious energies of Coupland's writing and best-selling politicized punks Green Day, Haynsworth identifies the re-emergence of a long-standing question: 'Is it possible to be subversive from within the system?'[16] The capacity of a free-market economy to exploit new and potentially subversive art forms is seemingly limitless. This idea surfaces in *Microserfs* as part of Susan's discussion of René Magritte and early-twentieth-century painting's exploration of the subconscious: she claims, 'if Surrealism was around today, "It'd last ten minutes and be stolen by ad agencies to sell long-distance calls and aerosol cheese products"'.[17] Similarly, in the self-consciously 'Gen X' movie *Reality Bites* (1994), Lelania Price's experimental video diary is turned into a crass sequence of micro-narratives on MTV sponsored by Pizza Hut.

This sense that generational identity itself has become a sly marketing scam is pursued in *Girlfriend in a Coma*: Linus, the novel's Transcendentalist *manqué*, regards the whole phenomenon of self-fashioning supposedly afforded by capitalism as bogus: 'Nobody believes the identities we've made for ourselves. I feel like everybody in the world is fake now' (*GIAC*, p. 82). Dag and Linus's shared suspicion of identity politics parallels Naomi Klein's argument that for those belonging to a rather nebulous 1990s youth culture – a group that might include teenagers and people on the cusp of their thirties – 'generational identity' had become 'a pre-packaged good'; for these young people, 'the search for self had always been shaped by marketing hype, whether or not they believed it or defined themselves against it'.[18] Describing her own adolescent ennui, Klein suggests that, in a consumer economy, rebellion always seems second-hand or appropriated, one's 'alterna-groove' borrowed from 'the secondhand bookstore, dusty and moth-eaten and done to death'.[19] Dag's provisional, equally spurious countercultural identity is the prelude to recognition that a quieter, more radical solution is required: the result is his migration to Palm Springs and the birth of the storytelling community. This narrative of personal transformation – from rampant consumerism to desert asceticism – embodies the strange interplay in the Western mind between hedonist and Puritan impulses.

A central issue in contemporary culture, as the editors of *The Consumption Reader* have argued, is the question of how 'the self-sacrifice and asceticism of the Protestants, whose work ethic defined the very spirit of capitalism' eventually 'mutate[d] into the kind of self-indulgent quest for gratification that underpins modern consumerism'.[20] Colin Campbell – whose ground-breaking study, *The Romantic Ethic and the Spirit of Modern Consumerism* (1987), has contributed to the shape of such debates – insists on the 'primary' historical connection between Puritan thought and pleasure-seeking cultures: the 'outright hostility to the "natural" expression of emotion' embodied in militant Protestant practice, he suggests, had the paradoxical upshot of helping to stimulate the 'split between feeling and action which hedonism requires'.[21] In *Generation X*, Tobias – an unrepentantly wealthy gatecrasher into Andy, Dag and Claire's peaceful world – embodies this hedonistic 'split between feeling and action'. Tobias wanders into the narrative as if from some other novel or film of the period: he has more in common with the yuppie colleagues of Bud Fox or Sherman McCoy from *Wall Street* (1988) and *Bonfire of the Vanities* (1989), or one of Patrick Bateman's dining companions (and future victims) in *American Psycho* (1989). Like Bret Easton Ellis's serial killer, Tobias, according to Andy, is 'smug', 'bland' and 'trades on [a] mask' (*GX*, p. 91). For all his crass materialism, however, Coupland allows this superficial individual a moment of narrative redemption in his own defining 'memory of Earth' (*GX*, pp. 104, 109). Andy and his dissatisfied friends are naive but the plot never punishes them for making a principled choice to reject affluence, whereas the shallow Tobias is expelled from the narrative. In some senses, the smart New Yorker is a doppelgänger for both Dag and Andy: he is actively sexual whereas Dag and Andy are – despite their own brief and ambiguous kiss – either repressed or abstemious. Tobias's pursuit of pleasure is unprincipled but, according to the logic of consumption, it is also perfectly rational, and in other contemporary narratives his behaviour would appear mundane.

The movement from Puritan self-denial to hedonist self-gratification frequently plays out in reverse in Coupland's narratives. In *Miss Wyoming* (2000), for example, John Johnson – a man bearing the most generic name possible – gradually recognizes that the incongruous financial 'rewards' harvested by his Hollywood movies are part of 'the delirium of excess' at the centre of contemporary life.[22] Johnson is certainly not immune to the seductions of his world – prostitutes, drugs and absurdly expensive houses are part of his daily experience – but, like Dag, his sudden revulsion from over-indulgence does not result in a more moderate lifestyle. Rather than reaching a compromise or accommodation with the culture, he rejects it absolutely. This vacillation between the ostensible binary oppositions of profligate indulgence and rigid, austere self-discipline might belong to an idiosyncratically American conception of consumption. 'Consume or die,' claims Jesse Detwiler in DeLillo's *Underworld*, is 'the mandate of the culture. And it all ends up in the dump.'[23] Clarke, Doel and Housiaux suggest that the most significant shift in patterns of consumer behaviour was brought about when 'consumption gradually freed itself from being functionally tied to 'needs' and 'necessities' to assume its distinctive character and purpose – propelled, above all else, by its own intrinsic *pleasurability*'.[24] 'Pleasure', like consumption itself, engenders a range of contradictory ideas in cultural debate: desire tempered by guilt, contentment undermined by dissatisfaction, and excess to disguise a sensation of lack are some of the crucial, mutually hostile pairings associated with the pursuit of gratification. 'The country with the highest per capita consumer debt and the greatest number of machine-made things,' states Twitchell, 'is the same country in which Puritan ascetic principles are most pronounced and held in highest regard.' Invoking the ghost of Henry David Thoreau, Twitchell notes that today's Puritan-Romantics, looking for solitude at Walden Pond, are likely to 'pack the sport utility vehicle with the dish antenna, the cell phone, the bread maker, the ashtray, the paddle ball'.[25]

An inverse image of John Johnson's born-again, rigid Puritan self-control is presented in *All Families are Psychotic* (2001). In a shabby Florida diner, the novel's oddest character, Florian, orders everything from the menu, informing the bemused waiter that his request is reasonable: 'Steven, my boy, having lots of fat people eating a lot of fattening food is a good, *good* thing for America.'[26] Excess, according to Florian's cartoon European decadent view, is not America's guilty secret but its function; intemperance means 'happiness and joy for all. Fatness ripples through the entire economy in a tsunami of prosperity' (*AFAP*, p. 234). Janet Drummond – the level-headed, moral conscience of the novel and a counterpoint to Florian's excess – reflects that living in a time of plenty, free from war and the depredations of poverty, has not made her now adult children particularly wise or perceptive: 'A life of abundance had turned her two boys into an element other than gold – lead? – silicon? – bismuth?' (*AFAP*, p. 2). This motif of reverse alchemy echoes Dag's scatological interpretation of marketing as an industry founded on the recycling of 'poop'.

Florian, by contrast, heir to a fortune made in the pharmaceutical industry, depends on a culture of self-destructive pleasure-seeking to proliferate his financial standing. Yet he cannot escape the illusory world of commodity fetishism. A comic sub-plot – and a possible allusion to Edgar Allan Poe's classic short story 'The Purloined Letter' (1844) – is set in motion by his idiosyncratic Anglophile desire to secure a sealed letter addressed to 'Mummy', that may or may not have been stolen from the coffin of the Princess of Wales. Florian's sentimental desire for a piece of private correspondence resonates with Jean Baudrillard's description of 'the consecrated ideology of consumption' in which the 'rapturous satisfactions' of the consumer experience 'cling ... to objects as if to the sensory residues of the previous day in the delirious excursion of a dream'.[27] This bizarre conspiracy takes on a 'delirious' logic, and the competitive folly that Coupland orchestrates around this apparently unique document is a heightened version of senseless consumer capitalism. Similarly, in *Miss Wyoming*, Marilyn's fanatical consumption is represented as a kind of delirium: she 'spent like a drunk in a casino gift shop ... she simply thrilled with the burst of power each time a piece of loot that once belonged to somebody else suddenly belonged to *her*' (*MW*, p. 285).

Coupland's writing does not ignore the bizarre trend of 'retail therapy' or 'shopping as leisure'. Bug, who possesses the most cynical voice in the extended *Microserfs* family, reflects that 'you can put *any*thing on a label and people will believe it. We are one sick species' (*MS*, p. 84). In his 'Postcard from the former East Berlin (Circus Envy)', one of the wistful 1990s epistles included in *Polaroids from the Dead*, Coupland suggests that the defining political question for the West at the end of the twentieth century emerged from dissatisfaction with consumer culture: 'What is it we can . . . desire now that things, objects – *stuff* – has failed us?'[28] As a mildly guilt-ridden, middle-class *flâneur* wandering the streets of the recently reunified city, a space that once symbolized the violent split between communist and capitalist regimes, Coupland encounters the resentments of those living in the former East who have not been 'nourished' by the novel experience of free-market consumption. The mundane act of buying the '*new R.E.M. album*', from the kind of music superstore that would not have existed in the district five years earlier, becomes a metaphor for post-cold war uncertainty regarding global culture and the price of freedom (*PD*, p. 90). The name of the band whose new album Coupland wanted to buy is significant: REM is a description of dream sleep and, in this evocation of a culture clash, the name becomes a subtle signifier of the American dream. The postcard narrates the reconfiguration of 'former ideological showplace' architecture – the era of socialist modernity – as it collides with the postmodern architecture of theme restaurants and luxury hotels (*PD*, p. 90). Motifs of detritus – this time ruined and recycled buildings – again dominate the narrative. Coupland faces a dilemma – one shared by many Westerners frustrated with the excesses and waste generated by the free market – regarding what he suggests is the 'hollowness' that lies at the 'core' of a society that defines itself solely around purchase power (*PD*, p. 92). The beast image in the postcard from East Berlin recalls – perhaps consciously – Yeats's apocalyptic poem 'The Second Coming' (1921).

Can 'new models of desire' – forms of aspiration that are creative, rewarding and liberating – be manufactured as an alternative to mere shopping (*PD*, p. 93)? The writer recognizes that 'the dream of consumption' is not sustainable but neither does his work propose the revival of communism as a viable alternative. Social historians recognize that there is a palpable difference between the productive, labour-intensive era inhabited by our nineteenth- and early twentieth-century ancestors and the 'post-industrial' moment of the early twenty-first century. That shift, for Bauman and others, is primarily determined by the alternative roles that people in these two (broadly defined) eras have been required to perform: where our ancestors were expected, primarily, to be 'producers' – members of a vast industrial workforce – the most pressing social obligation for dwellers in today's world is to enact 'the role of the consumer': 'The norm our society holds up to its members is that of the ability and willingness to play it.'[29] It is very easy to denounce such a society – to rail against the manipulative, monolithic reach of advertising and the deceptions of brand culture – but far harder to find an alternative way of life, free from corporate influence or the seductions of capitalist life. This is the world in which Douglas Coupland's novels are situated – the plots take place principally in the same year that they were written or published, and his characters' memories rarely reach back earlier than the late 1960s or early 1970s – and the dilemmas of his key characters tend to be those that living in such a time generates. As one of the young coders in *Microserfs* reflects: 'we're rapidly approaching a world composed entirely of jail and shopping' (*MS*, p. 261). Yet do Coupland's novels challenge, actively or implicitly, this hybrid carceral/commercial logic? Is the unconscious message of these fictions one of political nihilism?

If *Generation X* seems to advocate withdrawal from mainstream culture, *Shampoo Planet* might, superficially, be read as a celebration of consumer appetite. The pleasure that Tyler, the ultra-modern narrator, derives from talking about his favourite merchandise might fuel concerns that Coupland, like Bret Easton Ellis, is obsessed with the surface details of consumerism at the expense of more substantial narrative concerns. Tyler's passion for style rather than substance seems to resonate with the image-obsessed nation evoked in Jean Baudrillard's postmodern travelogue, *America* (1988): 'You wonder whether the world itself isn't just here to serve as advertising copy in some other world.'[30] However, in place of the excess of 'real' world commodities, corporate logos and gossip about minor celebrities that were available to the writer, the novel revels in the fabrication of imagined brands, fake products and imitation movie stars. Tyler is an expert on 'designer knock-off merchandise': his car and trip to Europe were both funded by his brief, lucrative trade in fake brand goods.[31] The novel's riot of manufactured trademarks – including hair care products named PsycoPath® and Monk-On-Fire® – prevents *Shampoo Planet* from descending into an exercise in literary product placement, and underlines its incipient anxieties about a simulated world (*SP*, p. 7). Tyler is caught between the possession-free ideals of his mother's hippie generation and a desire to succeed according to the materialistic rules of contemporary culture; he is aware that he must live in the present rather than an idealized past. He is also sensitive to the human capacity for squandering prosperity. Indeed, suspicion of the novel's apparent collusion with laissez-faire politics is undermined by its subtle evocation of the end of the Reagan era. Although this Zeitgeist-embracing narrator is too young to have the historical knowledge or critical vocabulary to offer a political critique, his lyrical reflections on early 1990s America are marked with a sense of loss and longing: 'We had plenty, and we blew it. I guess human beings just weren't cut out for plenty. Well, *most* human beings. *I* sure am, but where did plenty go?' (*SP*, p. 145).

Microserfs is similarly shaped by the legacy of so-called 'Reaganomics' and the rise of powerful corporations. The title itself is an *Adbusters*-style reappropriation of one of the most famous brand names of the globalized era, suggesting subversive intent. Microsoft, the narrator reflects, is either 'the foundry of our culture's deepest dreams' or, in a more sceptical mode, simply 'a great big office supply company' (*MS*, pp. 3, 35). However, the narrative constitutes Coupland's most politically ambivalent, morally complex work to date. Todd, the youngest of Daniel Underwood's co-workers and housemates, a uniquely body-conscious programmer – whose intensely religious upbringing and attraction to moral or political absolutes are discussed in Chapter 5 – is gifted some of the most significant, if accidentally arrived-at, philosophical insights in the novel. Casually flexing his muscles as he gazes at a TV screen that carries only the snowy haze of a disconnected signal, he unexpectedly reflects that there 'has to be more to existence than . . . "*Dominating as many broad areas of automated consumerism as possible*"' (*MS*, p. 60). This moment of near epiphany, related amidst the ambient noise of modern entertainment technology, symbolizes the difficulty that Coupland's younger characters experience in constructing the personal convictions that they hope might give life a meaningful shape or a sense of purpose. Todd, apparently a roguish sensualist, is surprisingly sensitive to a bigger socio-economic picture than that conveyed by life at Microsoft's Redwood campus.

Rob Latham isolates Todd's ominous concept of '*automated consumerism*' as fundamental to Coupland's critique of corporate America. The novelist's narration of the tide of social change precipitated by commerce is not exclusively dystopian – in vital instances, such as Mrs Underwood's post-stroke rehabilitation, new technology is identified as a possible force for enlightenment and amelioration – but his fiction, from *Generation X* onwards, is concerned with the ways in which 'this sinister regime' of perpetual electronic advertising' ensures that 'the deepest private responses of consumers are synthetically programmed'.[32] Todd is aware of his complicity in generating software that will simply extend the influence of an already pervasive brand but, like many of Coupland's characters before him, he is unsure how to disentangle his life from the seductive – and potentially pioneering – sphere of commercial technology. Does a viable political alternative to the entrepreneurial but financially alienated world of Bill Gates exist?

The ambivalence of Todd's worldview – trapped between stereotypical 1990s youth culture appetites and a yearning for the transcendent – echoes the split sensibilities of Tyler in *Shampoo Planet*. In Todd's unpredictable search for the point at which '*morality* enter[s] our lives', Coupland explores a 'deep-seated need to believe in something' that inflects a generation who were supposed to be content with a secular utopia of prosperity and classless social ease (*MS*, p. 60).

However, Todd and Dusty's brief embrace of a range of Marxist and anti-capitalist ideologies is neither taken seriously by their friends and co-workers at their new, supposedly more democratic start-up company, nor, we might suspect, by Coupland himself. This engagement with political ideals is sincere but ephemeral and, by the novel's conclusion, has been quietly forgotten. Indeed, despite an antipathy for unbridled consumerism, the politics of protest are rarely taken seriously in Coupland's fiction. Actively political figures are uncommon and, when they do appear, their conduct is represented neither as heroic nor as likely to bring about substantial social change. In *All Families are Psychotic*, for example, Bryan and Shw, two of the novel's most psychologically damaged individuals, meet in Seattle 'during the World Trade Organization riots': 'She helped Bryan set fire – I believe – to a stack of pastel colored waffle-knit T-shirts in a Gap . . . then a few months ago they met again destroying a test facility growing genetically modified runner beans' (*AFAP*, p. 8).

Despite Coupland's implied scepticism about the value and motivation of radical social action, *Microserfs*, in particular, features a more subtle critique of consumer culture than would be possible in a clear-cut manifesto. One recurrent focus is the way in which powerful corporations are in the process of rewriting time as another commodity. The implications of this temporal shift for narrative are discussed in Chapter 2. In terms of the present focus, however, a number of Coupland's novels display ambivalence about the phenomenon of leisure time. In *Microserfs*, Dan notes that 'we *all* have so much free time now' between 'product group assignment[s]'. He and his colleagues 'sit around . . . feeling deflated and just plain exhausted. We forget about clock- and calendar-type time completely'. Todd muses on the alarming prospect of 'internal clocks' set 'to *product cycles*': 'We got nostalgic about the old days, back when September meant the unveiling of new car models and TV shows' (*MS*, p. 55).

This phoney or 'Legislated Nostalgia' is not merely for another phase of the commercial or commodified era but for one in which a sense of time had not entirely evaporated. In *Generation X*, before Dag quits his job and junior yuppie lifestyle, he has a conversation with an older colleague who reflects that the 'only reason we all go to work in the morning is because we're terrified of what would happen if we *stopped*. "We're not built for free time as a species. We think we are, but we aren't"' (*GX*, pp. 28–9). Similarly, Reg Klaasen, the final narrator of *Hey Nostradamus!* (2003), and ostensibly Coupland's least sympathetic character, reflects that in his harsh, puritanical childhood, he 'was raised to believe that the opposite of labor is theft, not leisure'.[33] Surprisingly, Coupland has identified this austere position as his own, using identical words to the melancholy, broken Reg. In response to the question, 'What makes you most happy?' he states: 'Working. The opposite of labour is theft. Leisure is just a cheesy marketing ploy.'[34] Coupland's own attitude to work, consumption and time is ambivalent: in his fiction, labour with a more personal purpose – art, non-corporate software engineering or running a small hotel in Mexico, for example – is represented as valuable, even when it necessarily includes a compromise with a pernicious economic system.

The central characters in *Microserfs* are all aware that, increasingly, identity is being predicated by the whims of a few powerful corporations – including, presumably, Microsoft – and Interiority, as a company, is an alternative to life within that world. Consumption is supposed to define identity – to generate playful and liberating difference but, as Karla reflects, the reverse appears to be true: 'Everybody looks so Gappy and identical' (*MS*, p. 146). The semiotics of clothes from Gap is a frequent topic of conversation: this focus both dates the novel and turns its potential political critique away from a vague humanism to a more specific concern about the insidious power of brands to reconfigure time, place and identity: 'We . . . figured that Gap clothing isn't about *place*, nor is it about *time*, either', reflects Dan.

In an age when 'diversity' is championed – and consumer freedom is ostensibly the mechanism for defending a multi-cultural civilization – the major brands seem to shrewdly erase distinctiveness. Clothes from a store with a global market like Gap 'allow you to look like you're from nowhere in particular, it also allows you to look as though you're not particularly from the *present,* either' (*MS*, p. 269). When all but one of the coders admits to sporting at least one item of Gap clothing during their earnest deconstruction of the brand, Dan invokes a semi-ironic image of 'the hungry jaw of bar-code industrialism' and his fears of a 'McNuggetized' future, though there is no suggestion that he plans to fight against this featureless, commercial world (*MS*, p. 270).

These anxieties about brand blandness are explored with a more political edge in Coupland's non-fiction. In 'Nowhere = Anywhere', one of the short essays in *Souvenir of Canada* (2002), Coupland reflects on the incursion of American brand goods into other cultures (for example, he notes that it 'is astonishingly difficult to assemble a pile of purely Canadian goods'). He writes about a visit to Chile where he was shocked to encounter a country that had been 'culturally gutted', and found that it was apparently impossible to buy anything not made in 'an American branch plant' and that 'while it's evil to not wish abundance for your fellow man, Santiago had the sci-fi texture of a land where a ghastly price had been extracted in return for effortless plenty. In the case of Chile, I think it was its sense of itself, which is just plain sad' (*SOC*, p. 78). This antipathy for 'corrosive colonization' raises questions about the ways in which identity and difference are produced. Does it matter if consumer products are the same the world over? '[T]here is something deeply wrong with a place where nothing for sale is *from* there' (*SOC*, p. 78). 'All of us are doomed to the life of choices,' argues Zygmunt Bauman, 'but not all of us have the means to be choosers.'[35] Coupland's fiction focuses on those who, for the most part, 'have the means to be choosers' but who are profoundly unsatisfied with a world 'composed entirely of jail and shopping' (*MS*, p. 261).

'Deletia': The afterlife of objects (I)

'I'm interested in objects that people no longer want,' reflected Coupland in an interview that was published under the headline, 'Why is Douglas Coupland fascinated by garbage?'[36] This concern with the afterlife of objects – as well as the ethereal future of human beings –

is vital to his engagement with the seductions, possibilities and limits of contemporary consumerist culture. The spectre of rubbish haunts the literal and figurative landscape of Coupland's fiction. In *Generation X*, Dag gives Claire a mysterious jar of green sand from the deserts of New Mexico: the beautiful jade crystals are, in fact, potentially radioactive residues from an early nuclear test site. This bizarre gift – accidentally smashed on the floor of Claire's room – is emblematic of a contemporary world that is structured from increasingly trash-dominated, polluted landscapes. 'Plastics Never Disintegrate' is the title of a later chapter that features Dag's elaborate and refreshingly naive solution for disposing of radioactive waste; it includes the neologism 'Dumpster Clocking', which delineates the contemporary habit of guessing how long man-made objects will take to decay (*GX*, p. 188). Significantly, the trash aesthetic of *Generation X* is developed in relation to Tobias, the yuppie interloper: Andy describes this moneyed, East Coast acquaintance in the language of waste; he is imagined as a scavenging eagle – a trash artist, of sorts – who pilfers 'cheap, vulgar, toxic items that will either decompose in minutes or remain essentially unchanged until our galaxy goes supernova' (*GX*, p. 91).

The majority of Coupland's novels, including self-consciously modern works such as *Shampoo Planet* and *Microserfs* – fables that seem immaculate in their sensation of newness – feature transformative encounters with rubbish. In *Microserfs*, Daniel even describes his own body in the language of abandoned objects. When Karla touches his long-ignored body 'she . . . removed the abandoned refrigerators and couches and sacks of garbage from underneath [his] skin' (*MS*, p. 205). Tyler Johnson, *Shampoo Planet*'s enthusiast for all things new, deploys a similar set of trash motifs in his narrative: 'Cat scabs are documents, too . . . Just like piss and shit are documents . . . Everything is a document' (*SP*, p. 169). Rubbish, Tyler suggests, is a set of codes that demands interpretation. The principal business of Tyler's home town (Lancaster, Washington State) is the production of nuclear energy and – necessarily – the generation of dangerous waste: 'Lancaster was once the world's largest producer of, how shall I say, *forbidden substances* . . . substances more wicked than your darkest secret times a billion' (*SP*, p. 11). These 'forbidden substances' have a specific connection with consumer culture since Lancaster's workforce is made up of those employed either at 'the Plants' or the 'Ridgecrest Mall': the continued prosperity of the mall is dependent on the success of the environmentally damaging energy company. 'Garbage reveals the market's relation to nature,' claims Heather Rogers. 'It teases out the environmental politics hidden inside manufactured goods.'[37] The Lancaster Plants themselves have become obsolete, though their toxic remnants have a legacy that will outlast many human generations. This sinister inheritance is constituted not only in impending ecological ruin but it also shapes ways of looking at the world. For example, a rubbish-derived lexicon haunts Tyler's vernacular: the diner that he and his 'mallrat' friends frequent is nicknamed the 'Toxic Waste Dump' (*SP*, p. 34). At the novel's end, Tyler's sister and her slacker boyfriend, Murray, are happily employed – with a proper medical and dental plan – on a project to 'detoxify' the wasteland surrounding the Plants. The future of consumer capitalist economies seems to depend on an evolving relationship with hazardous waste. Tyler's imagined pictures of the future, typically optimistic, are contested by Anna-Louise's intermittent dystopian fantasies in which the 'year 3001' is another 'Dark Age' with '[s]hit everywhere' and the built landscape reduced to 'rubble' (*SP*, p. 32).

Images of a ruined future – the prospect of an epoch of debris and an end to originality – anticipate the multiple descriptions of waste that punctuate *Girlfriend in a Coma*. Jared's description of an abandoned, decaying supermarket, one year after the world has ended, blends ecology and artifice. Animals have made their home amidst the plastic wilderness of a dead consumer civilization, and this simulated world now competes with the power of a previously subjugated natural order: 'Shit of all types splotches the floor . . . The smell of rot . . . is ebbing away, masked by the smell of shampoos and cosmetics' (*GIAC*, p. 218). This motif of detritus is not restricted to the novel's end-of-the-world section. In fact, trash is everywhere in the narrative: on a night in December 1979 when Karen slips into her seventeen-year coma, the principal characters witness a senseless, orgiastic 'house-wrecker' of a teenage party in which a suburban home becomes trash (*GIAC*, p. 14).

This wanton destruction is symbolic of the decadent consumer culture that Coupland's protagonists are forced to question. Richard later describes odd, defamiliarizing encounters with trash: during a dangerous walk through an unlit train tunnel, he briefly glimpses random, ordinary disposed items including a wine bottle, a used nappy and a newspaper: 'These objects flashed briefly and vanished like fleeting shivers of shame . . . these castaway things deep inside the Earth, never to return to the surface' (*GIAC*, p. 59). The moralizing vocabulary – in which trash becomes synonymous with degradation or 'shame' – unconsciously parallels the doctor's description of Karen's 'virtually clean' state as she became comatose. A quasi-religious rhetoric of purity, defilement and ruin informs judgements of Karen and her friends: 'Almost clean. But *not* clean. Dirty. Tainted. Soiled and corrupted' (*GIAC*, p. 27). When Richard tells Megan the truth about her mother, this rites-of-passage event is again haunted by trash motifs. The life-changing conversation coincides with the 1987 stock crash in which Richard's investments become worthless; similarly, the forest in which Richard and Megan talk is a ruined paradise, in which the naturally decomposing vegetation is covered with 'uncountable cigarette packs, weather-yellowed pornography, candy wrappers, condoms . . . and clusters of stolen Mercedes hood ornaments' (*GIAC*, p. 66).

These sites of environmental squalor foreshadow the ruined, post-plague landscape that Richard and Karen will inhabit in the novel's third and final section. Jared even describes his listless friends as 'useless sacks of dung' as they kill time at the end of the world by 'an endless string of videos' (*GIAC*, p. 209). They are surrounded by once priceless objects that no longer have value – 'a parody of wealth' – as art and currency have become trash: 'They have money fights, lobbing and tossing Krugerrands, rubies and thousand-dollar bills . . . they make paper airplanes from prints by Andy Warhol and Roy Lichtenstein and shoot them into the fireplace' (*GIAC*, p. 209). Even personal, prized possessions stored in the 'safety deposit boxes at the Toronto Dominion Bank in Park Royal' are described as resembling the 'stuff you'd expect to find left over after a garage sale' (*GIAC*, pp. 238–9). These consciously grotesque images of postmodern plenitude and comfort mock an overwhelming sense of moral or spiritual absence.

Coupland's T. S. Eliot-like eye for the aesthetic possibilities of consumer waste is also evident in *Miss Wyoming*. Jenny Turner has observed that Coupland's fiction – 'full of lists of unloved objects, clothes and gadgets' – uses violent moments of upheaval to 'bring objects together in striking ways'.[38] The scene of the aeroplane crash, from which Susan uncannily walks away without injury, provides the most shocking sequence of trash images in any of Coupland's novels. After the bodies – or, more accurately, human remains – have been cleared from the fields, Susan Colgate returns to the crash site of Flight 802. A site of trauma becomes strangely aestheticized: 'the jet fragments resembled plaza sculptures at the feet of Manhattan bank towers' (*MW*, p. 73). This image of devastation inevitably generates associations with the terrorist destruction of the World Trade Center on 11 September 2001, despite its prior publication.

Other, less disturbing, but similarly visceral motifs of rubbish are used in the narrative: John Johnson's pedestrian journey across America is interspersed with 'time-expired hot dogs' and a landscape of 'sun-rotted condoms' (*MW*, p. 172). John survives his Kerouac-style road trip by making use of wasted junk food but the trip also comes to an end after he eats an abandoned hamburger and collapses: 'He began to shit and vomit as though all the cells in his body were screaming to empty themselves of toxins' (*MW*, p. 173). Consumer culture takes an odd, liberating revenge on John, both reducing him to a state of abjection and freeing him from his quixotic search for authenticity.

Just as John's quest ends in a heap of putrid human waste, so is Susan's young life transformed by a haphazard encounter with flying faeces. During her unpleasantly regimented adolescence, a 'meteorite' destroys Susan's family home. However, what her mother assumes to be a 'miracle', 'an omen' and a 'sign from the Lord above' is, in fact, a ball of frozen human excrement, jettisoned from an aircraft. Named the 'shitsicle' by Susan's laconic stepfather, this 'meteorite' is emblematic of contemporary modes of consumption, modernity's emphasis on speed and the farcically contingent relationship between human beings and the things that they create (*MW*, pp. 153–4). The financial settlement reached after this random collision allows Marilyn to pursue her consumer dreams. *Eleanor Rigby* (2004) features an uncanny reworking of this episode: Liz Dunn discovers what she believes to be a meteorite – 'steaming . . . like dog shit on a cold winter day' – and secretly keeps it as a blessed artefact.[39] However, the curious, metallic fragment is neither a meteorite nor, on this occasion, is it faeces; it is, more worryingly, dangerous radioactive waste. Liz's tragic-comic misreading of the object is both devastating and transformative: she faces an untimely death but also recovers a lost sensation of wonder at the miraculous qualities of life.

What is the significance of these frequently reiterated encounters with trash in Coupland's fiction? Robert McGill, citing instances of road- or rail-side detritus in *Generation X* and *Girlfriend in a Coma*, suggests that the novelist's distinctive lists of 'products . . . as litter' serve to emphasize 'the meaninglessness of modernity's project' and that 'The hodgepodge of debris, which Coupland notably associates with travel, is a postmodern image of modernity's destructiveness in its obsession with movement.'[40] In *Hey Nostradamus!*, Reg reflects that '[l]ists only spell out the things that can be taken away from us by moths and rust and thieves' (*HN*, p. 238). This motif of ruin consciously echoes Jesus' advice in Matthew's Gospel against hoarding worldly wealth that is similarly subject to 'moths', 'rust and thieves' (Matthew 6. 19).

'Trash is central to commercial culture,' observes Twitchell, because it constitutes 'the remains of our incomplete love affair with stuff'.[41] If the characters in Coupland's fiction are rarely convincingly political, they are frequently moved to abandon lives defined by the incessant acquisition of the latest consumer goods or the parallel collection of sensory experiences. Casual sex, exotic travel and cheap transcendence through the narcotic of fame are all represented as phenomena that fail to constitute lives of substantial, satisfying meaning. Andy Palmer, for example, tells his younger (and candidly money-orientated) brother that he does not want a Christmas present because he is 'getting rid of all the things' in his life (*GX*, p. 123). Yet the relationship between idealistic, reborn individuals like Andy and the wholly imperfect world that they inhabit is always brokered via such 'things'. In this instance, the paratext of Coupland's narrative destabilizes the purity of Andy's motivation. The margin presents us with a gloss for the phenomenon of 'Conspicuous Minimalism': 'A life-style tactic . . . The nonownership of material goods flaunted as a token of moral and intellectual superiority' (*GX*, p. 122). Divesting oneself of belongings still signifies a relationship with the world of objects.

The ritualistic shedding of personal property is a practice that occurs in a number of Coupland's novels. When Dan and his fellow coders take up Michael's job offer in *Microserfs*, they hold a garage sale and attempt to rid themselves of their 'worldly crap . . . or at least try starting from scratch again' (*MS*, p. 94). Coupland again uses the motif of garbage – or 'objects that people no longer want' – to signify regeneration. Disposing of worldly goods – as random as 'antique Ghostbuster squeeze toys' and, oddly, a collection of Styrofoam packing materials – is a rite of passage that allows its participants to generate a new identity (*MS*, p. 94). This decision is a return to the desire for 'lessness' articulated by Andy in *Generation X*; Daniel is a kind of 2.0 upgrade of Andy in some ways – his relief at becoming 'virtually possessionless' and the 'liberating' sense of having 'nothing' is an echo of Andy's rejection of a life dominated by advertising (*MS*, p. 95).

In *Miss Wyoming*, John Johnson gives away everything in an attempt to mutate into something real and new; similarly, in the same novel, Susan Colgate walks away from her life of minor celebrity 'without credit cards, cash, a driver's license or any other link to the national economy' (*MW*, p. 73). At the end of *Eleanor Rigby*, Liz Dunn confides that in order to change her life radically, she intends to 'throw away everything I own and sell my condo to the first person who bites. I'm trying to think of anything I want to keep, but come up blank' (*ER*, p. 247). Similarly, as *Girlfriend in a Coma* reaches its quietly apocalyptic conclusion, Richard believes his revolutionary work in the world can only begin when he '*jettison*[s] *everything*' (*GIAC*, p. 279).

Personal possessions, machinery, former luxury goods and ideas are not alone in being subject to the depredations of time-expiry. In a consumer economy people or, to use the current employment euphemism, 'Human Resources' reach a sell-by date and become 'obsolete' with alarming swiftness. Linus, discussing the ethics and consequences of modern life in *Girlfriend in a Coma*, argues that the 'highly competitive society' of consumer capitalism is dependent upon both 'glittering prizes' and 'terrible consequences for not obeying the rules'. 'There *must* be losers' (*GIAC*, p. 80).

In *Microserfs*, Daniel Underwood's father, part of the resented 'baby boomer' generation, is the clearest example of this process as observed in Coupland's fiction: a former college professor who, in the 1980s, followed the exodus out of academia for the more profitable world of industry and finds himself adrift in a world of new technology. Like his son, Mr Underwood worked in information technology but, shortly after Dan begins his electronic journal, IBM, the one-time Goliath of the computer industry, makes him redundant.

This predicament signals Coupland's ongoing negotiation with the idea that 'History' has reached its 'end': Francis Fukuyama's hypothesis is contradicted not only by ideological wars that rage around the world but in the experience of relatively prosperous, middle-class Westerners. In an idiom that Dan jealously notes is derived from Michael – at twenty-six his exact contemporary and a Bill Gates-style entrepreneur – Mr Underwood engages explicitly with Fukuyama's paradigm: 'We old folks mistake the current deluge of information, diversity, and chaos as the "End of History." But maybe it's actually the Beginning' (*MS*, p. 203). The motif of second-hand or salvaged goods is vital to this discussion: just as the new world pillages the old for ideas and inspiration, Dan's father reverses the paradigm by recycling language and ideas from a man thirty years his junior.

He later reflects on the sense of disorientation to which he and other 'newly obsolete humans' are subject (*MS*, p. 203). In other words, human beings are simply another natural resource that will be exploited until a quicker, better and more profitable generation emerges. This idea resurfaces in *All Families are Psychotic*: Ted Drummond, like Mr Underwood, is a man with a commercial scientific background – in this case as an engineer – but his eldest son is dubious about his father's future: 'What *would* the world have to offer Ted Drummond . . . a man whose usefulness to the culture had vanished somewhere around the time of Windows 95?' (*AFAP*, pp. 91–2). This impersonal process is a newly accelerated version of social Darwinism. The postmodern world – the era of late capitalism – seems scarcely more forgiving or sympathetic, whatever the superficial emphasis on choice and flexibility. In *Microserfs*, Dan redeploys a term derived from e-mail, a relatively new, not yet time-expired form of communication technology. 'Deletia' is a term included in a piece of mail to indicate that material has been cut. 'It stands for everything that's been lost,' states Dan (*MS*, p. 190). This, suggests Dan's highly educated but now de-skilled father, is a term that aptly describes his own invisible position in the modern, electronic economy (*MS*, p. 204). 'Ephemerality,' claims David Harvey, 'has always been fundamental to the experience of modernity.'[42] This phenomenon of transience and disposability applies as stringently to people as it does to the consumer objects that they are so often forced to resemble.

Rubbish reborn: the afterlife of objects (II)

Can exhausted, broken and discarded materials be made to live again? 'There's nothing new anymore,' complains Pam in *Girlfriend in a Coma* (*GIAC*, p. 238). This dejected recognition – made rather too late, after history itself has come to a catastrophic end – signifies a culture's chronic addiction to novelty and an inability to understand the consequences of unrestrained consumption. 'Quit Recycling the Past' proclaims one chapter title in *Generation X*: the severe, quasi-Modernist instruction reflexively admonishes the writer, his reader and an entire culture for its predilection for repetition. Yet this distinctively New World desire for originality and its anticipation of the cool, clean smoothness of the future as a blank slate – or as desert space – is continually problematized by the novelist's crowded, debris-strewn narratives. These fictions for an age of egregious consumption represent an ongoing negotiation between innovation and repetition, permanence and perishability, 'creation' and 'theft' (*GX*, p. 33). Zygmunt Bauman has argued that recycling, 'which blends preservation with renewal, rejection with affirmation' erodes the 'opposition between conservatism and creation, preservation and critique'.[43] 'Cultural rubbish', states John M. Ulrich, 'is subject to being "picked" and recycled, put to use in another form or context' and the multiple forms of 'hybrid, pastiche, collage, nostalgia' that emerge from the waste ultimately constitute 'the postmodern cultural landscape'. Ulrich argues that the label 'Generation X' has itself been redeployed, in multiple guises, as an example of cultural recycling.[44]

This fictive 'postmodern cultural landscape' features an abundance of characters, idioms, stories and things that are constantly reprocessed and reused.[45] Similarly, it is unsurprising that novels generated within such a cluttered world deploy tropes of recycling. These motifs have been part of Coupland's narrative world since the earliest chapters of *Generation X*. When Dag abandons his marketing job, he is able to imagine a moment of potential aesthetic redemption, as he visualizes a successor holding one of his abandoned personal possessions – a photograph of a wrecked whaling ship trapped in Antarctic ice – and re-evaluating his personality before throwing it away (*GX*, p. 31). The trash imagery is doubled – both the ship and the photograph become detritus – and the act of salvation fails. This peculiar reverie, however, signals the possibility of the imaginative redemption of objects.

Hey Nostradamus! features a parallel image of recuperated loss. The austere, emotionally forbidding Reg Klaasen remembers his childhood in the British Columbian wilds of Agassiz, constantly aware of the natural world's cycle of birth, death and decay. He was, he recalls, surrounded by tangible reminders of mortality: 'And then there was spring – always the spring – when the mess and stink and garbage of the rest of the year were redeemed by the arrival of the flowers' (*HN*, p. 232). In this instance, it is the processes of nature rather than a cultural intervention that implies the possibility of redemption. Similarly, *Shampoo Planet* presents a counter-intuitive collision of organic and synthetic spheres: in a rare moment of solitude, Tyler, ostensibly addicted to the pleasures of plastic, plunges his hands into a compost box. This spontaneous, sensual gesture – a hygiene-obsessed character's brief encounter with a *nostalgie de la boue* – is an act designed to precipitate connection and, perhaps, epiphany. The 'hot, living breathing pulp' stains his pristine clothes but the embrace of dirt reminds him of a mysterious reality that persists without reference to the transient contemporary ethos of desire and disappointment (*SP*, p. 127).

Coupland's recurrent reconfiguration of rubbish – including metaphorical refuse, such as discarded memories or displaced, unwanted people – exemplifies the complexity of his imaginative response to consumer culture. For a writer and artist who is primarily concerned with representing the experience of life in the kinds of advanced capitalist societies that are saturated with objects, ideas and images, piles of decomposing refuse – typically less pure than Tyler's compost box – are an unavoidable element of the post-industrial landscape. Yet encounters with rubbish are, for a number of Coupland's characters, more often the foundation of pleasant memories than they are evidence of a blighted environment. In 'Patty Hearst' (1994), for example, the narrator offers a 'snapshot' recollection of a carefree moment with his now missing sister. He recalls that they 'rummage[d] through Chinatown dumpsters for cool stuff' including 'discarded calendars'.[46] This image of time redeemed – the rescued calendars are figurative of a more ludic, innocent period destroyed by experience – connects waste with the transfiguring processes of memory.

All Families are Psychotic features a comparable imaginative reclamation of rubbish. Janet Drummond's recollections of the Second World War are dominated by images of everyday waste – 'bacon fat, tin cans, rubber' – that suddenly became not just salvageable but precious. Indeed, her 'most enjoyable childhood memories were of sorting neighborhood trash in the alleys, in search of crown jewels, metal fragments and love notes from dying princes' (*AFAP*, p. 12). Trash becomes treasure in these animated (and perhaps romantic) memories of an era before the experience of prosperity and surplus were routine aspects of middle-class, suburban life.

Shampoo Planet features a particularly audacious – or sublimely bizarre – model of recycling. Tyler may not be afflicted by the nostalgia of his parents or peers, but his business acumen prompts him to exploit the trend of historical yearning. In a piece of outrageous plotting, the young entrepreneur manages to secure his longed-for career with the Bechtol corporation, after sending its CEO a proposal to 'develop a nationwide chain of theme parks called *HistoryWorld*™' (*SP*, pp. 199–200). Tyler proposes that rubbish – a commodity that America stores in vast quantities – might provide the most vivid connection with history. This absurd scheme – a hybrid of Andy Warhol's passion for the ordinary, Walt Disney's shrewd imagination and Jean Baudrillard's wildest visions of a wholly simulated America – is both hallucinatory and, in terms of US patterns of consumption, entirely rational. As an engagement with the past, however, Tyler's artificial vision embodies a cynical, money-oriented branch of the heritage industry rather than a recuperation of vanished history.

Does Coupland's novel manage adequately to critique this commodified past? In an echo of the Pop Art aesthetic to which Coupland is so indebted, *Shampoo Planet* blurs the division between satire and authenticity in a way that is likely to alienate readers searching for a more explicit critique of consumerism. Indeed, Coupland himself has been more publicly critical of *Shampoo Planet* than any of his other novels: 'I guess it was just too much of a contrivance . . . there wasn't enough . . . honesty in it,' he suggested in one interview.[47]

Tyler's playful paradigm for a literally trashy, theme-park past is not, however, a unique proposal. *HistoryWorld*™ anticipates one of the ideas explored in DeLillo's *Underworld*: during a visit to a landfill, Jesse Detwiler, the tenured trash theorist, claims that this abysmal landscape, constructed on the gradually decomposing, spoiled remnants of civilization, represents 'the scenery of the future'. Detwiler suggests that detritus holds a nostalgic appeal and claims that this odd phenomenon is part of the human 'capacity for complex longings'. Like Tyler, DeLillo's 'maverick' prophet of waste predicts that people will happily pay to encounter a vista of dangerous but aestheticized trash:

> The more toxic the waste, the greater the effort and expense a tourist will be willing to tolerate in order to visit the site. Only I don't think you ought to be isolating these sites. Isolate the most toxic waste, okay. This makes it grander, more ominous and magical . . . Make an architecture of waste . . . Bus tours and postcards, I guarantee it.[48]

However, the reification of rubbish – trash as commodified object or currency – does not constitute the radical reclassification of waste embodied in other pivotal motifs in Coupland's fiction. The amateur junk artist – a figure who might redeem broken and unwanted objects – appears in various incarnations in a number of Coupland's plots: the trinity of tale tellers in *Generation X* construct their 'bedtime stories', both peculiar and mundane, from the flotsam and jetsam of personal and popular memory. Daniel Underwood's creation of a 'Subconscious' file on his PowerBook, discussed in more detail in Chapter 2 – a list of 'random words' that dart, unbidden, through his mind – becomes text-based art in the novel: pages of apparently arbitrary words, phrases and mini-narratives are interleaved throughout the narrative, interrupting Daniel's 'real' journal but also constructing a counter-story from the debris floating in his unconscious. In *Eleanor Rigby*, Jeremy Buck's scrawled notes, recording fragments of his visions and impressionistic ideas, take on an auratic quality for his mother (*ER*, p. 139).

Shampoo Planet, for all of its concern with sleek, sparkling new commodities, features a stark, unembellished mode of junk art that is far from the designer trash promised by *HistoryWorld*™. Tyler describes the subcultural space surrounding Lancaster's Free Clinic, populated by drug addicts – a body of people who share none of Tyler's desperate desire for material success – and encounters a bizarre and estranging piece of art made by these dispossessed individuals: in 'letters built of IV needles attached to the cement with soiled bandages and wads of chewing gum' is the defiant phrase 'WE LIKE IT' (*SP*, p. 72). Toxic, addictive and potentially infectious materials are remodelled as an improvised, confrontational sculpture. Tyler and Stephanie's later dalliance with text-based art – when they scribble Jenny Holzer-like slogans on dollar bills, turning currency into an aesthetic form – is an echo of this destabilizing image.

Miss Wyoming is both pervaded by motifs of junk and populated by various kinds of trash artist. John Johnson, producer of blockbuster movies, is figuratively tagged a 'sleazebag' (*MW*, p. 4). The speculative, sci-fi film script that John buys from Ryan, a video store clerk, is predicated by images of destruction and exploding trash. John's partner notes that the script would be good for testing new film technologies – including those developed by George Lucas's special effects company – that specialize in representing 'flying debris and litter' (*MW*, p. 122). This is a consciously absurd image: a world replete with trash is prepared to invest in simulated debris that appears to be more authentic than the real thing. Ryan himself seems to be obsessed with rubbish: he has constructed a semi-ironic shrine to Susan Colgate from old magazine clippings, candy bars, pill bottles and broken toys (*MW*, p. 115). The odd synergy that the novel proposes between trash and art coalesces in Eugene Lindsay, a former television star, who has settled into a reclusive lifestyle, making 'art from household trash' as he bathes in the glow of the TV screen (*MW*, p. 134). This eccentric hobby was inspired by the theft of discarded documents by Susan's mother; this potentially career-wrecking incident of blackmail both perpetuated paranoia and shaped a new faith in the magical value of waste. Eugene – a former local television meteorologist, minor celebrity and sometime beauty pageant judge – is a kind of Andy Warhol of the suburbs. His art projects include a sculpture made from 'thousands of the past decade's emptied single-portion plastic tublets of no-fat yogurt, their insides washed squeaky clean, stuffed inside each other, forming long wavy filaments that reached to the ceiling like sea anemones' (*MW*, p. 135). This once acquisitive individual remakes ordinary consumer items into art that exists for its own sake; it is decadent but not commercial, synthetic and strangely romantic.

Eugene's trash sculptures both encode *Miss Wyoming*'s aesthetic practice – it too appropriates ordinary, clichéd details of everyday life and reshapes them into a narrative that might engage critically with that culture – and replicates Coupland's experiments in visual art. His 'Canada House' exhibition, for example, explored the contours of evolving national identity via multiple trash-based sculptures: dumped synthetic materials were redeployed as new aesthetic objects, including furniture fashioned from Kraft food boxes, quilts made from NHL-logo drapes and great hunks of foam 'found on the tidal flats beneath Vancouver's Lions Gate Bridge' reshaped as *inuksuk*, a form of Inuit sculpture (*SOC 2*, p. 49). Coupland has expressed enthusiasm for other artists, including Tony Cragg, whose work similarly explores the implications of rubbish. This fervour for the forgotten also extends to his idiosyncratic pursuit of art supplies:

> I was out in the Queen Charlotte Islands about ten days ago . . . There's one beach that faces the northwest and the currents bring down everything from Japan and Korea. I got there when the tide was just right and found maybe 400 fishing floats, whisky bottles, shampoo bottles. This pile of treasure . . . I had a great time with all this leftover plastic. I really love an interesting object with an interesting history. I like things that are mass-produced because there's a sort of democracy in it.[49]

This mini-narrative might be construed as an accidental manifesto for a new aesthetics of rubbish. Certainly, Coupland is remarkably insouciant about art's loss of 'aura', famously attributed by Walter Benjamin to the transformative processes of mechanical reproduction in the modern world.[50] Mass production, in this instance, however, is viewed not as a sign of civilization's moral decline but as emblematic of democracy. Almost a decade before Coupland's beachcombing excursion to the wilderness of northern Canada, he narrated a similar, fictional experience, in '1,000 Years (Life After God)'. Scout and Kristy, frustrated by the superficial shape of their lives, drive out to where 'the Fraser River meets the ocean and the river turns to salt' and look for 'drift-stuff'. The shared encounter with 'sticks and bits of plastic and old logs and pieces of old plywood and bits of broken boats and wooden doors' encourages a new sense of the importance of memory (*LAG*, p. 333). This moment of recuperated innocence allows Scout and Kristy to make connections with time and the movements of history. These piles of debris are a reminder of mortality and that life has rhythms that exist beyond human control.

If many of Coupland's protagonists seek to recycle or retrieve memory via tactile encounters with disposed objects, so too does the novelist make use of 'cultural rubbish' to constitute the worlds of his fiction. *Girlfriend in a Coma*, as we have seen, features multiple images of debris. However, perhaps more importantly, the structure and the idiom of the novel itself are dependent on its author's mischievous, self-conscious recycling of song names, movie motifs and television plots. Not only does the title reuse the name of a Morrissey-Marr composition from The Smiths' final album, the dialogue and narrative themselves are littered with song titles: in describing a ravaged, post-historical landscape, for example, the spectral Jared invokes songs by Pink Floyd and REM that were released after his death ('Another Brick in the Wall', 'The End of the World As We Know It') (*GIAC*, p. 4). 'Big-mouth strikes again,' apologizes Richard, in another anachronistic, unconscious reference to a Smiths song (*GIAC*, p. 9). A catalogue of self-conscious references to Hollywood genre movies – particularly those involving environmental catastrophe, alien invasion or zombies – television sci-fi serials and millennial fictions intensify this pattern of cultural recycling. For McGill, the multiplicity of film references acts as a deliberate reminder that the novel is 'not apocalyptic' but a 'response to apocalyptic literature'.[51]

These allusions might simply be a knowing in-joke for a savvy, pop culture-literate readership. However, the intertextual patterns of the novel also have deeper and darker implications. Pam and Hamilton, for example, are rendered psychologically and spiritually inert by their debilitating addiction to the language of the most crass, commercially motivated elements of the entertainment industry. Their retro, gossip-culture saturated conversation is like a parody of Coupland's early novels or common assumptions about the kind of fiction that he once wrote: unable to cope with reality or the experience of time, they bury themselves in ironic fantasies of life in a parallel universe of minor celebrities (*GIAC*, p. 238). Their addiction to heroin – also known as 'junk' – is one more crippling symptom of emotional blankness and a lack of faith in anything new. Jared – a spectral reminder of a lost innocence that is, at least in part, illusory – confronts the couple's childish dependence on television programmes to describe life. History, for Pam and Hamilton, has become a figurative prison of commodified memories. As Robert McGill suggests, the aimless lives of these characters have become a 'conglomeration of modern myths with no confidence in the enabling power of those myths'.[52]

However, the daydream logic of the novel allows Jared to free his friends from their addictions in an inexplicable, healing gesture. This moment both echoes the kind of absurd narrative devices that typifies uninspired TV fantasy – dire consequences are averted by a magical solution, with only minutes before the final credits roll – and recuperates the energy of miraculous language. A splinter of cultural trash – a motif from genre TV movies – is made strange and rejuvenated in this act. Coupland's determined reprocessing of familiar images and plot lines embedded in cultural memory – most of which belong to a democratized, low-cultural milieu – indicates the subversive possibilities of imaginative recycling. Indeed, the novel's final image is constructed around a vocabulary of transfiguration. Richard believes that his friends, transformed by their sublime experience, will 'change minds and souls from stone and plastic into linen and gold' (*GIAC*, p. 281). This emphasis on collective endeavour unravels the American myth of superhuman individualism and suggests a bolder critique of consumerism. The motif of alchemy is, in some sense, metafictional: Coupland uses the 'plastic' materials of contemporary culture to produce something finer.

A similar set of trash and transfiguration tropes are used to represent Susan Colgate's symbolic rebirth in *Miss Wyoming*. The garbage motif is subtly introduced when Susan leaves the empty suburban home she occupies after the crash: she begins to leave her identity behind in the mundane action of throwing 'a plastic bag of her week's garbage into a stranger's trash can' (*MW*, p. 24). As she walks across an anonymous, commercial landscape (discussed in more detailed in Chapter 4), Susan has a bizarre, transformative encounter with trash. Hungry and penniless, Susan, like John Johnson, scavenges for disposed but edible junk food. She climbs into the 'dumpster' of a fast-food restaurant replete with 'fully wrapped, unsold, time-expired burgers' (*MW*, p. 78). This dumpster becomes a temporary prison, or a kind of mechanical womb, when it is locked and Susan is forced to spend the night in it. This reeking bin – locked to protect valuable waste – becomes a luxuriant interior space in which she is reborn. The description of Susan's sensation of weightlessness 'while tumbling into a truck bed, pelted with waste, the morning sun blinding her' invokes a collision of the miraculous with the mundane (*MW*, p. 98). The fact that she comes close to death for a second time, as the dumpster is hurled into a trash compressor, intensifies the biblical motif of resurrection: Susan's farcically undignified experience echoes, in particular, the story of Jonah, who is swallowed and emerges, reborn, from the belly of a whale (Jonah 1. 17). As she comes 'to rest on the crown of a crest of a heap of trash' encountering a new sense of liberation, Susan, once an unwilling participant in the culture of consumer excess, is transfigured amid the ordinary waste of America (*MW*, p. 98).

'Rubbish,' claims Heather Rogers, is both 'a border separating the clean and useful from the unclean and dangerous' and 'the text in which abundance is overwritten by decay and filth'.[53] Coupland's writing, however, frequently blurs the 'border' between trash and treasure in its fascination with the potential of junk to be made new. His novels and visual art display a peculiar sensitivity to the perishable quality of most human activity. Dan's speculation in *Microserfs* that 'Microsoft's corporate zest for recycling aluminium, plastic and paper is perhaps a sublimation of the staff's hidden desire for immortality' exemplifies the perplexing, superstitious attitude to rubbish at play in ostensibly rationalist, post-industrial societies (*MS*, p. 16). Values that we might associate with Naomi Klein's style of left-leaning critique are apparent throughout Coupland's work: antipathy for greed and exploitation, disillusion with corporate life and a refusal to believe that wealth provides any meaningful consolation, for example, are vindicated as rational positions to adopt in world of social and spiritual anomie. Similarly, the ruined landscapes of *Girlfriend in a Coma* and the litter-strewn wilderness of *Miss Wyoming* suggest environmental unease. Household trash, the deliberately forgotten residue of everyday life, becomes auratic in Coupland's work: damaged goods can be redeployed creatively. Enthusiasm for banal litter might imply that this twenty-first-century artist is happy to make a fetish out of consumed products. Yet Coupland's approach to junk – washed up on distant beaches, abandoned by the roadside or given away – seems to stem from an attempt to reconnect contemporary fragmentation with history: waste matter is part of a shared story, a set of narratives that become erroneous if we fail to represent the material consequences of production and consumption.

Notes

1 Douglas Coupland, *Girlfriend in a Coma* (London: Flamingo, 1998), pp. 4–5. All subsequent references will be given parenthetically as *GIAC*, followed by page reference.
2 Douglas Coupland, *Souvenir of Canada 2* (Vancouver: Douglas & McIntyre, 2004) includes an extended section on the exhibition's origins and individual exhibits, pp. 42–69. The exhibition included, for example, 'Fishing Float Lamps', constructed from floats gathered in Newfoundland (p. 47). All subsequent references will be given parenthetically as *SOC 2*, followed by page reference.
3 James B. Twitchell, *Lead Us Into Temptation: The Triumph of American Materialism* (New York: Columbia University Press, 1999), p. 4.
4 Don DeLillo, *Underworld* (London: Picador, 1999), p. 791.
5 Sheryl Garratt, 'Why is Douglas Coupland Fascinated by Garbage?', *Word* (October 2003), 25.
6 Heather Rogers, *Gone Tomorrow: The Hidden Life of Garbage* (New York: The New Press, 2005), p. 2.
7 Douglas Coupland, *Generation X: Tales for an Accelerated Culture* (London: Abacus, 1992), p. 47. All subsequent references will be given parenthetically as *GX*, followed by page reference.
8 Jefferson Faye, 'Canada in a Coma', *The American Review of Canadian Studies*, 31.3 (2001), 501–10 (506).
9 Alan Bilton, *An Introduction to Contemporary American Fiction* (Edinburgh: Edinburgh University Press, 2002), p. 223.
10 Douglas Coupland, *Souvenir of Canada* (Vancouver: Douglas & McIntyre, 2002), pp. 38–9. All subsequent references will be given parenthetically as *SOC*, followed by page reference.
11 Zygmunt Bauman, *Globalization: The Human Consequences* (Cambridge: Polity, 1998), p. 79.
12 *The Consumption Reader*, ed. by David B. Clarke, Marcus A. Doel and Kate M. L. Housiaux (London and New York: Routledge, 2003), pp. 1–2.
13 David Lyon, *Jesus in Disneyland: Religion in Postmodern Times* (Cambridge: Polity Press, 2000), p. 12.

14 Karen Ritchie, *Marketing to Generation X* (New York: Simon & Schuster, 1995), p. 149.

15 Ibid., pp. 152, 159.

16 Leslie Haynsworth, '"Alternative" Music and the Oppositional Potential of Generation X Culture', in *GenXegesis: Essays on Alternative Youth (Sub)Culture*, ed. by John M. Ulrich and Andrea L. Harris (Madison: University of Wisconsin Press, 2003), pp. 41–58 (p. 42).

17 Douglas Coupland, *Microserfs* (London: Harper, 2004), p. 44. All subsequent references will be given parenthetically as *MS*, followed by page reference.

18 Naomi Klein, *No Logo: Taking Aim At the Brand Bullies* (London: Flamingo, 2000), p. 66.

19 Ibid., p. 63.

20 Clarke *et al.* are glossing Colin Campbell's pioneering study, *The Romantic Ethic and the Spirit of Modern Consumerism* (1987). Clarke *et al.*, p. 29.

21 Colin Campbell, 'Traditional and Modern Hedonism', in Clarke *et al.*, eds pp. 48–53 (p. 51). Extract derived from *The Romantic Ethic and the Spirit of Modern Consumerism* (1987).

22 Douglas Coupland, *Miss Wyoming* (London: Flamingo, 2000), p. 127. All subsequent references will be given parenthetically as *MW*, followed by page reference.

23 DeLillo, p. 288.

24 Clarke *et al.*, p. 27.

25 Twitchell, p. 2. Twitchell cites Juliet B. Schor, *The Overworked American: The Unexpected Decline of Leisure* (New York: Basic Books, 1991), p. 126, as the source of his statistics.

26 *All Families are Psychotic* (London: Flamingo, 2001), p. 234. All subsequent references will be given parenthetically as *AFAP*, followed by page reference.

27 Jean Baudrillard, 'The Ideological Genesis of Needs' (originally published in *Cahiers Internationaux de Sociologie* (1969)), *For a Critique of the Political Economy of the Sign*, trans. C. Levin (St Louis: Telos Press, 1981), pp. 63–8. Essay reprinted in *The Consumption Reader* (2003), pp. 255–8 (p. 255).

28 Douglas Coupland, *Polaroids from the Dead* (London: Flamingo, 1997), p. 93. All subsequent references will be given parenthetically as *PD*, followed by page reference.

29 Bauman, p. 80.

30 Jean Baudrillard, *America*, translated by Chris Turner (New York: Verso, 1989), p. 32.

31 Douglas Coupland, *Shampoo Planet* (London: Simon & Schuster, 1993), p. 37. All subsequent references will be given parenthetically as *SP*, followed by page reference.

32 Rob Latham, *Consuming Youth: Vampires, Cyborgs, and the Culture of Consumption* (Chicago: University of Chicago Press, 2002), pp. 170–1.

33 *Hey Nostradamus!* (London: Flamingo, 2003), p. 232. All subsequent references will be given parenthetically as *HN*, followed by page reference.

34 Jon Butler, 'Writing His Own Rules', interview with Douglas Coupland in British paperback edition of *Eleanor Rigby* (London: Harper Perennial, 2005), p. 8.

35 Bauman, p. 86.

36 Garratt, p. 25.

37 Rogers, p. 231.

38 Jenny Turner, 'Top of the World', *London Review of Books*, 22.12 (22 June 2000), www.lrb.co.uk/v22/n12/turn03_.html (10 November 2005).

39 *Eleanor Rigby* (London: Fourth Estate, 2004), p. 156. All subsequent references will be given parenthetically as *ER*, followed by page reference.

40 Robert McGill, 'The Sublime Simulation: Vancouver in Douglas Coupland's Geography of Apocalypse', *Essays on Canadian Writing*, 70 (2000), 252–76 (261).

41 Twitchell, p. 3.

42 David Harvey, *The Condition of Postmodernity: An Enquiry into the Origins of Cultural Change* (Oxford: Blackwell, 1989). Reprinted in *Postmodernism and the Contemporary Novel: A Reader*, ed. by Bran Nicol (Edinburgh: Edinburgh University Press, 2002), p. 40.

43 Zygmunt Bauman, *Life in Fragments: Essays in Postmodern Morality* (Oxford: Blackwell, 1995), p. 77.

44 John M. Ulrich, 'Introduction: Generation X: A (Sub)Cultural Genealogy', in *GenXegesis: Essays on Alternative Youth Culture*, ed. by John M. Ulrich and Andrea L. Harris (Madison: University of Wisconsin Press, 2003), pp. 3–37 (p. 10).

45 See Daniel Bell's exploration of these issues: 'Modern culture is defined by this extraordinary freedom to ransack the world storehouse and to engorge any and every style it comes upon. Such freedom comes from the fact that the axial principle of modern culture is the expression and remaking of the "self" in order to achieve self-realization and self-fulfillment. And in its search, there is a denial of any limits or boundaries to experience. It is a reaching out for all experience; nothing is forbidden, all is to be explored.' *The Cultural Contradictions of Capitalism* (London: Heinemann, 1979), pp. 13–14. Cited in *Religion in Modern Times: An Interpretive Anthology*, ed. by Linda Woodhead and Paul Heelas (Oxford: Blackwell, 2000) p. 376.

46 Douglas Coupland, *Life After God* (London: Simon & Schuster, 1994), p. 235. All subsequent references will be given parenthetically as *LAG*, followed by page reference.

47 Douglas Coupland, interview with Kim France, *Elle* magazine (September 1993). Reprinted in *The GenX Reader*, ed. by Douglas Rushkoff (New York: Ballantine, 1994), pp. 11–16 (p. 15).

48 DeLillo, p. 286.

49 Garratt, pp. 24–5.

50 Walter Benjamin, 'The Work of Art in the Age of Mechanical Reproduction', translated by Henry Zohn, in Benjamin, *Illuminations: Essays and Reflections*, ed. by Hannah Arendt (London: Jonathan Cape, 1970).

51 McGill, p. 270.

52 Ibid., p. 262.

53 Rogers, p. 3.

4

Nowhere, anywhere, somewhere: Coupland and space

> I fly more than most people . . . I've flown across Canada a conservative total of fifty-five times, most likely more . . . There's just all of this *land* down there, blank and essentially uninhabited, no roads or power lines . . . Will these vast refrigerated stones someday harbour modern cities and societies? Corner malls with a Lenscrafters and a Baskin-Robbins on Baffin Island? . . . What does it *mean* for Canadians that we own these huge rocks if there's really not much we can do on them?[1] (*Souvenir of Canada*, 2002)

Souvenir of Canada, Coupland's first explicit reading of the national consciousness, begins with an aerial vision of the country's unpopulated, wild northern lands. Gazing at the enigmatic landscape, the writer lists places that, apart from the colonial act of naming, appear to be untainted by human intervention ('Hudson Bay and the Ungava Peninsula, Ellesmere Island, Baffin Island') and starts the work of rethinking his own relationship with geography. Cocooned in the memory of one or many aeroplane cabins – an interchangeable tourist space emblematic of modernity's uninhibited penchant for constant motion – Coupland attempts to connect the knowable and malleable (sub)urban reality which he inhabits with an apparently unchanging and incomprehensible terrain. These vast, empty territories constitute most of the landmass that Canadians cautiously – and perhaps conditionally – call home. Coupland's visual narrative, inflected with Romantic nostalgia and distinctively late modern ecological concern, echoes what is probably the most famous twentieth-century literary description of early European contact with the 'American' landscape. At the end of *The Great Gatsby* (1926), Nick Carraway, F. Scott Fitzgerald's disenchanted narrator, gazes out from an East coast shore and attempts to visualize how seventeenth-century colonists might have viewed the now populous land:

[T]he inessential houses began to melt away until gradually I became
aware of the old island here that flowered once for Dutch sailors' eyes –
a fresh, green breast of the new world. Its vanished trees . . . had once
pandered in whispers to the last and greatest of all human dreams; for a
transitory enchanted moment man must have held his breath in the
presence of this continent, compelled into an aesthetic contemplation he
neither understood nor desired, face to face for the last time in history
with something commensurate to his capacity for wonder.[2]

This melancholy, modernist synthesis of cultural memory is an
attempt to reconstruct the 'new world' as a fallen paradise. Fitzgerald's
vocabulary is markedly gendered – the 'fresh, green breast' of land
suggests a feminized space that will be violated by the commercial,
masculine interests of the settlers. Yet the narrative makes a still more
disturbing connection between the apparently innocent, adoring gaze
of the traveller-spectator and the eventual desecration of the land. A
similar fear troubles Coupland's description of the Northern territories:
how long can such immaculate space defy human incursion?

The pristine visions at play in the memories of an early twentieth-
century fictional narrator and a twenty-first century writer afford their
reader-spectators a virtual experience of the wilderness; they are spaces
that both invite and resist human contact. The extracts simultaneously
evoke a sense of the impermanence of human interventions in any
landscape and the environmental threat posed by the relentless and
often destructive forces of progress. Whilst Fitzgerald was examining
the imaginative repercussions of a lost innocence – America's built
landscape is equated with an Eden from which his characters
are eternally exiled – Coupland's essay limns the more ambiguous
postmodern experience of space. Air travel, the writer implies, might
revise our familiar perception of the world: it grants passengers the
illusion of having achieved a near-miraculous God's-eye view of
creation; the experience also promotes a disorienting sense of human
transience. Panoramic visions such as this are fleeting, but, for the
narrator and many other nomadic, economically privileged citizens of
the early twenty-first century, the frequent repetition of flight can alter
deep-rooted beliefs about self, society and nation. A desolate vista, like
that of Baffin Island, inscribed with notions of limit and infinity,
requires a way of understanding human identity that differs markedly
from standard notions of historical and social being.

This airborne encounter with uninhabited territory is indicative of
Coupland's evolving geographical imagination. Despite his abiding

interest in narrating the experience of time, the novelist's most distinctive contribution to contemporary literature might be viewed as spatial rather than temporal: a crucial element of his fiction is shaped by an endeavour to re-imagine the specifics of space at the so-called 'end of history'. A cameo or *mise en abyme* of this concept is perceptible in a computer game devised by Michael in *Microserfs* (1995): this piece of electronic narrative imagines a 'beautiful kingdom on the edge of the world that saw time coming to an end'; the kingdom has found a way to transform 'its world into code . . . bits of light and electricity' and, simultaneously, to grant itself eternal life 'after time had come to an end'.[3] In the mystic-entrepreneur's speculative game, eternal peace is secured only after territory has been displaced by virtual space.

Coupland's turn to a space-oriented mode of thought echoes the objectives of Edward Soja's groundbreaking and polemical study, *Postmodern Geographies* (1989). Soja critiques the elevation of 'time and history' which '[f]or at least the past century' have been privileged 'in the practical and theoretical consciousness' of the social sciences (and Marxism, in particular) to the detriment of spatial concerns.[4] This claim is emphatically not anti-historical but rather constitutes a reassertion of the powerful force that a politicized geography has in shaping human agency: 'My aim is to spatialize the historical narrative, to attach to *durée* an enduring critical human geography'.[5] What Soja has named the 'spatial hermeneutic' is at play in Coupland's fiction. This chapter explores Coupland's representation of three distinctive – but interconnected – forms of space. The first section addresses the built landscape, including those most obviously postmodern spaces described by James Howard Kunstler in *The Geography of Nowhere* (1993) as 'Capitals of Unreality'.[6] These powerfully simulated locations are defined by artifice and a sense of illusion, exemplified in Coupland's recurrent references to the Disney theme parks and the dreamlike, gambling town of Las Vegas. The section concludes with Coupland's evocation of domestic space and, in particular, the much maligned world of suburbia. Why does Coupland attempt to rewrite the perceived blandness of the middle-class periphery? The second section explores the impact of travel on space with particular reference to the boundary genre of the road story. Many of Coupland's meandering road stories take detours into the wilderness or desert. The last section explores the novelist's engagement with these barren spaces. What position can unscripted, blank wilderness occupy in the cultural imagination of an era defined by 'accelerated' commercial activity?

'Something larger than just a landscape': from Disney World to the suburbs

'"Place" is a joke' states Coupland, in a mock-ominous description of the bland, undifferentiated scenery of the globalized era.[7] His fiction is often located in a rather anonymous landscape: *Generation X* (1991) takes place on the indistinctive periphery of a wealthy, resort town in California. *Shampoo Planet* (1992) moves between the melancholy, polluted and recession-hit Lancaster in Washington State and the illusive promise of Los Angeles. 'Eighty percent of everything ever built in America has been built in the last fifty years, and most of it is depressing, brutal, ugly, unhealthy, and spiritually degrading', claims James Howard Kunstler, in his unforgiving account of late twentieth-century architecture.[8] How does this nightmarish image compare to Coupland's reading of the synthetic spaces that dominate contemporary Western terrain?

Alan Bilton suggests that a fundamental dilemma of Coupland's work is spatial: as an heir to the Pop Art movement we would reasonably expect the writer to 'prefer a world of plastic to a world of mud'.[9] Yet how does a penchant for Nick Carraway-like 'aesthetic contemplation' operate in an environment that is largely artificial? The manufactured landscape against which Kunstler and others have issued appalled warnings, elicits a much more ambivalent response from Coupland. In *Microserfs*, Abe speculates that 'the '90s will be a decade with no architectural legacy or style', suggesting that the rapid progress and sophistication of computer code has become a virtual alternative to real buildings and design (*MS*, p. 23).[10] At the end of the decade, however, in a short article for *Architectural Record*, Coupland offered a very different perspective on the legacy of the 1990s. The article celebrates the revivification of Modernism and 'the volumes of vigorous, innovative, and compelling architecture for which this decade will happily be remembered'.[11]

Coupland's fiction vacillates between Abe-style scepticism and intermittent displays of enthusiasm for the new. In *Miss Wyoming* (2000), for example, the novelist represents alternative experiences of contemporary American architecture: certain encounters with the built environment are dismal whilst others generate a bewildering sensation of euphoria. During his peripatetic flight across America, John Johnson recalls an earlier uncanny experience of space. Driving across the crest of 'the Hollywood Hills' John catches sight of the strange, iridescent city of Los Angeles and witnesses 'something larger than just a landscape'.[12] An ordinary visual memory becomes a moment of revelation: John now perceives this scene of a city famous for its self-conscious approval of the artificial – an urban centre that has no natural place in the landscape – as evidence of human creativity rather than a penchant for environmental destruction. John's ecstatic, sensuous embrace of the synthetic embodies one aspect of Coupland's writing of the constructed landscape.

Yet Susan Colgate's parallel trek across Ohio is much bleaker. She strolls through a 'sidewalk-free' strip – her senses overwhelmed by garish fast-food restaurants and exhaust fumes – 'as if seeing her country for the first time' (*MW*, p. 78). Her journey evokes a bland panorama, in which desire culture displaces beauty, and space is transformed by advertising. The 'dead' Susan has a renewed, estranged perspective on the tyranny of an advert-soaked America. This defamiliarized view parallels the acute observations of 1990s culture made by Karen McNeil in *Girlfriend in a Coma*, when she wakes up from her near twenty-year loss of consciousness. Susan's recent encounter with mortality similarly renders her more aesthetically sensitive.

An antipathy for generic, environmentally unsympathetic archi-tecture is displayed in a number of Coupland's novels. Shopping malls, in particular – a major component of what Kunstler irritably describes as the 'destructive, wasteful, toxic, agoraphobia-inducing spectacle' of capitalist progress – are a vital feature of his fictional landscape.[13] One of the neologisms in *Generation X* – 'The Emperor's New Mall' – describes the bizarre assumption that 'shopping malls exist on the insides only and have no exterior'.[14] Fastidious consumers, Coupland implies, are encouraged to play a game of architectural *Fort/Da* in order to tolerate vast, generic structures that blight the landscape. 'The mall is the television version of place,' suggests G. P. Lainsbury. 'It represents the victory of commerce over utopian ideology.'[15]

In *Shampoo Planet*, by contrast, Tyler Johnson's natural habitat is the Ridgecrest Mall; he displays no disdain for its characterless, utilitarian form but instead proclaims 'love' for the rather forlorn commercial centre of his town: 'At the mall people are interested only in staying as modern as possible, continually forgetting the past while envisaging a shinier more fabulous future.'[16] This bright promise, for Tyler, is caught up with a need to preserve commodified space. Indeed, one of Tyler's few melancholic moments occurs during his European jaunt, when deprived access to shopping as leisure: finding the mall in a Parisian suburb closed ('primitive!'), this impatient *flâneur* is overwhelmed by 'a sensation of rootlessness . . . of being untethered' (*SP*, p. 113). Tyler is homesick in the absence of a powerful surrogate for happy domestic space: the haven of the shopping mall. He enjoys the 'elegant hysteria of Paris', protected, like other American travellers, by 'the absolution of youth' (*SP*, p. 105). This freedom, symbolically recognized amid the tombs of the famous in Père Lachaise cemetery, is conferred as much by the imagined freshness of American national identity compared to Europe's mysterious, deep history as it is by his own adolescence.

During a later journey west, Tyler encounters the 'necklace of futuretowns' beaded across the Silicon Valley: his rapturous response to such avant-garde environments suggests that they are not really 'places' but 'documents'. These nameless, futuristic suburbs 'are the foundries of our deepest desires as a species. To doubt them is to doubt *all*' (*SP*, pp. 218–19). This description, fusing technophilia with religious ecstasy, anticipates the description, in *Microserfs*, of the Microsoft campus in Washington as 'the foundry of our culture's deepest dreams' (*MS*, p. 3). Tyler's fascination with the plastic world – or 'Shampoo Planet' – also parallels Coupland's more critical interest in the increasingly fictional landscape of America.

Trips to the strange, simulated town of Las Vegas – with its 'Lego-pure' fantasy architecture – are undertaken in a number of the novels (*MS*, p. 337). In *Girlfriend in a Coma*, for example, Linus, the romantic drifter, does not pitch up on the banks of Walden Pond with the collected works of Thoreau, but instead is found working as a waiter in the Nevada gambling resort.[17] Wade Drummond, on the run from a betrayed husband, similarly finds brief refuge as a 'hockey player in a trashy casino'.[18] Encounters with this 'capital of unreality' frequently foreshadow transformative events: Linus, on a quest for truth, is later caught up in miraculous, sublime events in his home city, Vancouver. Wade also makes an impulsive, sentimental journey back to Vancouver but stumbles upon paternal violence – he is shot by his father within hours of his homecoming – rather than divine revelation (*AFAP*, p. 32). Jason Klaasen, another Vancouverite and the most troubled narrator of *Hey Nostradamus!* is twice secretly married in Las Vegas;

the first of these surreptitious ceremonies takes place shortly before the indiscriminate high-school shooting that ends Cheryl's life and decimates Jason's future.

During a business trip to the resort in *Microserfs'* final chapter, Dan offers an apt simile for this hallucinatory space as 'the subconsciousness of the culture exploded and made municipal' (*MS*, p. 339). Dan and his colleagues are in Las Vegas symbolically to gamble on the future of their own economic dreams. In this narrator's eyes the theme hotels, casinos and gaming environments incarnate the increasingly simulated nature of American life. The novel plays with the carnivalesque possibilities of this post-industrial paradise, described as the expectation of 'sleazy adventure divorced from consequences' (*MS*, p. 342). However, the news that Dan's mother has suffered a stroke provides a cruel reminder of the real world of flesh and blood human suffering. The seductive idea that Las Vegas-style simulation might entirely displace reality is weakened, though the city's over-abundance of virtual reality apparatus also prefigures the more benevolent possibilities of this technology that are deployed in Mrs Underwood's rehabilitation.

Las Vegas is only the second most famous fictive space frequently alluded to in Coupland's fiction. Walt Disney, whose set of trademarks are almost universally recognizable, is name checked in chapter titles in *Generation X* ('Adventure without Risk is Disneyland') and *Polaroids from the Dead* (1996) ('The 1960s Are Disneyland'). In the first chapter of *Shampoo Planet*, Tyler, sitting in an LA airport hotel, reflects on his proximity to 'the legislated memories of Disneyland' (*SP*, p. 5). Mildly disparaging citations of Disney are also made in the non-fiction, particularly with reference to Vancouver: in *Polaroids from the Dead*, the Nitobe Japanese Gardens, at the University of British Columbia, are 'still beautiful' despite being a 'manufactured version of wilderness, like a seventeenth-century Disneyland' (*PD*, p. 81). By contrast, Coupland expresses relief that Vancouver's airport has avoided becoming 'a sort of Disney version of Vancouver style'.[19]

The Disney phenomenon has become a useful, if overworked shorthand, for critics of advanced capitalism: Eleanor Byrne and Martin McQuillan, for example, claim that its power 'as an ambassador of . . . American strategic interests, lies in its ability to make itself an object of desire' rendering it 'the *objet petit a* of the late twentieth century'.[20] For David Lyon, 'The Magic Kingdom' corresponds with 'popular perceptions of the postmodern' because it 'is all about fantasy, illusion, slippery surfaces, revised realities, multiple meanings'.[21] Coupland's numerous references to the Disney Corporation are slightly less iconoclastic than the politicized analysis of contemporary theory. However, he does deploy these references, like Lyon, to test the 'revised realities' and 'multiple meanings' of contemporary life.

The absurd adventures of *All Families are Psychotic*, set in Florida, almost inevitably include an interlude in Disney World. Wade's visceral dislike of the theme park becomes Coupland's most sustained critique of America's escalating rejection of reality: '*No newspapers. No litter. No evidence of the world outside its borders . . . It could be 2001, it could be 1986, and it could be 2008.*' Far from being pleasantly recreational, the erasure of history renders this illusory space bland and dreamless. '*All you can get out of a place like this*', reflects the displaced Canadian, '*is a creepy little tingle that lets you know your kid is never going to be anything more than a customer – that the whole world is being turned into a casino*' (*AFAP*, pp. 93–4). The dark compulsions of Las Vegas and the infantilizing pleasures of Disney's escapist playgrounds, Coupland suggests, are dangerously similar. Wade's cynical interpretation of the Disney experience echoes Jean Baudrillard's analysis of its Californian incarnation: 'Disneyland is presented as imaginary in order to make us believe that the rest is real,' he argues, 'whereas all of Los Angeles and the America that surrounds it are no longer real.'[22]

Plastic utopias or 'capitals of unreality', according to this argument, are also shaping contemporary domestic space in the West. A few miles away from the Beverly Hills restaurant where Coupland scheduled John Johnson and Susan Colgate's first coincidental meeting, is where the not-quite suburb of Brentwood is located. Coupland's evocative, multi-genre 'Brentwood Notebook' represents this prosperous adjunct to the sprawling, daydream city of Los Angeles as embodying a blandness that paradoxically verges on eccentricity. Illusion tied to a laboured credibility provides the skewed, makeshift architecture of life in this chimerical world, inhabited by celebrities and those wealthy enough to evade economically diverse communities, exemplifying what Coupland names the West Coast's 'laboratory of denarration' (*PD*, p. 180). Brentwood, with its perfectly manicured lawns and plethora of neatly spaced trees, participates in the peculiarly American myth that '*Heaven is manufacturable*' yet is also a place that 'does not exist . . . technically' since according to maps it is nothing more than a postal district ('ZIP code: 90049') (*PD*, pp. 147, 164). Robert McGill – in a sophisticated examination of what he calls Coupland's 'geography of apocalypse' – suggests that the 'Californian impulse is to live up to its utopian mythology, through pretence if not through fact'. Drawing on Jean Baudrillard's *America* (1988) – a suitably genre defying comparison for the 'Brentwood Notebook' – McGill notes that the hyperreality of this landscape 'engenders a depthless mode of existence that seeks to simulate the unachieved utopia without having a realized model on which to base itself'.[23] Coupland implies that Brentwood itself is a paper-thin story, a mirage of the perfect, heavenly space rather than the thing itself. Brentwood, as a faux utopian urban space apparently at the end of history, had enjoyed a 'covenant of invisibility' (*PD*, p. 162), but it has also gained a distinctly postmodern kind of fame from its association with the bizarre deaths of two of its celebrity residents: Marilyn Monroe, the 30th anniversary of whose apparent suicide coincides with Coupland's visit and Nicole Brown, the former wife of O. J. Simpson, murdered together with another man, only weeks before the composition of this 4 August 1994 notebook.

This distinctly dystopian view of what briefly became the most infamous North American suburb parallels the widespread contemporary antipathy for middle-class ways of life. Indeed, in an article on the 'Brentwood Notebook', David Hamers argues that one way of reading Coupland's postmodern scrapbook is to see it as 'a pessimistic argument in which a cultural diagnosis of postmodern pathology is linked up with a nostalgic desire for community'. In fact, Hamers proposes that the piece would be more profitably read as 'an experiment with time and place' but it is difficult to deny that Coupland prioritizes a critique of Californian artifice.[24] 'It is hard to find anyone with a good word to say about surburbia', claims Susan Brook, asserting that the 'image of the suburbs as homogenous and conformist is pervasive' in both popular culture and literary criticism.[25] Images of the middle-class periphery in fiction, film and television emphasize the correlation between monotonous, repressive conservatism and private decadence or violence. This allegedly bland mode of community, integral to the post-industrial landscape, is regularly deployed in contemporary narrative as a signifier of mediocrity, imaginative lack and spiritual futility. *American Beauty* (1999), Ang Lee's adaptation of *The Ice Storm* (1997) and the television series *Desperate Housewives* (2004–) perpetuate an apparently highly marketable myth of shallow suburban serenity that masks clandestine moral corruption.

The alleged sterility and blandness of suburban life, however, holds a paradoxical sense of creativity and mystery for Coupland. In fact, the aversion to Brentwood might originate in his desire to re-enchant the suburbs of North America. 'For millions of Canadians,' Coupland observes, 'the suburbs are life's main experience' but they are rarely referred to without 'disdain'. '[S]uburbanites' represent 'the bulk of Canadian society, yet history books come to a screaming halt at the well-mowed edges of a subdivision, a light-industrial-park or a big-box mall' (*SOC*, p. 107). If the youth culture emphasis of Coupland's early fiction easily fits his designation as reluctant spokesperson for a nameless generation, it might now be more appropriate to read him as a literary advocate of a *space* that similarly lacks a unique identity: his work is generating an ambivalent poetics of the North American suburbs.

Miss Wyoming – paralleling Coupland's airborne vision of the unknowable wilderness in *Souvenir of Canada* – features an unfamiliar vision of suburbia from the sky. Gazing down from a plane that will shortly plummet to earth, Susan Colgate reflects on the banality of 'just another American town that bought Tide, ate Campbell's soup and generated at least one weird, senseless killing per decade' (*MW*, p. 15). This dismissive description is balanced by Susan's brief, secluded contentment in the Ohio town where the plane crash-lands. Susan seeks out the empty, cool and manufactured interior space of an ordinary suburb home. This is the kind of domestic space – much disparaged in the elitist cultural imagination – that her own soap-opera style childhood and subsequent acting career has denied her. It is no coincidence that Susan's most famous television role was in a long-running sitcom called *Meet the Blooms*, the kind of sentimental show that fortifies the mythology of suburban contentment: the loss of this simulated reality, her ejection from the virtual paradise of television, allows her to seek a corollary in the 'real world'. The 'normalcy' of the empty house that Susan lets herself into is 'so extreme' she has the sensation of having travelled hundreds of years into the future and having entered a 'diorama recreating middle-class North American life in the late twentieth century' (*MW*, p. 19). The ordinariness of the suburbs evaporates and the banal is remade as a magical space. The illicit occupation of the house is thrilling for Susan and its monotonous stability a reminder of her own transience. This motif is repeated in *Eleanor Rigby*, when Liz Dunn, as a self-conscious child, finds her greatest pleasure in 'being all alone' after compulsively breaking into temporarily vacated homes, feeling 'like a ghost who had come back . . . to remember the world as it once was'.[26]

Liz's pseudo-spectral status, like Susan's 'death' in the plane crash and her resurrection in the suburban home, are emblematic of a wider search for stable identity. *'I live on the border, between two states'*, writes Simon Armitage in *All Points North* (1999), a lyrical exploration of regional identity.[27] This liminal sensibility is important for Coupland's many dwellers of suburbia. In *Girlfriend in a Coma* (1998), for example, Richard Doorland and his circle of friends are conscious that their lives are trapped between disparate worlds: growing up in the suburbs of North Vancouver, a space that connects the progress of the 'city of glass' and the organic worlds of the wilderness and timeless forests. Similarly, in *Hey Nostradamus!*, Heather describes the liminal but 'ludicrous' position of a fraudulent medium's house: 'at the top of a mountain . . . a yodel away from pristine wilderness, an existence made possible only through petroleum and some sort of human need for remaining remote while being relatively close to many others'.[28]

The protagonists in *Girlfriend in a Coma* not only occupy a literal geographical midpoint but are also brought up as children of 'the middlest of middle classes' and as 'middle-class dull to the point of scientific measurability' (*GIAC*, p. 39). Yet the suburbs, apparently the last place to merit revelation, become the space in which Coupland chooses to play out dreams of apocalypse.[29] This end-of-the-world fantasy is foreshadowed in '1,000 Years (Life After God)', when Dana – former model for dubious adult publications and now a zealous, if unlikely, convert – earnestly tells the narrator that 'God is descending into the suburbs, Scout.'[30] This might be the opportunity for suburban spiritual satire but the specifics of the location are important: the divine is caught up in the everyday, in the banal, and suburbia, rather than being excluded or mocked, is at the centre of the story. Part of popular culture's anti-suburban rhetoric relates to its lack of history: the suburbs typically have neither the splendour of age nor the pristine purity of brand new, metropolitan architecture.

Yet in his primarily Vancouver set narratives, Coupland emphasizes the aesthetic possibilities of the suburbs. He has cheekily noted that one of the reasons why so many US movies and television shows are now filmed in the suburbs of Vancouver and Toronto is because these peaceful neighbourhoods resemble 'the way the United States was *supposed* to have turned out . . . When people dream the American dream, they're often dreaming of Canadian suburban mainstays' (*SOC,*

p. 110). Suburban Canada has mutated into a simulation of the 'dream' that is somehow more viable than that nurtured in its nation of origin, the United States. In '1,000 Years (Life After God)', sitting outside a house in North Vancouver that is 'about as suburban as suburban gets', Scout states that 'the city before us will glow gold, a dozen construction cranes transforming its profile almost by the hour' (*LAG*, pp. 286–8). Similarly, in *Girlfriend in a Coma*, Vancouver and its suburbs are figured as places of promise. At the beginning of the novel, Richard stands on top of Grouse Mountain 'overlooking a shimmering city below, a city so new that it dreamed only of what the embryo knows, a shimmering light of civil peace and hope for the future' (*GIAC*, p. 6).

   'My own theory about Vancouver,' states Coupland in his collaborative, pictorial celebration of home, *City of Glass* (2000), 'is that we're at our best when we're experimenting with new ideas, and at our worst when we ape the conventions of elsewhere.' In fact, Coupland's Vancouver, for all its malleability when it becomes a variety of simulated North American cities for the big screen, is dynamically different from the United States. The writer accentuates the 'liberating' quality of the city's 'lack of historical luggage' that 'dazzles with a sense of limitless possibility' (*COG*, p. 58). This fascination with place – even the supposedly static suburbs – as a dynamic, shifting form is most explicit in Coupland's writings of the road.

'The romance of the road': Coupland and travel-space

'Travel dissolves you', reflects Liz Dunn in *Eleanor Rigby*, during her second, rather surreal excursion to Europe. During Liz's first, adolescent trip – a mostly disappointing high-school visit to Rome – she became pregnant; almost thirty years later, her presence accidentally causes an international incident at Frankfurt airport and, in a spirit of ambivalent happy endings, reunites the hapless narrator with the father of her son. Journeys, Liz suggests, precipitate the need to 'rebuild yourself' and force 'you to remember where you're from' (*ER*, p. 204). One of the essays in *Souvenir of Canada* similarly explores 'the psychic vulnerability caused by travel' and, like Liz, concludes that, in the indeterminate journey space, 'identity dissolves' (*SOC*, p. 27). In the same volume, Coupland describes the transformative impact of a rare train journey that he took from Vancouver to Toronto: personal and national memories fuse in his 'visions of the pioneers and locusts and bison and 1930s gangsters'; the traveller and the journey become inseparable in his narration as he becomes 'part of the road and part of the journey' conscious that 'the prairies' are 'unfolding even as you read this, for someone else is making that exact same trek across the land' (*SOC*, p. 91).

A number of Coupland's narratives explore the alternative relationships to space generated by travel and its implications for identity. Most of the novels include significant plane journeys. Quixotic references to space flight – a residue of the cultural memories from a more optimistic age – are another motif of mobility. Claire's story of Buck the Astronaut in *Generation X* and Richard Doorland's Hallowe'en costume in *Girlfriend in a Coma*, 'a silver Apollo astronaut's suit', are reminders of a vanished New World confidence associated with the space race (*GX*, p. 46; *GIAC*, p. 101). *All Families are Psychotic* extends this motif with Sarah Drummond's imminent NASA mission: '*Space knows no limitations*,' reflects her mother, born in a pre-Second World War age when this way of conceptualizing the universe was barely credible (*AFAP*, p. 6).

Coupland's interest in travel, however, does not normally transcend the limits of earth-bound gravity. Road stories – in a sense, the classic North American genre – are frequently included in his fiction. Coupland, like Jack Kerouac and other Beat writers, is enthralled by the mixed blessing of what John Johnson in *Miss Wyoming* names 'the romance of the *road*' (*MW*, p. 52).

One particular expanse of road from Coupland's native Vancouver – the Lions Gate Bridge, linking the city of Vancouver with its North Shore – is a recurrent presence in both his fiction and non-fiction: this structure connects more than the districts of a city; for Coupland this 'fairy-tale bridge' becomes a 'a structure so potent and glorious' that it has become 'the actual *architecture*' of his imagination. In his tribute to the bridge – originally published in *Vancouver Magazine* but subsequently reprinted in both *Polaroids from the Dead* and *City of Glass* – Coupland invites the reader to consider if their home has 'a structure through which all of your dreams and ideas and hopes are funneled' (*PD*, p. 69). A view of the bridge at night, delicately illuminated, generates memories of Coupland's youth as he anticipated his sixteenth birthday and would be able to 'drive into that magic city bathed in light' (*PD*, p. 73). In spite of his critique of modernity and its penchant for speed, the writer does not escape the tendency to make a fetish of the automobile. However, the 'bridge's very existence', he observes, 'is a metaphor for journey' (*PD*, p. 70). Coupland is unable to view this construction as 'merely a tool, a piece of infrastructure that can be casually deleted' and, relating stories from his own and the city's past to Lions Gate, he ponders the consequences 'its vanishing might have on our interior lives' (*PD*, p. 74). Similarly, in 'Life After God (1,000 Years)' the experience of driving over Lions Gate Bridge becomes a proxy for creative thinking: 'the act of endless motion itself a substitute for any larger form of thought' (*LAG*, p. 272). For Coupland hectic, car-crammed roads are not just a banal part of an environmentally ruined landscape; like the apparently dull suburbs, they are filled with romantic and imaginative potential.

Fictions of the road are particularly significant in *Generation X*, *Shampoo Planet* and *Miss Wyoming* but most of the novels incorporate transformative journeys. In *Microserfs*, for example, the ex-Microsoft staffers leave Washington for the (postmodern) Promised Land of the Californian Silicon Valley. The trip to Palo Alto – a kind of pastiche exodus – is, in a sense, a regressive journey for Dan, since it involves a return to his family home. It is also a return to the odd ambience of the suburbs. In gaining independence from Bill Gates – a powerful father-surrogate – he is simultaneously relinquishing autonomy by moving in with his biological parents, though he has collected a diverse troupe of surrogate siblings during his adventures in Washington. Bug, the most fractious of his pseudo-brothers, 'romanticiz[es]' the trip even before it has begun, insisting on 'playing that old '70s song, "Convoy"' (*MS*, p. 97). In this quotation from an earlier, rather clichéd road story – an allusion that stands somewhere between irony and idealization – Coupland craftily reminds his reader of a pop culture tradition of comic travelling.

Other members of Dan's extended family have their own idiosyncratic fascination with roads: Susan and Karla, for example, become infatuated with a 1975 *Handbook of Highway Engineering* and its captivating illustrations of new, empty roads: 'So clean and pure and undriven' (*MS*, p. 53). This fascination parallels work in software engineering that, in the mid-1990s, was helping to generate the virtual road of the 'information superhighway' (*MS*, p. 47). Significantly, the novelty of the Internet seems less appealing to these decidedly IT-literate characters than the 'real' space of the open road. When an earthquake strikes Los Angeles in January 1994, Ethan – a local boy – actually sheds tears when he sees images of his 'beloved freeways' in ruins (*MS*, p. 223). He even replicates a 'freeway cloverleaf' in Lego with the odd – and perhaps puritanical – intention of demolishing and rebuilding the plastic structure (*MS*, p. 231).

Katie Mills has examined the ways in which Coupland re-scripts the road story in *Generation X* for a changing America, proposing that the novel 'alters the . . . genre by uniting the Beats' romantic urge to escape with its own postmodern romanticism'.[31] Bug's appropriation of 'Convoy' – a popular movie as well as a hit song – emphasizes that tradition of 'postmodern romanticism'. Mills's argument makes particular reference to Andy's story – 'a failure when I told it . . . a few months ago "The Young Man Who Desperately Wanted to Be Hit by Lightning"' (*GX*, p. 201). This unresolved tale of the search for adventure and significance amid the dangers of nature, Mills notes, parallels its narrator's own quest. The novel ends with Andy on the road – travelling to meet his friends in Mexico – and, following an epiphanic experience (examined in more detail in Chapter 5), he is both physically wounded and spiritually enlivened by the journey (*GX*, p. 208).

If Andy and Bug both idealize the experience of travel – their wanderlust intensified by private or popular stories of the road – Tyler Johnson has an unashamedly (and unsurprisingly) consumerist approach to travel. The self-assured narrator of *Shampoo Planet* – an impatient young man who is unlikely to cherish battered copies of Beat novels – reflects that road trips 'are like fast-forwarding through life, zapping out the boring bits, fulfilling my (according to Anna-Louise last Christmas during a long bout of zapper-intense TV-channel trolling) male need for magic' (*SP*, pp. 221–2). This idiom of enchantment that couples the supposedly real space of the road with the illusory realm of multi-channel television is revealing: in the heavily mediated, MTV-lit world of Tyler's mind, the journey remains an imaginative as well as a literal experience. Tyler's confident, unreflective belief in mobility as a kind of given resonates with Zygmunt Bauman's observation that 'distance' is no longer perceived as a significant obstacle: 'Sometimes it seems that it exists solely in order to be cancelled; as if space was but a constant invitation to slight it, refute and deny.'[32] Coupland's fiction registers these issues – as a 'Global Teen' Tyler is part of a generation of Westerners who view the world as a playground – but it does not offer a substantial account of the disappearance of distance or of its economic consequences of globalization and social mobility for those from the economically oppressed Two-thirds World.

Generation X and *Shampoo Planet* both feature rites of passage journeys from the United States into Canada: these border-crossing narratives embody Coupland's interest in the complexities of contemporary national identity and in the atavistic compulsion to travel. Coupland's debut novel begins with Andy's recollection of his first significant solo jaunt, aged fifteen, to observe a total eclipse in Brandon, Manitoba (*GX*, p. 3). This recollection subtly connects the modern predilection for mobility with the search for timeless emotion and experience: Andy is intuitively aware that his rare encounter with this elliptical light connects him with young people throughout history.

In *Shampoo Planet*, Tyler – whose destination, like the former Microserfs, is California and the hope of riches – begins his journey with a trip into the country of his birth. On board a 'ferry headed from Port Angeles, Washington, toward Vancouver Island', Tyler is thrilled at the realization that he has 'crossed an invisible line – a border – into Canada' (*SP*, p. 187). Tyler is accompanied by Stephanie – a character from the 'Old World' of European hierarchy and tradition – and his response to this symbolic journey borders on religious ecstasy: 'My past lies behind me like a bonfire of anchors and I am freed from the trappings of identity . . . I feel unpredictable and shockingly new' (*SP*, pp. 187–8). This sensation of renewal echoes puritan hopes for the New World (discussed in more detail in Chapters 2 and 5), and myths of the frontier. The elation of this encounter with the Canadian landscape inverts the sensation of Tyler's trip to Europe – narrated in flashback – in which he encountered the 'the jaded, elegant hysteria of Paris' (*SP*, p. 105). Indeed, as he gazes over a cliff, at 'the end of the world', Tyler, this child of the New World, is delighted by the vista's difference from 'Europe's overhistoried countrysides dusted with charcoal and laced with unmoving gullies of pureed smoker's lung' (*SP*, p. 191).

Tyler is an inheritor of a world that has already been mapped and colonized, but, as a reasonably financially independent (though, by US standards, not rich) individual, he is able to replicate old journeys into the unknown. For Tyler, like Dan in *Microserfs*, the journey constitutes a reverse migration, the brief visitation to his place of birth an attempt to recover a more stable sense of origin (*SP*, p. 189). Transience – a consequence of social mobility – is the novel's dominant sensation. *Shampoo Planet* – in common with *Generation X* and *All Families are Psychotic* – begins in a motel bedroom. This is space that might bear the scent of other personal histories, if they were not chemically erased every day; the motel room is a dumb witness to a culture in flux. Janet Drummond, awaking in her rather seedy motel, finds the space disorientating, making 'her feel slightly too transient' (*AFAP*, p. 5). Tyler, by contrast, professes enthusiasm for hotel and motel rooms because they free their occupants from the burdens of history: 'There is no past' and they become, therefore, 'most ideal places indeed to be' (*SP*, pp. 30–1).

Flight from the past is a vital theme of *Miss Wyoming*, the closest that Coupland has come to writing a novel that sits explicitly within the 'road story' tradition. *Generation X* and *Shampoo Planet* explore the phenomenon of travel, and the protagonists of the former, in particular, are aware of the possibilities represented by escape. However, in Coupland's sixth novel, multiple forms of road narrative converge in the parallel peripatetic stories of John Johnson and Susan Colgate. Some of these plots include cross-state car journeys but the novel's principal mode of transport is distinctively old-fashioned or even un-American: John and Susan pursue their initially separate retreats from the civilized world on foot. John's journey – following an apparent nervous breakdown – is later dismissed as a 'disastrous experiment in hobodom' (*MW*, p. 55). Whatever its success, the journey's trajectory is significant: in modern American mythology, travellers reach their destination in California after a long journey West; John reverses this narrative by beginning his expedition in Los Angeles and then walking towards the East.

Before he leaves his lucrative, comfortable life behind – a radical departure in which he declares that he will no longer be American but a 'citizen of *nowhere*' – John idealizes the romance of the road: 'Adventures every ten minutes . . . No crappy rules or smothering obligations' (*MW*, pp. 51–2). Despite John's desire to lose his citizenship, the pursuit of a new beginning – and a blank space in which to rewrite identity – is a peculiarly American tradition. His wish to become a 'sensate creature walking the country's burning freeways . . . its gashes of wilderness' and, in particular, 'its lightning storms', makes John a direct literary descendant of Andy Palmer's imaginary 'Young Man Who Desperately Wanted to Hit by Lightning' (*GX*, p. 201).

One of the problems with John's 'Kerouac routine' – his life as 'a dharma bum' – is that it is not new (*MW*, pp. 60, 62). The desire to find answers on the road has a long history in American literature; James Fenimore Cooper's Natty Bumppo, Mark Twain's Huck Finn and Jack Kerouac's Sal Paradise from *On the Road* (1957) have all strolled across the land first. The trope of dropping out and taking to the open road is a further point of continuity and, in terms of interpretation, a radical difference between Coupland and his precursors in the Beat generation. Since a literary model of aimless, bohemian wandering already exists – and, in the minds of his peculiarly conformist, commercially successful friends in Hollywood, it is a romantic ideal that has lost all credibility – John's journey seems condemned to failure before he undertakes it. 'The road is *over* . . . It never even *was*', claims his closest friend, Ivan. This cynic unflatteringly compares John's project to adolescent fantasies of escape, mocking the naive belief that Kerouac held a secret alternative to the bruising, dull realities of everyday life (*MW*, p. 52). Is the narrative itself as cynical as Ivan about the 'road' and endeavours at self-discovery on the journey? John, like a number of Coupland's restless wanderers, longs for the unmapped, indeterminate wasteland. His search belongs to what David Jasper has described as the quasi-theological pursuit of 'the Other, found in the immensity of vast open space for which we yearn in our contracting world'.[33] Can the supposedly vacant, clean spaces of the desert or the vast American wilderness transform disillusion into something more substantial? Why does this unforgiving landscape continue to retain its mystique for the contemporary imagination?

'Blank space at the end of a chapter': the desert experience

When John Johnson 'nose-dive[s] deeper into the American landscape' he is both pursuing independence and searching for a form of miraculous, vanishing space (*MW*, p. 170). 'What haunts me', states Naomi Klein, 'is not exactly the absence of literal space so much as a deep craving for metaphorical space: release, escape, some kind of open-ended freedom'.[34] The pursuit of this 'metaphorical space' is a vital theme in much late twentieth- and early twenty-first century fiction tagged postmodern. In Don DeLillo's *Americana* (1971), David Bell – who, like John Johnson, works in the entertainment industry – attempts a journey 'into the depths of America, wilderness dream of all poets . . . westward to match the shadows of my image and my self'.[35] It is a delirious quest that results in picaresque adventures but little evidence of enlightenment.

'[T]he longing to escape an overly complex and materially corrupt civilization', suggests Alan Bilton, is both '*the* great American theme'

and the defining issue of Coupland's work.[36] He argues that Coupland
is rewriting 'America's seemingly inexhaustible pastoral ideal' and
particularly the concept that the wilderness represents 'redemption,
salvation from the corrupting influence of civilization'.[37] Henry David
Thoreau's idealistic project of self-sufficiency at Walden Pond certainly
finds an echo in *Generation X*. Andy, Dag and Claire's escape to the
periphery of society, on the border between the hyperreal space
of Californian civilization and the wastes of the desert is a kind of
unconscious Walden-style project, though their storytelling is a far
more relaxed iteration of transcendentalism.

Their Californian destination reimagines a long-standing European-
American myth: the journey West by a group hoping to find sanctuary.
Palm Springs, replete with shopping malls and cosmetic surgery clinics
is, however, a rather ironic refuge. More significant, for Andy, is their
proximity to the scorched, barren, abandoned land of the desert: 'the
equivalent of blank space at the end of a chapter' (*GX*, p. 19). The
storytellers' expectations of the desert are not specific and, as such,
they are not truly capable of disappointment. Is there any difference
between the assumed sublime of the 'blank' wilderness and the
anonymity of the suburbs? John M. Ulrich has used Baudrillard's claim
that 'the whole of America is a desert' to explore the function of the
wilderness space in Coupland's first novel.[38] Unlike Baudrillard's
vision of the apocalyptic, Ulrich argues that Coupland's 'desert
functions not as the aesthetic form of superficiality but as its *negation
and erasure*'. Andy, Dag and Claire's desert is 'born of the desire to
recover the social and the sentimental, to reinscribe it in a new space
that, rather than ecstatic and visible, remains subtle and private'.[39] For
this group, storytelling recuperates the parched, infertile landscape:
the desert resists commerce and human intervention but promotes
imaginative endeavour.

John Johnson's solitary experience is, initially at least, far bleaker. As
he collapses in the wilderness, John looks at 'this landscape so savage
and broken . . . this desert, this blank space' and recognizes that future
generations will neither understand nor tame the land that 'would
always outsmart them, always be just one notch more cruel' (*MW*,
p. 173). Unlike the hopeful protagonists in *Generation X*, the wilderness
encountered by John Johnson is not just literally arid; it is also an
imaginative disappointment: the purity of the 'blank space at the end
of the chapter' is not, after all, what this exile hoped to find. Johnson

later bitterly reflects that his experience of the 'road was a sham . . . His exercise in going solo was a cosmic joke' (*MW*, p. 174). 'Over and over again in Coupland's work, the faithful pilgrim returns from the wilderness disappointed and unenlightened', notes Bilton.[40] The experience of disillusionment is visceral but it is also often a temporary sensation; indeed, disenchantment might even be a vital form of interior 'desert' experience in itself.

The anonymous narrator of 'In the Desert', Coupland's most focused wilderness fiction, is more terrified than enlightened by his encounter with the 'Nothingness' of the Mojave Desert (*LAG*, p. 167). In *Girlfriend in a Coma*, Linus spends four years pursuing 'romantic solo wanderings'; like John Johnson's peripatetic flight, his journey is a deliberate 'venture into nothingdom' (*GIAC*, p. 76). The road is not the place of revelation that Linus hoped it might have been; his friends are frustrated that he had no 'revelation' on his long trip across North America. Yet for John and Linus the road and the wilderness are a prelude to a more substantial change: these characters, in spite of their frustrations, are capable of connecting with other people more sympathetically and creatively than before. The disorientated driver of 'In the Desert', who faces death in an arid wasteland, has a still deeper encounter with otherness. Rescued by a mysterious, taciturn stranger, he is left with a memory of a 'windburned face' and the too scarce 'possibility of forgiveness and kindness' in the desert of the wider world (*LAG*, pp. 212–13).

'The present epoch will perhaps be above all the epoch of space', speculated Michel Foucault in 'Of Other Spaces' (1986), his succinct but highly influential contribution to human geography.[41] Coupland, in Foucault's terms, might be both a 'descendant of time' – an inheritor of the nineteenth-century fascination with temporality and narrative – and a 'determined inhabitant of space', an artist who is sensitive to the limits imposed on individuals and societies by governing concepts of location and environment. 'How much a part of us is the landscape, and how much are we a part of it?' asks the narrator of 'In the Desert' (*LAG*, p. 210). Implicit in Coupland's writing is the call for a spatialized rather than a purely linear, time-bound imagination. Coupland is continually fascinated by both cluttered, hyperreal terrain and the desert spaces in which 'endless pioneers' continue to forge delicate identities 'along the plastic radiant way' of a world that is no longer new (*MW*, p. 311).

Notes

1 Douglas Coupland, *Souvenir of Canada* (Vancouver: Douglas & McIntyre, 2002), pp. 4–5. All subsequent references will be given parenthetically as *SOC*, followed by page reference.
2 F. Scott Fitzgerald, *The Great Gatsby* (London: Penguin, 1990), p. 171.
3 Douglas Coupland, *Microserfs* (London: Harper, 2004), p. 24. All subsequent references will be given parenthetically as *MS*, followed by page reference.
4 Edward W. Soja, *Postmodern Geographies: The Reassertion of Space in Critical Social Theory* (London: Verso, 1989), p. 1.
5 Ibid., p. 1.
6 James Howard Kunstler, *The Geography of Nowhere: The Rise and Decline of America's Man-Made Landscape* (New York: Touchstone, 1993). 'Capitals of Unreality' is the title of Chapter 12.
7 Douglas Coupland, *Polaroids from the Dead* (London: Flamingo, 1997), p. 112. All subsequent references will be given parenthetically as *PD*, followed by page reference.
8 Kunstler, p. 10.
9 Alan Bilton, *An Introduction to Contemporary American Fiction* (Edinburgh: Edinburgh University Press, 2002), p. 222.
10 For a detailed discussion of this idea and 'the cultural impact of living in a software age' see Graham Thompson, ' "Frank Lloyd Oop": *Microserfs*, Modern Migration, and the Architecture of the Nineties', *Canadian Review of American Studies*, 31 (2001), 119–35.
11 Douglas Coupland, 'Nostalgia's dead', *Architectural Record*, 187.2 (1999), 39–40 (39).
12 Douglas Coupland, *Miss Wyoming* (London: Flamingo, 2000), p. 106. All subsequent references will be given parenthetically as *MW*, followed by page reference.
13 Kunstler, p. 10.
14 Douglas Coupland, *Generation X: Tales for an Accelerated Culture* (London: Abacus, 1992), p. 80. All subsequent references will be given parenthetically as *GX*, followed by page reference.
15 G. P. Lainsbury, '*Generation X* and the End of History', *Essays on Canadian Writing*, 58 (1996), 229–40 (236).
16 Douglas Coupland, *Shampoo Planet* (London: Simon & Schuster, 1993), p. 141. All subsequent references will be given parenthetically as *SP*, followed by page reference.
17 Douglas Coupland, *Girlfriend in a Coma* (London: Flamingo, 1998), p. 71. All subsequent references will be given parenthetically as *GIAC*, followed by page reference.
18 Douglas Coupland, *All Families are Psychotic* (London: Flamingo, 2001), p. 23. All subsequent references will be given parenthetically as *AFAP*, followed by page reference.

19 Douglas Coupland, *City of Glass: Douglas Coupland's Vancouver* (Vancouver: Douglas & McIntyre, 2000), p. 151. All subsequent references will be given parenthetically as *COG*, followed by page reference.

20 Eleanor Byrne and Martin McQuillan, *Deconstructing Disney* (London: Pluto Press, 1999), p. 174.

21 David Lyon, *Jesus in Disneyland: Religion in Postmodern Times* (Cambridge: Polity Press, 2000), p. 11.

22 Jean Baudrillard, *Simulacra and Simulation*, translated by Sheila Faria Glaser (Ann Arbor: University of Michigan Press, 1994), p. 12.

23 Robert McGill, 'The Sublime Simulation: Vancouver in Douglas Coupland's Geography of Apocalypse', *Essays on Canadian Writing*, 70 (2000), 252–76 (260).

24 David Hamers, 'Having arrived, time to move on: Coupland's Brentwood with space and time', *Environment and Planning A*, 33.12 (2001), 2109–25 (2110).

25 Susan Brook, 'Hedgemony? Suburban space in *The Buddha of Suburbia*', in *British Fiction of the 1990s*, edited by Nick Bentley (London: Routledge, 2005), pp. 209–25 (p. 209).

26 Douglas Coupland, *Eleanor Rigby* (London: Fourth Estate, 2004), p. 45. All subsequent references will be given parenthetically as *ER*, followed by page reference.

27 Simon Armitage, *All Points North* (London: Penguin, 1999), p. 1.

28 Douglas Coupland, *Hey Nostradamus!* (London: Flamingo, 2003), p. 209. All subsequent references will be given parenthetically as *HN*, followed by page reference.

29 For a more detailed discussion of Coupland's imaginative use of Vancouver and accumulated myths of the West in reimagining a postmodern sublime see McGill's highly persuasive article, cited above.

30 Douglas Coupland, *Life After God* (London: Simon & Schuster, 1994), p. 298. All subsequent references will be given parenthetically as *LAG*, followed by page reference.

31 Katie Mills, '"Await Lightning": *How Generation X Remaps the Road Story*', in *GenXegesis: Essays on Alternative Youth (Sub)Culture*, ed. by John M. Ulrich and Andrea L. Harris (Madison: University of Wisconsin Press, 2003), pp. 221–48 (p. 223).

32 Zygmunt Bauman, *Globalization: the Human Consequences* (Cambridge: Polity, 1998), p. 77.

33 David Jasper, *The Sacred Desert: Religion, Literature, Art and Culture* (Oxford: Blackwell, 2004), p. 64.

34 Naomi Klein, *No Logo: Taking Aim At the Brand Bullies* (London: Flamingo, 2000), p. 64.

35 Don DeLillo, *Americana* (London: Penguin, 1990), p. 341.

36 Bilton, p. 220.

37 Ibid., p. 221.
38 John M. Ulrich, 'Introduction: Generation X: A (Sub)Cultural Genealogy', in *GenXegesis: Essays on Alternative Youth Culture*, ed. by John M. Ulrich and Andrea L. Harris (Madison: University of Wisconsin Press, 2003), pp. 3–37 (p. 15).
39 Ulrich, p. 16.
40 Bilton, p. 227.
41 Michel Foucault, 'Of Other Spaces', translated by Jay Miskowiec, *Diacritics* 16 (1986), 22–7 (22). Quoted in Soja, p. 10.

5

'You are the first generation raised without religion': Coupland and postmodern spirituality

> I began to wonder what exactly I had believed in . . . Precisely articulating one's beliefs is difficult. My own task had been made more difficult because I had been raised without religion by parents who had broken with their own pasts and moved to the West Coast – who had raised their children clean of any ideology in a cantilevered modern house overlooking the Pacific Ocean – at the end of history, or so they had wanted to believe.[1] (*Life After God*, 1994)

Belief, or its absence, haunts Douglas Coupland's most dispirited protagonists. The wilderness reflections, for example, uttered by the anonymous narrator of 'In the Desert' – one of the thematically interconnected narratives in *Life After God* – pivot around a sensation of spiritual dissatisfaction that is shared by many individuals in Coupland's fiction. This desert sojourner's conviction that he was raised in a creedal vacuum, without fixed beliefs – a personal history 'clean of any ideology' – is optimistic but, as he suspects, not entirely credible. The blank-slate, zero history contexts that he and many of his contemporaries view as normative are, above all else, potent, if invisible, ideologies. A liberal capitalist, 'end of history' worldview attempts to inhibit any argument that disrupts the prevailing reality, including subversive spiritual codes that anticipate either an alternative world or a future that might supersede, rather than merely materially enhance, the present era. The unspoken ideals of this nameless narrator's upbringing echo one theologian's description of post-modernism as the triumph of the concept 'that the once hoped-for future of the human race has arrived'. 'It is not a new age because the ages have come to an end, and now everything that once was is to be recuperated and used – as we like – in our fashioning.'[2]

The confessional, first-person accounts of spiritual lack in *Life After God* should not be read as straightforward autobiographical narratives. However, Coupland has acknowledged that his own childhood was similarly free of specific religious values. 'Imagine the year is 1970 and you are eight years old. Imagine that you have no religion', he asks the reader in an essay on his childhood admiration for James Rosenquist and pop art. 'Imagine that the houses lived in by you and your friends are all built by contractors and furnished with dreams provided by *Life* magazine. Imagine that you inhabit a world with no history and no ideology.'³

Why would any citizen of such an apparently liberated, post-ideological, post-historical world need to make use of a religious vocabulary? For many avant-garde writers of the early twentieth century, a life without religion represented a distant utopia that might be glimpsed only in dreams. In novels such as *Life After God* and *Girlfriend in a Coma* (1998), however, the lack of access to a shared idiom that has been considered sacred – even one that may have been repudiated in adult life – renders articulation of spiritual concerns difficult, even if those crises are momentary. The restless narrator of 'In the Desert', for example, spends much of his wilderness chronicle 'trying to understand the notion of Belief' and, in spite of his alienation from the disembodied, fundamentalist Christian voices that boom from the car radio, he at last makes the unexpected confession that he too believes 'there is a God' (*LAG*, p. 210). This intimate, fragile affiliation between faith and scepticism embodies the complex engagement with religious ideas in Coupland's fiction.

In a 1994 interview with *USA Today*, the novelist, then celebrated for his postmodern cynicism and acute satires of the consumerist Zeitgeist in *Generation X* (1991) and *Shampoo Planet* (1992), made the surprising declaration: 'Everything I write or think about now seems, in the end, to veer toward the religious . . . This wasn't something I ever expected to happen.'⁴ Coupland's reputation in the early 1990s was as a hip prophet with an acute sensibility for the pleasures and disappointments of pop culture, yet since the beginning of his literary career, his writing has been suffused with a sense of *Weltschmerz*, a desire for a world beyond ephemera and sensation. This chapter explores the unpredictable religious impulse that informs Coupland's fiction in the light of Zygmunt Bauman's notion of the postmodern condition as one of 're-enchantment'. For Bauman, a defining characteristic of postmodernity has been a restoration of the capacity for wonder in Western value systems and a rejection of modernity's absolute faith in rationalism and the narrative of unfettered human progress:

> All in all, postmodernity can be seen as restoring to the world what modernity presumptuously, had taken away; as a *re-enchantment* of the world that modernity tried hard to *dis-enchant*. It is the modern artifice that has been dismantled; the modern conceit of meaning-legislating reason that has been exposed, condemned and put to shame. It is that artifice and that reason, the reason of the artifice, that stands accused in the court of postmodernity.[5]

Where does a liberal and ostensibly secular writer fit into this apparent resurgence of 'enchanted' worldviews? Unsurprisingly, there is certainly no enthusiasm in Coupland's fiction for a return to a pre-Enlightenment world of superstition and the doctrinaire regimes of religious or secular hierarchies. Neither do his narratives of our 'accelerated culture' demonstrate misplaced nostalgia for an age in which morality was easily and absolutely safeguarded by ecclesiastical authority. Yet his novels actively and explicitly mourn for those 'who once knew what profoundness was, but who lost or became numb to the sensation of wonder – people who closed the doors that lead us into the secret world' and maps routes towards the possibilities of faith (*LAG*, p. 51). The perceptible evaporation of traditional religious ideas and practices from the everyday rituals of mainstream Western life in the twentieth century also raises questions about the relationship between popular culture and spirituality. If consensus has been obliterated, can the postmodern novelist tell tales of religious or political significance? Can contemporary novels that explore spiritual questions transcend accusations of fashionable flirtation with low-commitment, elastic religion?

'[S]ociety has lost a shared set of references gleaned from a particular text or texts, by which it could identify and articulate the spiritual quest', observes Paul Fiddes.[6] For the late capitalist world that Coupland narrates, any 'shared set of references' is unlikely to derive from a single, self-proclaimed authoritative body of scriptures such as the Bible. This idea is emphasized in the epigraph to 'In the Desert'. 'You are the first generation raised without religion' (*LAG*, p. 161). The statement is deliberately neutral; the absence is both blessing and curse, suggesting liberation and lack. As an axiom it consciously mimics the text-based public art of Jenny Holzer, whose work, discussed in the introduction, Coupland admires and whom he cites in *All Families are Psychotic* (2001). It is also an unmistakable rewriting of Gertrude Stein's famous declaration to the group of American authors, including Ernest Hemingway and F. Scott Fitzgerald, who emerged in the hedonistic, post-war and pre-Depression era of the 1920s: 'You are all a lost generation.' Hemingway famously used this desolate sobriquet as an epigraph for *The Sun Also Rises* (1926). Importantly, however, he placed it alongside an extended quotation from Ecclesiastes, which is also the source of the novel's American title.[7] Hemingway's self-destructive characters live amid a riot of alcohol and despair but the novel's appropriation of religious tradition implies that their present existential suffering has a sense of theological depth. By contrast, Coupland's characters are rarely able to draw directly on the consolations of a forgotten religion.

Where does a so-called secular writer find the resources to explore 'sacred' questions? Coupland's critique of materialism is informed by an ongoing negotiation with a variety of distinctive religious traditions: visionary or apocalyptic elements of biblical Christianity vie with ideas popularized by American Romantic or 'Transcendentalist' thinkers such as Ralph Waldo Emerson. The absence of a cohesive established religion in Western life and lack of residual religious memories becomes a defining trauma in Coupland's fiction. Few of Coupland's characters – with the exception of central figures in *All Families are Psychotic, Hey Nostradamus!* (2003) and *Eleanor Rigby* (2004) – openly profess conventional religious beliefs.

Many of the least obviously devout individuals in these narratives, however, ultimately confess that their secret hope is to find a meaningful, generous belief in something not shaped by consumer appetites. All of Coupland's novels, from *Generation X* onwards, are inflected by his characters' search for meaning and identity, but with the evolution of his work, this quest has assumed an increasingly theological shape. Many of the narratives feature explicit or covert images of conversion, baptism and parable, and the theme of apocalypse – both in the material sense of cataclysmic ending and as an echo of biblical traditions of revelation, a divine uncovering of mystery – is central to Coupland's reading of the postmodern landscape. Yet as a writer from an avowedly secular background, Coupland's relationship with the Christian tradition is neither one of disillusion nor of reclamation.[8] Rather, his work seeks a new sacred vocabulary constructed from the detritus of an obsessively materialist culture and represents a serious attempt to read an apparently godless world in spiritual terms.

The religious identity of Coupland's work is impossible to accommodate to a single paradigm and its complexity has inspired various contradictory labels: in the mid-1990s one Canadian journalist concluded that the writer was 'dedicated to a kind of agnostic spiritual quest'.[9] More recently, in an interview with Coupland, Brian Draper asserted that the novelist 'is a man who has been trying earnestly, since the early 1990s, to introduce the spirit of the age to the Holy Ghost, and get them talking'.[10] The search for faith in Coupland's fiction is most explicitly articulated by Scout, the narrator of the concluding story in *Life After God*, who wrestles with the absence of orthodox faith from his world and with a life that is apparently beyond belief: 'we are living creatures – we have religious impulses – we *must* – and yet into what cracks do these impulses flow in a world without religion? It is something I think about every day. Sometimes I think it is the only thing I should be thinking about' (*LAG*, pp. 273–4).

This post-secular journey into a new engagement with religious ideas is undertaken not only by Coupland's characters, but also by their creator. What Robert Detweiler has named 'religion-oriented readings' of ostensibly secular texts are, I would argue, entirely appropriate for Coupland's narratives of quest and redemption.[11] This chapter explores the evolving representation of religious belief in Coupland's work via three connected areas of discussion. The first section locates his fiction in the wider context of the apparent 'sacred turn' in contemporary culture. The argument then focuses on the most frequently recurring manifestation of Coupland's spiritual sensibility in his use of epiphany as a structuring motif in a number of the novels including *Generation X*, *Life After God*, *Girlfriend in a Coma*, *Miss Wyoming* (2000) and *Eleanor Rigby*. These visionary encounters are related to concepts of apocalypse and the final section examines the theological and cultural implications of Coupland's representation of 'end time' narratives.

Life after: Coupland and the 'sacred turn'

'LET'S JUST HOPE WE ACCIDENTALLY BUILD GOD', proclaims one of the many slogans scrawled by Tyler Johnson on a stack of one-dollar bills in *Shampoo Planet*.[12] In Coupland's fiction, a desire for the divine frequently manifests itself in the most secular of transactions. Tyler is a self-confessed materialist, determined to succeed according to worldly standards, yet even his acquisitive attitude is unsettled by a latent religious sensibility. The novelist's evocation of an active spiritual pulse – one that persists even in an ostensibly rationalist, demystified moment – exemplifies a bigger cultural phenomenon that emerged almost imperceptibly in the last decade of the twentieth century. John D. Caputo, a principal advocate of this 'sacred turn', has argued that:

> To the great astonishment of learned despisers of religion everywhere, who have been predicting the death of God from the middle of the nineteenth century right up to Y2K, religion in all of its manifold varieties has returned. Even to say that is misleading, since religion was reported missing mostly by the intellectuals; no one outside the academy thought that it had gone anywhere at all.[13]

Even 'learned despisers' of the religious have reassessed perspectives on the importance of faith to contemporary culture. Fredric Jameson, committed to a thoroughly materialist worldview, claimed in his celebrated study of 'the Cultural Logic of Late Capitalism' that 'the modern age' had witnessed 'the extinction of the sacred and the spiritual'.[14] More recently, however, in his response to Jacques Derrida's engagement with the legacies of Marxist thought, Jameson has argued that 'religion is once again very much on the agenda of any serious attempt to come to terms with the specificity of our own time'.[15] Indeed, many ostensibly secular fields of philosophy – including Derrida's deconstruction, Michel Foucault's post-structuralism and debates in French feminism – have been re-examined in terms of their possible religious affinities.[16] This theoretical reappraisal arises from a perceived crisis in secular identity and uncertainties regarding the fate of religion in the western world. 'The assumption that we live in a secularized world is false,' argues Peter L. Berger, a sociologist of religion: 'The world today, with some exceptions . . . is as furiously religious as it ever was, and in some places more so than ever.'[17]

The alternative, protean forms that postmodern religion takes – and the ways in which this variety of spiritualities might shape a social practice such as literary fiction – cannot be easily accommodated to a single theory or set of beliefs. As Caputo suggests, religion 'is too maddeningly polyvalent and too uncontainably diverse for us to fit it all under one roof'.[18] John McClure has explored the emergence of heterodox post-secular thinking in American culture in the surprising shape of Thomas Pynchon's novels.[19] Arresting spiritual fiction, in the traditions of modern anglophone writing, has rarely been produced by traditional believers. Ironically, many of the most theologically dynamic novels of the last twenty years have been produced by candidly sceptical writers: Philip Pullman, Jim Crace and Salman Rushdie, for example, set themselves at a critical distance from monotheist belief but write powerfully – and empathetically – of the relationship between belief in the miraculous and ordinary life. In fact, the idea that the supposedly disparate phenomena of 'secular' and 'religious' cultures might find themselves colliding to produce an alternative mode of experience is identified by sociological studies as vital to the narrative of contemporary belief.

Paul Heelas, for example, suggests that 'it is arguably the case that dedifferentiation has taken place with regard to the secular–sacred boundary. In measure, the religious has become less obviously religious, the secular less obviously secular.'[20] Grace Davie – writing specifically of the British context but with a sense of its wider implications – makes a similar claim about the mobility of religious ideas in the late twentieth century and beyond:

> The sacred starts to spill over into everyday thinking. Indeed, in many respects, things seem to be turning full circle. If, in the 1960s the sacred borrowed somewhat indiscriminately from the secular, the reverse may – perhaps – be true in the last decade of the twentieth century as the sacred is plundered by the secular. At the very least, the lines between the two categories are undoubtedly becoming increasingly blurred.[21]

Coupland's narratives continually turn to the 'blurred' space between sacred intention and secular activity. However, these fictions rarely idealize the intersection of holy and worldly narratives. One of the neologisms that footnote *Generation X* delineates the novelist's scathing classification of contemporary spirituality:

> **Me-ism:** A search by an individual, in the absence of training in traditional religious tenets, to formulate a personally tailored religion by himself. Most frequently a mishmash of reincarnation, personal dialogue with a nebulously defined god figure, naturalism, and karmic eye-for-eye attitudes.[22]

Although the definition ironizes religious tourism, it also proposes that the need to believe has not dissipated. 'Me-ism' echoes Reginald Bibby's concern that religion 'has become a neatly packaged consumer item – taking its place among other commodities that can be bought or bypassed according to one's consumption whims'.[23] The eclectic 'mishmash' of philosophies might result in a self-serving and inconsistent creed but it is also a sign of quest, the desire to seek something greater than oneself. In Coupland's narratives, the distinctively fuzzy spirituality of the postmodern moment arises from an anxiety of choice – a parody of freedom that has degenerated into coercive consumerism – that is also a consequence of the lack of coherence at the heart of a postmodern world. Spirituality, he implies, has not been erased but rewritten by the ruthless, vampiric economics of consumerism. 'Belief', Michel de Certeau has argued, has been devalued by its displacement into a cacophony of distinctively temporal, non-transcendent commodities. Trust in merchandise, artificially produced, analysed and marketed by agents of commerce, compromises the whole concept of religious faith: 'There are now too many things to believe and not enough credibility to go around.'[24]

'Me-ism' constitutes what the British theologian, Graham Ward, has described as a religion transformed into 'special effect'. Theological commitment and a tradition of worship are displaced by an illusory mode of transcendence 'inseparably bound to an entertainment value' that merely trades on a religious tradition's 'symbolic capital' to avoid 'the profound uncertainties, insecurities and indeterminacies of postmodern living'.[25]

A detraditionalized, commercial mode of spirituality might trouble conservative believers such as Ward, but it also worries many of Coupland's uncommitted, agnostic seekers. *Hey Nostradamus!* features a charlatan psychic whose supposed 'channel into the afterworld' is simulated solely for financial reward.[26] Similarly, in *Miss Wyoming*, the apparently 'harmless nonsense' of Dreama's numerology is a business.[27] Liz Dunn, the disenchanted narrator of *Eleanor Rigby*, is careful to distance herself from superstition or New Age mysticism in her description of the Hale-Bopp comet in 1997:

> I first saw it just past sunset while standing in the parking lot of Rogers video . . . Sure, I think the zodiac is pure hooey, but when an entirely new object appears in the sky, it opens some kind of window to your soul and to your sense of destiny. No matter how rational you try to be, it's hard to escape the feeling that such a celestial event portends some kind of radical change.[28]

Liz, an instinctive sceptic, is confident in her logical dismissal of astrology but, against expectation, the sight of the comet undermines her seemingly impermeable rationalism.

This tension between reason and faith, hard-hearted scepticism and candid optimism is explored in one of the parable-like 'bedtime stories' in *Generation X*, in the chapter 'Leave Your Body'. Claire Baxter, an acerbic and practical presence in the novel, narrates the conversion of a 'poor little rich girl named Linda' who tires of her inherited wealth and seeks to unlock 'the mechanisms of her soul' by following the disciplines of a Himalayan sect of monks. By meditating in silence and isolation for seven years, seven months, seven days and seven hours, Linda hopes to achieve an ecstatic release and new wisdom. She reaches the end of this punishing period but is informed by a monk from the order that she has misunderstood the exercise and the calendar of the sect; it should, according to the Christian calendar, have lasted 'just over one year': 'You children from Europe . . . from America . . . you try so hard but you get everything wrong – you and your strange little hand carved religions you make for yourselves' (*GX*, p. 147). The fable is partly a satire of the modish and superficial flirtation of bored, godless Westerners with Eastern religions. Linda's misinterpretation is symbolic of a *fin de siècle* tendency for excess: she simply exchanges material decadence for a form of obsessive ascetic inwardness. However, the transformative ending, in which Linda dies and undergoes a 'supernatural conversion', also suggests a sense of respect for those who are prepared to seek an alternative to the seductions and banalities of the consumerist West: 'the piece of light that was truly Linda vacated her old vessel, then flitted heavenward, where it went to sit . . . on the right hand of her god' (*GX*, p. 148).

Claire's curious parable of the rewards and consequences of spiritual experimentation echoes the quest story in which she, Andy and Dag are the leading players. How does a post-religious generation, raised to trust only the visible, construct a worldview that can accommodate the ineffable and the uncanny? If Claire's narrative suggests that citizens of the contemporary West are condemned always to fail in their efforts to construct a sacred worldview, Coupland's later novels are tenacious in their pursuit of transcendence amid the mundane business of everyday life.

'I think we've always wanted something noble or holy in our lives, but only on our own terms', reflects the emotionally inhibited – and spiritually confused – narrator of *Girlfriend in a Coma*.[29] Richard Doorland – whose surname, as Robert McGill has observed, emphasizes that he stands 'at the threshold of another place' – begins to detect 'new sensations' in what he tentatively names his 'soul'.[30] This nascent mysticism surfaces when, via various serendipitous accidents, he is working as part of the production crew for a television serial, closely modelled on *The X-Files*, that follows investigations into paranormal events. In lieu of theology or traditional religious ritual, Richard and his friends are 'exposed . . . day in, day out, to a constant assembly line of paranoia, extreme beliefs, and spiritual simplifications' (*GIAC*, p. 90). The fact that this group of childhood friends, after randomly reconvening in their home city, all now work in the entertainment industry and, coincidentally, are all employed on this pseudo-mystical programme has a symbolic resonance: they are passively participating in the construction of an alternative or surrogate mythology, a counterfeit sacredness that none of them positively 'believes' but for which they have no alternative narrative. Coupland's protagonist is cynical enough to view this manufactured simulation of the sacred as a fraudulent substitute for something finer. The virtual spirituality of Zeitgeist-chasing, paranoid, genre television engenders questions that are unfamiliar to his comfortable (and perhaps complacent) secular education. Indeed, this hesitant and unexpected craving for life to take on an authentic holy significance is formalized amidst a mode of pop culture that is distinctively artificial. What McGill calls 'the ruthless fictiveness of *Girlfriend in a Coma*' – its constant reminders of the illusory world in which its protagonists live and which, via their television work, they now help to fabricate – heightens the desire for an experience of the world that is real.[31] All of the novel's key characters – with the obvious exception of the titular heroine – are involuntarily immersed in pop culture lore but a number of these lost thirty-somethings, particularly Richard and Linus, a thwarted mystic, are suspicious of the mass media's impact on their capacity to sustain a profound interior life.

Is the virtual world of screen idols, shaman-like rock stars and paperback spiritual gurus an obstruction to the transcendent? Tom Beaudoin, a self-styled Generation X theologian, contends that popular culture, regarded by conservative critics as the antithesis of humanity's potential for sensitive spiritual awareness, has become a viable alternative space for the sacred. Television, pop music and film are the 'amniotic fluid that sustained' a generation which 'had a fragmented or completely broken relationship to "formal" or "institutional" religion'.[32] Similarly, Craig Detweiler and Barry Taylor distance their theological critique from 'those who decry the decline of Western civilization' and suggest that 'a profound, profane, honest discussion of God, the devil, death, and the afterlife is sweeping pop culture'.[33] '[I]mpropriety and irreverence', Beaudoin suggests, are the counterintuitive traits of a surreptitiously religious postmodern generation.[34] Coupland's fiction draws on a similar spirit of sacred irreverence as a way towards a renewed rather than inherited spirituality.

This mischievous (virtual) theology is revealed primarily in the novelist's improbable choice of spiritual seekers. In casting highly unlikely figures as the recipient or conduit of an invisible grace, Coupland is echoing the mode of other 'profane' religious writers, including John Updike and Graham Greene. The characters in Coupland's fiction who, ultimately at least, represent compassionate spiritual beliefs are rarely conservatively 'religious'. In the opening chapter of *All Families are Psychotic*, for example, Wade Drummond, a seasoned barfly and professional slacker, wakes up in a Florida jail, his blood-drenched clothes 'converted . . . into a skin of beef jerky'.[35] Overnight incarceration, the narrative implies, is not an exceptional experience for Wade, a man of many picaresque adventures, but the motivation for the bar-room brawl is more surprising. 'I got in a fight because this guy . . . was making fun of God' (*AFAP*, p. 3). In a later conversation with his mother, he confesses that he has a strange dream of becoming a superhero who can 'shoot lasers' that would enable people to 'see God': 'I'd be Holy Man – that'd be my name . . . A super power like *that* is almost too much power for mere human beings. But then maybe I could try and see God myself, and maybe once I did, I'd be firing lasers in all directions all the time, a non-stop twenty-four-hour God transformer' (*AFAP*, p. 270).

This collision of radical, mystic religion with the iridescent imagery of American comic-book heroism generates a defamiliarizing iconography of late modern belief. Wade's bizarre, consciously adolescent religious language represents a kind of pop art sacramentalism. This phenomenon of an off-centre iteration of the holy is developed further in the more melancholy plot of *Eleanor Rigby*. Jeremy Buck, the long-lost, twenty-year-old son of the narrator, is introduced into the novel moments after being declared 'technically' dead. This improbable resurrection – after a narcotic binge dressed in a decadent *Rocky Horror* costume of garish lingerie – anticipates the slightly surreal tone of the narrative: Jeremy, like Wade, is an unruly figure who blends self-destructive appetites with acute, specifically religious visions. His idiosyncratic impulsiveness brings about a conversion in his mother's lonely, disenchanted worldview to a renewed perception of the mundane.

In its emphasis on grief and loss, *Eleanor Rigby* also has strong affinities with the novel's immediate predecessor, *Hey Nostradamus!*, in which Coupland explores the relationship between belief and incomprehensible human suffering. In the earlier narrative, Jason Klaasen's life is wrecked by the murder of his girlfriend, along with many others, by three of their fellow high-school students. The irrational suspicion that falls on Jason – who, like his girlfriend, had a quiet, slightly rebellious faith – transforms him into a contemporary embodiment of Job. In the biblical narrative, Job is a holy man whose faith is tested by God after a wager with the devil: after many bereavements and personal ruin, Job emerges with a resolute faith. Jason's faith position is much more ambiguous. As his section of the narrative ends – before his mysterious, unresolved disappearance – this damaged individual contemplates the possibilities of divine meaning in an apparently random universe: 'Redemption exists, but only for others. I believe, and yet I lack faith' (*HN*, p. 135). Unconsciously echoing Scout in '1,000 Years (Life After God)', Jason refuses to accept that life has no purpose ('We're all born separated from God – over and over life makes sure to inform us of this . . . We mean something. We *must*'), but his own disintegration leads him to 'feel like the unholiest thing on earth' (*HN*, p. 146). Jason becomes a man of sorrows – the scapegoat for a guilty, bewildered community – and the possible source of redemption for his own viciously religious father. In this distinctively twenty-first-century narrative of random violence and spiritual despair, Coupland does not offer uncritical Christian doctrine as a simple palliative to the problem of evil. However, the allusions to the New Testament that border the narrative – the epigraph is taken from 1 Corinthians 15: 52–3 ('Behold I tell you a mystery; we shall not all sleep, but we shall all be changed') and the concluding image constitutes a conscious reworking of the parable of the prodigal son – are a symptom of the novelist's continuing absorption in the language and redemptive possibilities of religious tradition in a world exhausted by fundamentalism of all varieties.

Jason Klaasen is one of a small number of Coupland's wayward prophets who grew up with firm religious beliefs. Todd, the most socially confident of the young programmers in *Microserfs* (1995), described as both 'historically empty' and obsessed with body image, is another lapsed Christian now alienated from his 'ultra-religious parents.'[36] In a rare moment of introspection, he confides to the narrator that his 'body was just something that I could believe in because there was nothing else around' (*MS*, p. 244). Todd's search for something to believe in leads him to Marxism, Maoism and, eventually, into a silent, empty Californian Baptist church where he quietly reconnects with his early faith (*MS*, p. 282).

Coupland's use of these irreligious pilgrims unconsciously echoes a vital, controversial strand in twentieth-century theology. The crisis theology of Karl Barth, observes one commentator, 'insists on the "secularity" of the Word of God' and 'freely chooses worldly objects through which to reveal himself', although since these 'objects [are] completely unsuitable for the disclosure of divine glory, God is bound always to be veiled in the very act of self-unveiling'.[37]

'It must be nice to have something external to believe in', reflects Douglas Rushkoff in his introduction to *The GenX Reader*. The potential object of belief, is, however, not specific: 'Something that doesn't move. Something absolute. Having no such permanent icon (no God, no Country, no Superhero) we chose instead . . . to experience life as play.'[38] In Coupland's fiction, this nebulous yearning for the transcendent displayed by individuals who have no trace of religious training in their background – not even a conscious atheism – emerges in ways that ostensibly appear divorced from any religious tradition. In *Microserfs*, for example, Dan Underwood continually looks for signs of belief in a post-ideological age. Dan, like so many of Coupland's narrators, notes that he was 'raised without any beliefs' but his 'subconscious' PowerBook file covertly identifies him as a 'Godseeker'. '[M]aybe this whole Bill thing is actually the subconscious manufacture of God', he reflects (*MS*, pp. 15–16, 363). Dan, a Microsoft staffer, is mischievously (but sincerely) reflecting on the cult of Bill Gates ('a moral force, a spectral force, a force that shapes, a force that molds', *MS*, p. 3). In his notes made at a business seminar on interactive technology – as secular and banal a space as one can imagine – Dan concludes that

> Flight Simulation games are actually out-of-body experience emulators. There must be all of these people everywhere on earth right now, waiting for a miracle, waiting to be pulled out of themselves, eager for just the smallest sign that there is something finer or larger or miraculous about our existence than we had supposed (*MS*, pp. 142–3).

This counterintuitive insight resonates with Graham Ward's view that a 'culture that focuses upon the spectacular and attempts to produce endless intensities and excitements might be termed . . . a transcendental culture'.³⁹ The crucial difference between these interpretations is that for Dan the pursuit of transcendence in postmodern culture is not merely a simulated, monstrous or fake version of an authentic original. Computer-generated experiences become a viable analogue for a tradition of pilgrimage and mystical exploration, neither more nor less 'real' than older forms of prayer and worship. In fact, technology, in a number of guises, regularly takes on the force of the sublime for Coupland. In *Miss Wyoming*, for example, Eugene Lindsay constructs a list 'of things which would astound somebody living a hundred years before him' in order to 'persuade himself that he was living in a miraculous world in a miraculous time' (*MW*, pp. 133–4).

Similarly, in the non-fiction work *Souvenir of Canada 2* (2004), Coupland makes a specific connection between technology and the miraculous in an anecdote about his aunt's serendipitous discovery (via scanning equipment at a US-Canadian border) that her car harboured radioactive matter: 'The fact is that we truly do live in an age of miracles and wonders – there may be more darkness in the world, but there is more light, as well.'⁴⁰ This echoes the concluding images of *Microserfs* in which Dan's mother, paralysed by a stroke, is able to communicate with her family via software; new technology, in both instances, is a sign of hope rather than a warning of human obsolescence.

From one perspective, the optimism that Coupland displays regarding human innovations might be viewed as naive and surprisingly oblivious to the more destructive aspects of technology. Certainly, this marked technophilia exists in tension with the strong distaste for consumer excess embodied in most of his novels. The conflation of miracle and technology is a crucial aspect of the search for the mystical in the midst of an aggressively secular moment. However, Coupland's enthusiasm for scientific discoveries is desta-bilized by an inkling that, far from being a space of easy grace, the modern world is polluted by a human capacity for evil. As Cheryl Anway concludes her sepulchral retelling of her own murder she reflects that 'the sun may burn brightly . . . but in the air we breathe, in the water we drink and in the food we share, there will always be darkness in this world' (*HN*, p. 42). Cheryl's conviction that 'humanity alone has the capacity at any given moment to commit all possible sins' and that even 'those of us who try to live a good and true life remain as far away from grace as the Hillside Strangler' is suggestive of a puritan ghost that haunts Coupland's narratives (*HN*, p. 3). The possibilities of perceiving or receiving grace in such a 'fallen' world are rare and frail but the need to imagine such moments of gift and vision are vital to Coupland's exploration of the postmodern experience.

'Isolated little cool moments': interpreting epiphany

'I sometimes get hijacked by pictures', Jeremy Buck tells his estranged mother in *Eleanor Rigby* (*ER*, p. 42). These uncanny visions are moments of intense personal revelation that may or may not be a product of Jeremy's aggressive illness. This peculiar phenomenon is, however, far from exceptional in Coupland's fiction. Flashes of visual perception – real or imagined – are a defining motif across the writer's body of work. In his early fiction, in particular, such moments constituted rumours of grace amidst the ruins of consumer culture. These unexpected encounters, suggests Gordon Lynch, are an alternative to the type of 'elaborate philosophies of life' typically eschewed by Coupland's spiritual seekers: '[F]ragmentary experiences of meaning are not . . . things to be captured or created, but . . . are given to us in ways, times and places that are beyond our control.'[41] Sudden, unexpected, and not necessarily supernatural experiences such as these might be described as moments of epiphany, a phenomenon that Coupland has explored since his debut novel.

In *Generation* X, Coupland's first, unconventional postmodern family wish to resist the contemporary tendency to live 'life as a succession of isolated little cool moments' without coherence or meaning (*GX*, p. 10). Yet the novelist uses a series of these 'cool moments' as a way of structuring the narrative and suggests that the more purposeful sense of personal narrative that his protagonists crave is in turn dependent on such Wordsworthian 'spots of time'. Indeed, *Generation X* begins and ends with moments of epiphany experienced, Emerson-like, before nature. In the opening chapter, Andy describes a formative journey he undertook alone to Canada as a 15-year-old to watch a total eclipse of the sun, when the experience of watching the 'sky go out' engendered a new sense of 'darkness and inevitability and fascination' (*GX*, p. 4). The novel concludes with a journey to Mexico: leaving his car to gaze at a fire-ravaged landscape, Andy is grazed by a circling eagle; he is surrounded by a group of mentally-handicapped children, who hug him in an 'adoring, healing, uncritical embrace' (*GX*, p. 207). The ending returns to the sense of revelation that informs the novel's opening narrative but replaces the isolation of observing an eclipse with a new sense of inclusion in a wider world of human activity: 'this *pain* . . . this crush of love was unlike anything I had ever known' (*GX*, p. 207). It is an encounter that engenders a sense of connection with a wider world; it represents, in Lynch's terms, an experience of 'meaning that we occasionally glimpse if we can remain open to signs of kindness, beauty and care around us'.[42]

Applying the term 'epiphany' to such moments, loaded as it is with both Christian and modernist associations, is problematic. As a date in the church calendar, the Feast of Epiphany celebrates the appearance of the Christ child to the Magi, figures who might be read as symbolic of the Gentiles.[43] James Joyce, steeped in the language of Roman Catholicism, is responsible for the twentieth-century aesthetic appropriation and reinterpretation of the term. It has since become a kind of shorthand for any intense experience that reveals a new insight into the nature of the universe, sense of self or, as Ashton Nicholls notes, 'momentary manifestations of significance in ordinary experience'.[44] Yet epiphanies of any kind, both those that claim a specific religious meaning and those that emerge from secular contexts, are dependent on acts of narration after the event and are subject to the limits of human interpretation.

Epiphanies in Coupland's fiction are not always experienced in solitude or via engagement with nature after a flight into the wilderness. In a number of cases, the moment of revelation is engendered in a surprisingly suburban context. For example, Coupland explores the interpretative nature of epiphany in a chapter entitled 'Transform' in which Andy reluctantly returns home for Christmas. The chapter investigates the significance of a Christian festival celebrated by a family without religious beliefs. Andy creates a ritual, a moment of light and holiness, with thousands of candles that he places around the living room before inviting his parents and brother into the room:

> the three of them enter the room, speechless, turning in slow circles, seeing the normally dreary living room covered with a molten living cake-icing of white fire, all surfaces devoured in flame – a dazzling fleeting empire of ideal light. All of us are instantaneously disembodied from the vulgarities of gravity; we enter a realm in which all bodies can perform acrobatics like an astronaut in orbit . . . This light is also making the eyes of my family burn, if only momentarily, with the possibilities of existence in our time (*GX*, pp. 170–1).

The narration of the moment is crucial – it is another of the shared stories that structure the novel. It is an attempt to resacrilize Christmas, itself a festival that celebrates the divine becoming human and signals the possibility of redemption. In the absence of orthodox religious beliefs Andy, and by extension Coupland, is considering ways of satisfying a human need for ritual and, indeed, sacraments. Frederick Buechner has argued that a 'sacrament is the breaking through of the sacred into the profane' whereas 'a ritual is the ceremonial acting out of the profane in order to show forth its sacredness'.[45] The desire to find a sacrament from a simple ritual is clear in this passage: it is a new kind of ritual that connects an ancient symbol of light with the postmodern world of commerce and exchange; it is Andy's gift – a gift that does not require recompense – to a family with whom he cannot connect on the profound level he craves. The exalted vocabulary of Pentecost competes with a scientific discourse: the 'surfaces [are] devoured in flame' and the family are freed from the limits of 'gravity' as the experience makes them feel 'disembodied'. The moment is predicated on aesthetics – a moment of visual shock contrived by the narrator for his family and reader – but it signifies a desire to move beyond symbol.

Neither is it simply a New Age activity, a displaced Christian ritual without the need to believe – there is no invocation, no guru, no specific spiritual expectation. It is a secular sacrament that is created and offered for a small community as an expression of hope and the possibility of transformation. The candles are bought in a supermarket and the moment brings together the secular world of the late-twentieth century with less mundane spiritual aspirations. This brief moment of illumination, literal and spiritual, concludes rather ambiguously as the family return to their usual routines fundamentally unchanged. The narrator's vague sense of disappointment signals a desire for a truly transformative moment. Epiphany, he suggests, should signal a substantial change in the people privileged as its witnesses.

If Coupland's recurrent exploration of epiphanic motifs appeals to postmodern theologians such as Gordon Lynch, it has also provoked criticism. Alan Bilton has argued that 'the sheer number of epiphanies' in Coupland's work – and particularly in *Generation X* – 'smacks of creative desperation'.[46] In *Blank Fictions*, James Annesley argues that Coupland's representation of epiphany traduces the 'fundamentally commercial nature' of 'decadent' experience. Annesley suggests that, in *Generation X*, the narrative fails 'to recognize the commercialised nature of the types of sensations it celebrates' and therefore 'the text creates significant tensions between the illusion of transcendence and these inescapable material realities'.[47] This view seems to misread the novel's emphasis on the specifics of contemporary revelation – it takes place within a contemporary landscape, using contemporary symbols. In an interview on religious issues with Douglas Todd, Coupland has reflected that part of the failure of contemporary religion is its inability to engage with contemporary symbols and motifs: 'We're lost. But we have this unbelievable set of new symbols and meanings around us. And all we have to do is open our eyes and look a bit harder and figure out how they relate and what the new mythologies are.'[48]

One possibility for literary versions of private revelation is that their recipient misinterprets them: this mode of 'anti-epiphany' was regularly deployed by James Joyce as a way of exploring self-deception and the consequences of losing such illusions. Coupland's epiphanies also intimate the possibility of misinterpretation. A recurrent theme of Coupland's fiction is that in a 'denarrated' world, delusion has become an integral element of everyday experience. In *Miss Wyoming*, for example, his first novel of the twenty-first century, Coupland limns the hallucinatory world of LA star culture and the near-religious contemporary obsession with celebrity. The strange narrative of John Johnson, an emotionally wrecked movie producer, whose oeuvre includes the promisingly titled *Bel Air P.I.* and *Bel Air P.I. 2* ('one of the few sequels better than the original'), is engendered by a moment of misinterpretation that somehow typifies postmodern disorientation (*MW*, p. 25). On his first meeting with Susan Colgate, former beauty pageant queen, faded child star and the eponymous 'Miss Wyoming', Johnson relates a moment of life-changing vision. As he lies critically ill in hospital, he hears Susan's voice and sees her face and, in response, chooses to leave behind his indulgent and destructive celebrity lifestyle:

> But what happened was that months later, after I'd gone and completely chucked out all my old life, I realized I *didn't* have this great big mystical Dolby THX vision. I realized that there'd merely been some old episode of that TV show you used to star in playing on the hospital's TV set beside my bed. And it must have melted into my dream life. (*MW*, p. 11)

The collision of conventional religious discourse with commercial technology ('great big mystical Dolby THX vision') in John's description of an incident that did not quite take place indicates the inadequacy of contemporary language as an idiom through which to represent the sublime. This moment of fake epiphany is indicative of Coupland's ambivalent relationship with pop culture: although the visionary encounter was not genuinely mystical and has an utterly rational, indeed banal, explanation, the simulated revelation did precipitate a radical change in its witness.

Visions experienced in conjunction with medical crises or medication are now a familiar trope in Coupland's writing of epiphany: Richard experiences the 'only vision' of his life after taking a painkiller in *Girlfriend in a Coma* (p. 52). Similarly the strict rationalist, Liz Dunn, in *Eleanor Rigby*, is given a drug to relieve a blinding headache but also has a mystical encounter (*ER*, p. 248). If casual drug taking is largely derided in the novels, these accidental, analgesic-assisted visions are afforded an odd legitimacy as they seem to produce a beneficial transformation in their recipient.

John's resolution to relinquish his wealth and fame echoes accounts of Saul of Tarsus' conversion to Christianity on the road to Damascus; it also has precedents in the American literary tradition, as it rewrites Emerson and Thoreau's calls to a modest, non-materialistic way of life. The itinerant existence that John adopts after his delirious illness does not generate the solutions that he expects. However, his fleeting experience of transcendence is accessed not via a deliberate return to nature nor as a traditional moment of prayer but, more surprisingly, amongst the contingent mess of a mass media culture. John – who, after all, works in an industry that profits from the manufacture of shared illusions – has problems in distinguishing between the fictive and the real. This crisis of interpretation personifies David Lyon's definition of the postmodern experience as 'a debate about reality' in which the 'world of solid scientific facts and a purposeful history' engendered by the European Enlightenment becomes 'mere wishful thinking'.[49]

Unsurprisingly, John Johnson spends little time considering the legacy of the European Enlightenment but he is aware that the manipulative reach of debased and distorting commercial images increasingly compromises meaningful personal choices and 'a purposeful history'. His desire to change, to light out for the territories like a middle-aged, media-savvy Huck Finn and, finally, to find a story worth inhabiting, is an effort to recuperate reality and a repudiation of 'denarrated' postmodern life. John's initial quest ends in apparent failure – if we consider being rescued then filmed, naked and puking on the fringes of the desert to be something of a disappointment – but it is a prelude to his eventual ability to move beyond Hollywood and its burnished seductions.

A number of Coupland's most theologically informed novels offer strategies of resistance to what John McClure has called 'the quotidian impurities of consumer capitalism' and a still keener spiritual hunger.[50] In *Life After God*, Coupland's third full-length work of fiction, the distaste for the corrosive corruptions of global capitalism hardens into a resolve for personal and social transformation. The final, and semi-eponymous story in the collection, '1,000 Years (Life After God)', echoes the disillusion and desire for re-enchantment crucial to *Generation X*. Like the earlier novel, it too is narrated by a single, male narrator from a middle-class background who has no material cares but is burdened by a new, insistent need for belief in some greater truth.

Scout's narrative, which begins with an almost sacred memory of him and his friends in the days of adolescence, floating in a suburban swimming pool, recounts how each of their privileged lives has become devoid of meaning: 'Ours was a life lived in paradise and thus it rendered any discussion of transcendental ideas pointless' (*LAG*, p. 273). This materialist life was, he notes

> the life of children of the children of the pioneers – life after God – a life of earthly salvation on the edge of heaven . . . [but] I think there was a trade-off somewhere along the line. I think the price we paid for our golden life was an inability to fully believe in love; instead we gained an irony that scorched everything it touched. And I wonder if this irony is the price we paid for the loss of God. (*LAG*, p. 273)

The story concludes with the narrator abandoning his job, throwing away his antidepressants and driving deep into the forest, on Vancouver Island, where he begins to recover a more coherent, sharper sense of self: 'As long as there is wilderness, I know there is a larger part of myself that I can always visit, vast tracts of territory lying dormant, craving exploration and providing sanctity' (*LAG*, p. 344). The spiritual inclinations of the narrator are resonant of Thoreau in *Walden; or, Life in the Woods* (1846–50): 'We need the tonic of wildness . . . We must be refreshed by the sight of inexhaustible vigor . . . We need to witness our own limits transgressed, and some life pasturing freely where we never wander.'[51]

In the heart of the forest Scout undergoes a baptism-like ritual and the narrative ends with an echo of its opening memory of the swimming pool. Here, however, instead of a warm, suburban pool, accompanied by his friends, Scout plunges naked into a freezing and roaring stream, observed by no one but the reader. The suburban space of play, imaged as a mock conception ('We would float and be naked – pretending to be embryos, pretending to be fetuses', *LAG*, pp. 271–2), is replaced with one of a painful rebirth in the unruly peace of nature, his connection with the world reaffirmed in the shock of the glacial water.

A similar motif of baptism is used in *Hey Nostradamus!* Reg, who for much of the narrative is a self-righteous and brutally pious individual, remorsefully recollects wading into the treacherous Fraser River as a young man: 'I believed the maxim that should I lose my footing, God would come in and carry me wherever the river was deepest. The water felt like an ongoing purification, and I've never felt as clean as I did then' (*HN*, p. 231). Similarly, in *Life After God*, Scout frames the moment as devotional and transformative. '[T]his is the end of some aspect of my life,' he says, 'but also a beginning – the beginning of some unknown secret that will reveal itself to me soon. All I need do is ask and pray' (*LAG*, p. 352). The solitary nature of this 'baptism' is significant: unlike the storytellers of *Generation X*, Scout does not share the story or the moment of change with one of his friends; the intimacy is established, instead, with a stranger. It is the reader who is invited to act as a kind of priest-midwife with whom the narrator shares his confidence:

> Now – here is my secret:
> I tell it to you with an openness of heart that I doubt I shall ever achieve again, so I pray that you are in a quiet room as you hear these words. My secret is that I need God – that I am sick and can no longer make it alone. I need God to help me give, because I am no longer capable of giving; to help me be kind, as I no longer seem capable of kindness; to help me love, as I seem beyond being able to love. (*LAG*, p. 359)

This unambiguous emphasis on the need for the transcendent does not, of course, indicate the conversion of the novelist to a kind of evangelical Christianity or even an Emersonian belief in an Over-Soul. It does, however, signal a commitment in his literature to explore the language and possibilities of belief. This moment of confession resonates with Martyn Percy's claim that '[m]odern minds seem to have plenty of space for the unexplained, the ineffable, the sublime, worship, awe and wonder'.[52]

If epiphany is one mode of apocalypse emphasized in Coupland's novels – a potentially life-altering moment of revelation – Coupland is also interested in the alternative and more commonly recognized understanding of the term. 'Apocalypse' is now synonymous with a plurality of cultural representations of the end of the world. Indeed, the epiphanic moments that 'hijack' Jeremy Buck in *Eleanor Rigby* are of 'end time' visions of 'burning whales heaving themselves onto beaches, daisies that shatter, bales of money that wash up on shore; trees that go limp and deflate' (*ER*, p. 42). This final section focuses on the ways in which Coupland has reimagined 'end time' narratives.

This is the end: Coupland and apocalypse

'When you are young, you always expect that the world is going to end,' states an unidentified narrator in Coupland's short story 'The Wrong Sun' (*LAG*, p. 108). This fear-fascination of an incipient apocalypse is a defining element in the novelist's exploration of religious thought and the contemporary pursuit of meaning. One of the pop art-style illustrations in *Generation X* features a comic book figure (think Jimmy Olsen from a 1950s *Superman* illustration) shielding his eyes from a blazing glare of light: the first of two speech bubbles exclaims, 'OH NO! IT'S FINALLY HAPPENED! THE BLINDING FLASH OF LIGHT!' The second exclamation expresses relief: 'PHEW! IT WAS ONLY LIGHTNING' (*GX*, p. 152). In this pastiche of cold war, pop culture anxieties of annihilation, Coupland is also exploring an attendant fear of spiritual revelation. Nuclear apocalypse – annihilation without the hope of redemption – was a determining dread of life in a cold war culture. Coupland's is part of a generation who grew up surrounded by images, real and spectacular, of a coming end: 'Imagine what it was like to see the same scary movie . . . over and over again, every day for your entire upbringing. This is, in essence, what it was like to grow up during the Cold War.'[53]

Images of judgement and catastrophic endings torment many of Coupland's characters, and his early fiction features a recurrent narrative strand related to the end of the world: *Generation X, Shampoo Planet, Life After God* and *Microserfs* all include end-of-the-world stories. Todd, one of very few characters in Coupland's fiction to have a specifically and intensely religious background, is able to offer a different understanding of time to his colleagues: 'in Christian eschatology ("the study of the Last Things") it is always made very clear that time and the world both end simultaneously, that there is no real difference between the two' (*MS*, p. 195). 'How Clear Is Your Vision of Heaven?' and one of the 'postcard' essays in *Polaroids from the Dead* explore the possibility that mortality may not represent the true end to the human story: 'I wondered how I would be judged if just today were to be my entire life. Was I being good? Was I being evil? What sort of judgment would be passed on me?' (*PD*, p. 108).

Coupland's engagement with apocalypse is more urgent in *Girlfriend in a Coma*, which is predicated on the kind of eschatological framework that Todd outlines to his friends in *Microserfs*. The novel does not satirize chiliastic expectations but uses them to explore Coupland's perennial anxieties regarding the direction of the Western world. The plot itself is simple: at the end of the 1970s, a teenage girl, Karen McNeil, slips into a twenty-year coma after experiencing visions of the end-times; during these years she gives birth to a daughter and, shortly after she awakes, her visions become a reality. Her own crisis is inverted as the entire world, with the exception of her own small group of friends, falls asleep and dies. Although allusions to the final divine judgement prophesied in the book of Revelation are most explicit, there are also echoes of the flood. The majority of mankind succumbs to death, but one specific group of friends, like Noah and his family, are chosen to survive and, in turn, are commissioned with the task of renewing the world.

The first words of *Girlfriend in a Coma* – 'I'm Jared, a ghost' – signal a spectral return and make the novel's supernatural narrative explicit (*GIAC*, p. 3). A novelist who had previously worked within the conventions of realism offers his reader an alternative ontology, one that casually announces the presence of the supernatural within an otherwise recognizable contemporary landscape. The figure of a ghostly adolescent narrator established in this novel becomes a recurrent trope in Coupland's later narratives: the first section of *Hey Nostradamus!* is posthumously spoken by Cheryl Anway from a kind of limbo after she is shot by disturbed classmates ('I'm no longer a part of the world and I'm still not yet a part of what follows', *HN*, p. 9); *School Spirit* (2003), Coupland's collaboration with Pierre Huyghe, is narrated by a lonely teenage ghost who seems forever trapped in the halls of her school and between the pages of her yearbook; she has become a textual spectre doomed to be remembered only via their virtual memories of a book. The spectral narrator emerges elsewhere in contemporary fiction: Alice Sebold uses the device in *The Lovely Bones* (2002), for example, in which Susie Salmon, murdered at the age of fourteen by a neighbour on 6 December 1973, observes the continuing life of her family from a strangely godless heaven.

Jared's is a curious haunting: his first visitation is not to the world of his past, but as narrator to the reader, whom he informs that 'the world is over' (*GIAC*, p. 4). The end of Western civilization is represented as a world that has exhausted itself. Coupland engages in a millenarian fantasy, causing the consumer-driven world that appeared so inexorable in his earlier work to be erased. The narrator of this silent apocalypse is the most carnal of ghosts, and his fond memories of earthly appetite provide the paradox of the angelic role that he plays within the narrative. Even in his ethereal state he makes one of the characters pregnant. Neither is he merely a ghost; following the Greek term *angelos*, meaning messenger, he is also a rather shameless angel.[54] He is one of a number of debauched, earthly angels in late-1990s culture: Kevin Smith's *Dogma* (1999) included two distinctly Gen X members of the heavenly host in the form of Loki (Matt Damon) and Bartleby (Ben Affleck). 'Angels these days', laments Harold Bloom, 'have been divested of their sublimity by popular culture.'[55] Coupland is exploring this loss of aura via a figure placed deliberately between comic extremes of sanctity and worldliness. Jared was the school sports hero, a paragon of athletic ability, popular with men and women, and his death from leukaemia signals the end of innocence for his adolescent contemporaries. Jared's real function in the narrative is as a quasi-divine voice of wisdom. He is a kind of holy fool, a sepulchral voice eternally frozen at age 17 who is sent to warn his now middle-aged friends of their own folly and spiritual blindness: 'You think you've been forsaken – that the opportunity for holiness is gone, but this isn't true' (*GIAC*, p. 261).

The future, in Karen's dreams of *apokalypsis*, is not, as for Leonard Cohen, another Canadian with millennial presentiments, 'murder'. Neither is it a landscape ravaged by nuclear holocaust, nor one in which civilization has been obliterated by a rogue comet. Coupland teases his reader: before Karen falls into her coma at the end of 1979 she describes a future in which 'Russia isn't an enemy anymore' and 'sex is – fatal' (*GIAC*, p. 10). In the late 1990s and early twenty-first century, the end of the cold war and cruel reality of Aids are mundane truths. Yet, within the economy of the novel, the accuracy of these predictions corroborates the integrity and truth of Karen's sense of a coming judgement.

The scale of these dark epiphanies is at once smaller and more vast than most Western conceptions of the end-times. They do not, for example, offer the terrifying images of judgement and eternal damnation of John Martin's popular Victorian apocalyptic paintings, including *The Great Day of His Wrath* (1854). Rather, her dreams anticipate a world in which 'meaning ha[s] vanished' (*GIAC*, p. 10). 'The future', she tells her boyfriend, is '*not* a good place' (*GIAC*, p. 10). In these nocturnal visions people 'looked better' but have 'eyes without souls' (*GIAC*, pp. 10–11). The central anxiety of these dreams that become reality is that the elusive, defining quality of humanity, described by Karen as the soul, has been vanquished.

Coupland's warning is against the anaesthetic qualities of contemporary Western life. The implicit disapproval of drug taking, for example, is not so much a puritanical antipathy to the pleasures of the flesh as an embrace of a vigorous engagement with the world. The sleep into which the world of the novel falls parodies and reaffirms the evangelical 'Great Awakenings' of the United States in the eighteenth and nineteenth centuries. Coupland's religious or moral framework is, in one sense, far from the wrathful Calvinist God of Jonathan Edwards and eighteenth-century revivalism. Yet there are echoes and revisions of Edwards' theology. The physical salvation of Richard and his five friends as the sole survivors of the plague-sleep that destroys the rest of the world parallels the Calvinist belief in an elect, predestined by God to be spared the torments of hell and chosen to spend eternity in the renewed Kingdom. The elect of the novel, however, endure a banal 'new' world in which 'the air always smells like there's a tire fire half a mile up wind' (*GIAC*, p. 4). Nevertheless, the novel does not end with a bleak warning of annihilation. The 'elect' group of friends, who spend a year following the end of the world merely entertaining themselves, are reprimanded by Jared, who forces them to question their curious fate. A new awareness that they have 'no *evidence* of an interior life' is engendered (*GIAC*, p. 256).

Yet they are granted another chance and their world is subject to one further transformation. Coupland creates a miracle, as time is reversed, broken bodies are healed and the world is remade, his characters restored but their consciousness changed irrevocably. Their disillusion is changed to wonder and their worldly cynicism has become charity. As the postmodern 'God' of this particular narrative, Coupland allows his characters more than one 'second chance'. Bauman, similarly, has observed that postmodernity 'does not know of' a world with an 'inbuilt finality and irreversibility of choices'.[56] Indeed, it is evident that this happy ending quite explicitly owes as much to Frank Capra's *It's a Wonderful Life* (1947) as it does to New Testament eschatology. The celebrated film narrates a crisis in its hero's life, as a depressed George Bailey (James Stewart) is granted a vision of a world in which he had never been born, preceded by a glorious, if sentimental recreation of his small but significant life. For all of its manipulative romanticism, Capra's first post-war film anticipates the underlying political and religious ambiguity of *Girlfriend in a Coma*. '[I]n its day *It's a Wonderful Life* would have encouraged a more cynical and desperate disposition in its audience', suggests Jonathan Munby: 'Christmas was not good enough as a salve to the social and psychic wounds of the time; that Epiphany was a fanciful, even impossible, gesture of contrivance in the face of secular despair.'[57] Similarly, Coupland's use of divine intervention may indicate a rather despondent view of the human capacity for independent agency and change. Ironically, Capra's cinematic fable, traditionally screened in North America at Christmas, is the kind of narrative that has replaced conventional religious memories for Coupland's post-religious generation. His characters do not have the biblical knowledge to reimagine Lazarus' resurrection but they are able to remember James Stewart's joyful home-coming at the conclusion of the film.[58]

We might be tempted to read the conclusion as a simple parody of Capra's film and the sentimental, decadent nature of a Western culture that expects to be effortlessly forgiven for its transgressions. Coupland could be accused of flirting with religious mythology as a way of escaping history, and we might even, with Martin Jay, ask why 'apocalyptic fantasies' such as *Girlfriend in a Coma* have 'continued to thrive even in the ostensibly postreligious imaginaries we have called scientific and postmodern'.[59] The postmodern use of deus ex machina – a classical device involving a sudden, perhaps miraculous, narrative intervention that resolves apparently irreversible predicaments – may trouble readers for a number of reasons. In aesthetic terms, this narrative ploy is at odds with our expectations of non-genre contemporary fiction: allowing the last survivors on earth to return to their old world – albeit with changed priorities and a renewed sense of the sacred – seems to belong to an earlier narrative mode that created *The Wizard of Oz* or the Narnia stories of C. S. Lewis.

In fact, Coupland has deployed a similar trick to generate what Bilton names 'the outrageous wish-fulfilment ending' in a later novel: the idiosyncratic, Coen Brothers-style plot of *All Families Are Psychotic* concludes with two characters inexplicably being cured of Aids.[60]

Coupland's rather casual experiment with miraculous healing echoes Graham Ward's accusation that certain 'contemporary forms of customized transcendence' – perhaps including spiritually-inflected fiction – recklessly appropriate elements of religion to give their practice a superficial 'magical, mystical polish'.[61] A similar charge of spiritual dilettantism could be levelled at the conclusion of *Girlfriend in a Coma*. The fact that Jared's angelic intervention strips his friends of their capacity for irony and propensity to float commitment-free through life represents a major ethical problem. The characters, in Mark Forshaw's view, are offered the opportunity to escape 'not just from their post-apocalyptic predicament, but also from out of the ubiquitous *uncertainty* of life in the postmodern era'.[62]

Readers sympathetic to Coupland's aims – and spiritual emphasis in particular – should take these criticisms seriously. Charges of excessive sentimentality, cavalier mysticism and much-denied nostalgia are not entirely unfair. Yet there is an alternative way of interpreting Coupland's persistent representation of miracles and, in particular, his constant need to reimagine the apocalyptic end. The vision of a collective and literal resurrection of the body in *Girlfriend in a Coma* is, I would argue, a serious attempt to restate the need for a sense of the transcendent and the possibilities of transformation. The world is remade as a consequence of a willingness to change and a kind of repentance on behalf of Coupland's characters. Indeed, the final lines of the novel echo the great commission at the conclusion of the Gospel according to St John:

> You'll soon be seeing us walking down your street, our backs held proud ... Every cell in our body explodes with the truth ... We'll be begging passers by to see the need to question and question and never stop questioning until the world stops spinning ... We will change minds and souls from stone and plastic into linen and gold – that's what I believe. That's what I know. (*GIAC*, p. 281)

Coupland, who confesses no orthodox faith, concludes his millenarian fantasy with an affirmation of belief. This peroration would not be out of place in an evangelical sermon but, in spite of its debt to this revivalist tradition, Richard's speech transcends sectarian or theological histories and offers, instead, a broader hope of transfiguration. Far from closure, the ecstatic vision suggests an eternal messianic openness – a welcome to what is unknown and a rejection of undemanding acquiescence in banal certainty.

In resisting a single, nameable theological home, Coupland's work seems to draw yet closer to aspects of the Christian tradition of pilgrimage. His work simultaneously reflects a generational lack – the absence of spiritual training – and an odd ability to use superficially profane symbols to express a theological imagination – a new religious lexicon. But the increasingly intense spiritual mood of Coupland's fiction troubles some critics. Mark Forshaw, for example, is sympathetic to the questions that novels such as *Girlfriend in a Coma* elicit regarding 'the possibility and apparatus of resistance, political or otherwise' to a culture of endemic irony.[63] Yet the 'ideological ramifications' of the 'literary strategies' deployed by such spiritually inflected narratives also disturb him. Forshaw's identification of Coupland as 'at heart a theologian or a metaphysician' is not intended as praise.[64] These misgivings reflect the complexities of engaging with a theological vocabulary in an era when, in North American culture at least, any implicit sympathy for a sacred as opposed to a strictly materialist worldview is, perhaps understandably, too swiftly associated with the insidious rise of the now politically powerful religious Right. However, Coupland's exploration of ideas and images that emerge from the Christian tradition is not indicative of uncritical affinity with any specific form of religious practice.

Donna Tartt, author of *The Secret History* (1992) and *The Little Friend* (2002), a writer who, like Coupland, emerged in the early 1990s, has argued that a good novel 'enables non-believers to participate in a world-view that religious people take for granted: life as a vast polyphonous web of interconnections, predestined meetings, fortuitous choices and accidents, all governed by a unifying if unforeseen plan'.[65] For Douglas Coupland, a writer who is open about his sympathies to a theistic perspective, but who is also clear that he cannot 'join the revival tent', fiction has become such a space of religious possibility.[66] The uncertainties of the postmodern world have inspired him to negotiate the possibilities of finding truth, rather than to reject it as an obsolete quest. For Kevin Vanhoozer, '[p]ostmodernity has opened up breathing space once again to consider what is "other" to our theories'.[67] In this case, the 'other' is the return of a reinvigorated and – to many raised in a secular-materialist environment – deeply troubling theological vocabulary. Indeed the moral project of Coupland's fiction might best be described by the hope of one of his characters in *Life After God*: 'You know – I'm trying to escape from ironic hell: cynicism into faith; randomness into clarity; worry into devotion' (*LAG*, p. 286).

Notes

1 Douglas Coupland, *Life After God* (London: Simon & Schuster, 1994), p. 178. All future references will be given in the text with the abbreviation *LAG*, followed by page reference.

2 Gerard Loughlin, *Telling God's Story: Bible, Church and Narrative Theology* (Cambridge: Cambridge University Press, 1999), p. 5.

3 Douglas Coupland, *Polaroids from the Dead* (London: Flamingo, 1997), pp. 121–2. All subsequent references will be given parenthetically as *PD*, followed by page reference.

4 M. Snider, 'The X-Man//Douglas Coupland, from 'Generation X' to spiritual regeneration', *USA Today*, 7 March 1994. www.geocities.com/SoHo/Gallery/5560/usat1.html (5 January 2001).

5 Zygmunt Bauman, *Intimations of Postmodernity* (London: Routledge, 1992), p. x.

6 Paul S. Fiddes, 'Introduction: The Novel and the Spiritual Journey Today', in *The Novel, Spirituality and Modern Culture* (Cardiff: University of Wales Press, 2000), pp. 1–21 (p. 9).

7 The novel was republished in the UK in 1927 under the title *Fiesta*.

8 Coupland gave an illuminating interview on his religious background and ideas to Brian Draper, then editor of *Third Way*, in March 1997. 'Engaging in Reflection', *Third Way*. http://thirdway.org.uk/past/showpage.asp?page=52 (5 January 2001). See also Douglas Todd, *Brave Souls: Writers and Artists Wrestle with God, Love, Death and the Things That Matter* (Toronto: Stoddart, 1996), pp. 83–90.

9 Todd, p. 88.

10 Brian Draper, 'Novelist Who's Telling Us a Mystery', *The Church Times*, 26 September 2003. http://churchtimes.co.uk/churchtimes/website/pages.nsf/httppublicpages/1401D530D3 (17 November 2005).

11 Robert Detweiler, *Uncivil Rites: American Fiction, Religion and the Public Sphere* (Urbana: University of Illinois Press, 1996), p. 5.

12 Douglas Coupland, *Shampoo Planet* (London: Simon & Schuster, 1993), p. 219.

13 John D. Caputo, *On Religion* (London: Routledge, 2001), p. 66.

14 Fredric Jameson, *Postmodernism, or the Cultural Logic of Late Capitalism* (London and New York: Verso, 1991), p. 67.

15 'Marx's Purloined Letter' in *Ghostly Demarcations: A Symposium on Jacques Derrida's Spectres of Marx* ed. by Michael Sprinkler (London: Verso, 1999), pp. 26–67 (p. 53).

16 See, for example, Graham Ward, *Barth, Derrida and the Language of Theology* (Cambridge: Cambridge University Press, 1995); John D. Caputo, *The Prayers and Tears of Jacques Derrida* (Bloomington: Indiana University Press, 1997); Arthur Bradley, *Negative Theology and Contemporary French Philosophy* (London: Routledge, 2004); *Religion and Culture by Michel Foucault*, selected and edited by Jeremy Carrette (Manchester: Manchester University Press, 1999).

17 Peter L. Berger (ed.) *The Desecularization of the World: Essays on the Resurgence of Religion in World Politics* (Washington: Ethics and Public Policy Center; Grand Rapids: William B. Eerdmans, 1999) p. 2. Cited in *Religion in Modern Times: An Interpretive Anthology*, ed. by Linda Woodhead and Paul Heelas (Oxford: Blackwell, 2000), p. 434.

18 Caputo, p. 1.

19 J. A. McClure, 'Postmodern/Post-Secular: Contemporary Fiction and Spirituality', *Modern Fiction Studies* 41.1 (1995), 141–63. For a critique of McClure's argument see Brian D. Ingraffia, 'Is the Postmodern Post-Secular?', in *Postmodern Philosophy and Christian Thought*, ed. by Merold Westphal (Bloomington: Indiana University Press, 1999).

20 Paul Heelas, 'Introduction: On Differentiation and Dedifferentiation', in *Religion, Modernity and Postmodernity*, ed. by Paul Heelas, with David Martin and Paul Morris (Oxford: Blackwell, 1998), pp. 1–18 (p. 3).

21 Grace Davie, *Religion in Britain Since 1945: Believing Without Belonging* (Oxford: Blackwell, 1994), p. 41.

22 Douglas Coupland, *Generation X: Tales for an Accelerated Culture* (London: Abacus, 1992), p.145. All subsequent references will be given parenthetically as *GX*, followed by page reference.

23 R. W. Bibby, *Fragmented Gods: The Poverty and Potential of Religion in Canada* (Toronto: Stoddart, 1987), pp. 1–2. See also David Lyon, *Postmodernity* (Buckingham: Open University, 1994), p. 62. For research on the commercial nature of contemporary spirituality see Stuart Rose, 'Is the Term "Spirituality" a Word that Everyone Uses, But Nobody Knows What Anyone Means By It?', *Journal of Contemporary Religion*, 16.2 (2001), 193–207; Michael York, 'New Age Commodification and Appropriation of Spirituality', *Journal of Contemporary Religion*, 16.3 (2001), 361–72.

24 Michel de Certeau, *The Practice of Everyday Life*, translated by Steven Rendall (Berkeley: University of California Press, 1988), p. 179.

25 Graham Ward, *True Religion* (Oxford: Blackwell, 2003), pp. 132–3.

26 Douglas Coupland, *Hey Nostradamus!* (London: Flamingo, 2003), p. 208. All subsequent references will be given parenthetically as *HN*, followed by page reference.

27 Douglas Coupland, *Miss Wyoming* (London: Flamingo, 2000), p. 242. All subsequent references will be given parenthetically as *MW*, followed by page reference.

28 Douglas Coupland, *Eleanor Rigby* (London: Fourth Estate, 2004), p. 3. All subsequent references will be given parenthetically as *ER*, followed by page reference.

29 Douglas Coupland, *Girlfriend in a Coma* (London: Flamingo, 1998), p. 256. All subsequent references will be given parenthetically as *GIAC*, followed by page reference.

30 Robert McGill, 'The Sublime Simulation: Vancouver in Douglas Coupland's Geography of Apocalypse,' *Essays on Canadian Writing*, 70 (2000), 252–76 (265).

31 Ibid., p. 271.

32 Tom Beaudoin, *Virtual Faith: The Irreverent Spiritual Quest of Generation X* (San Francisco: Jossey-Bass, 2000), p. 21.

33 Craig Detweiler and Barry Taylor, *A Matrix of Meanings: Finding God in Pop Culture* (Grand Rapids: Baker Academic, 2003), p. 297.

34 Beaudoin, p. xiii.

35 Douglas Coupland, *All Families are Psychotic* (London: Flamingo, 2001), p. 13. All subsequent references will be given parenthetically as *AFAP*, followed by page reference.

36 Douglas Coupland, *Microserfs* (London: Harper, 2004), pp. 11, 34. All subsequent references will be given parenthetically as *MS*, followed by page reference.

37 Fiddes, p. 6. See Karl Barth, *Church Dogmatics*, English trans., ed. by G. W. Bromiley and T. F. Torrance (Edinburgh: T. & T. Clark, 1936–77), i/1, pp. 165–9.

38 Douglas Rushkoff, 'Introduction: Us, by Us', in *The GenX Reader*, ed. by Douglas Rushkoff (New York: Ballantine, 1994), pp. 3–8 (p. 7).

39 Ward (2003), p. 121.

40 Douglas Coupland, *Souvenir of Canada 2* (Vancouver: Douglas & McIntyre, 2004), p. 11.

41 Gordon Lynch, *After Religion: 'Generation X' and the Search for Meaning* (London: Darton, Longman and Todd, 2002), p. 98.

42 Lynch, p. 98.

43 Matthew 2: 1–12.

44 Ashton Nicholls, *The Poetics of Epiphany* (Tuscaloosa: University of Alabama, 1987), p. 1.

45 Frederick Buechner, *Listening to Your Life* (San Francisco: Harper, 1992), p. 57.

46 Alan Bilton, *An Introduction to Contemporary American Fiction* (Edinburgh: Edinburgh University Press, 2002), p. 227.

47 James Annesley, *Blank Fictions: Consumerism, Culture and the Contemporary American Novel* (London: Pluto Press, 1998), pp. 121–2.

48 Todd, p. 87.

49 David Lyon, *Postmodernity*, second edition (Buckingham: Open University Press, 1994), p. 2.

50 McClure, p. 155.

51 H. D. Thoreau, *Walden; or, Life in the Woods* (1846–50) in *Henry David Thoreau*, ed. Robert F. Sayre (New York: Library of America, 1985), p. 575.

52 Martyn Percy, *The Salt of the Earth: Religious Resilience in a Secular Age* (London and New York: Sheffield Academic Press, 2001), p. 53.

53 Douglas Coupland, *Souvenir of Canada* (Vancouver: Douglas & McIntyre, 2002), p. 22.

54 Gilles Néret, *Angels* (Köln: Taschen, 2004), p.5.

55 Harold Bloom, *Omens of Millennium: The Gnosis of Angels, Dreams, and Resurrection* (New York: Riverhead Books, 1996), p. 43.

56 Bauman, pp. 32–3.

57 Jonathan Munby, 'A Hollywood Carol's Wonderful Life', in *Christmas at the Movies: Images of Christmas in American, British and European Cinema*, ed. by Mark Connelly (London: I. B. Tauris, 2000), pp. 39–57 (p. 41).

58 See the discussion of the film in *Girlfriend*, p. 253.

59 Martin Jay, *Force Fields: Between Intellectual History and Cultural Critique* (London: Routledge, 1993) p.97. See also Detweiler, p.137.

60 Bilton, p. 234.

61 Ward (2003), p. 132.

62 Mark Forshaw, 'Douglas Coupland: In and Out of "Ironic Hell"', *Critical Survey*, 12.3 (2000), 39–58 (pp. 39–40).

63 Forshaw, p. 50.

64 Ibid., p. 50.

65 Donna Tartt, 'The Spirit and Writing in a Secular World' in Fiddes, pp. 25–40 (p.38).

66 Draper, 'Novelist Who's Telling Us a Mystery', *The Church Times* (26 September 2003), http://churchtimes.co.uk/churchtimes/website/pages.nsf/httppublicpages/1401D530D3 (17 November 2005).

67 Kevin J. Vanhoozer, 'Scripture and Tradition', in *The Cambridge Companion to the Bible and Culture*, ed. by Kevin J. Vanhoozer (Cambridge: Cambridge University Press, 2003), pp. 149–69 (p. 167).

6

Conclusion: *JPod* and Coupland in the future

I am thinking about the future.
I am optimistic about the future. (*Shampoo Planet*, 1993)[1]

'I don't believe in the future. I think we're all doomed'. (*JPod*, 2006)[2]

What do Douglas Coupland's abundant – and frequently conflicting – images of the future reveal about his worldview? Does his writing and visual art aspire to represent the innovative and the imminent, that is, to forge new ideas in a seemingly exhausted, derivative era? His novels occupy a perplexing hinterland between Tyler Johnson's irrepressible optimism 'about the future' and the everyday, apocalyptic paranoia expressed in *JPod*, the writer's most playfully surreal, exuberantly decadent and morally unsettling piece of fiction to date. This conclusion will use Coupland's highly self-conscious tenth 'novel' – though absurdist science-project or anti-art manifesto might be more appropriate terms – as a lens (admittedly distorting), through which to review his creative work and its aesthetic and ideological implications. Does the future have *any* future in the world according to Coupland?

In a strict, chronological sense, if we accept Fredric Jameson's historical model, this narrator of late twentieth- and early twenty-first century experience emphatically belongs to the postmodern moment.[3] Rampant consumerism, the loss of story and the breakdown of traditional, democratic politics all inform Coupland's work. Yet it is also inflected with unruly humour, a revived interest in mystical language, the benign possibilities of technology and a renewed confidence in smaller, personal narratives. Indeed, his simultaneous attraction to and disdain for the excesses of this belated epoch, a condition that Jameson once somewhat optimistically named 'late capitalism', is an anxiety represented throughout his fiction.[4] However, for a writer and artist so fascinated by the possibilities of the new, postmodernism is a problematic label.

Is it even accurate to locate Coupland within the tradition of avant-garde, intellectualism associated with post-1960s American fiction? Mark Forshaw insists that he 'has never been a post-modern writer in the sense that we think of Paul Auster . . . or Donald Barthelme, as being postmodern writers'. It would be more accurate, he argues, to read Coupland as a 'novelist who writes *about* postmodernity' and one who has 'done so . . . with increasing distaste for both its cultural and its economic manifestations'.[5] However, this 'distaste' is sometimes beguilingly unclear. Where *Girlfriend in a Coma* (1998) and *All Families are Psychotic* (2001), for example, deploy the tropes of romance or parable to propose radical ways out of spiritual bankruptcy, *JPod* insouciantly strides into a world that has little interest in remedying any such malaise. Its two immediate predecessors, *Hey Nostradamus!* (2003) and *Eleanor Rigby* (2004), are structured around melancholy, introspective and, ultimately, redemptive plots that eschew self-conscious experiment or playfulness. Although *JPod* shares their contemporary Vancouver setting – frequently a signifier of a more solemn, contemplative mode than the chaotic comedy of Coupland's US set fictions – its atmosphere is boisterous, irreverent and cheerfully lawless.

JPod specifically revisits the new technology-focus of *Microserfs* – indeed, it has been marketed as '*Microserfs* for the age of Google' – and wilfully demolishes the utopian hopes and expectations of Coupland's fourth novel. Ethan Jarlewski, *JPod*'s witty but rather cold narrator, is a twenty-something, highly skilled but powerless employee of a successful (and anonymous) software company. In Coupland's earlier fiction of the 1990s tech-boom, Microsoft staffers were both exhilarated and exhausted by the intellectual demands of shipping deadlines. By contrast, in its 2006 equivalent, the inhabitants of the titular jPod are bored and frustrated when charged with 'retroactively' including 'a charismatic cuddly turtle character' into a skateboard game ('BoardX') (*JP*, p. 16). Yet unlike the extended, technogeek family from the Redmond, Washington Campus, the jPodders have few illusions about the possibility of escape. The arbitrary, bureaucratic process that placed these programmers together – all have surnames beginning with the letter J – is a symptom of their anonymous, affectless world. JPod is another subculture – a world within a world – rather like a corporate, and more dispirited, version of the storytelling community of *Generation X*.

The calculated stylistic mimicry of the earlier work – its Pop-Art feel generated by a textual riot of visual word games, pages of prime numbers and mock eBay entries, for example – only heightens a palpable change in mood. The typographical flair of *Microserfs* reflected a mid-1990s buoyancy and willingness to experiment; Daniel Underwood's PowerBook diary entries – including the random words of the 'subconscious' file – were designed 'to try to see the patterns in [his] life'.[6] By contrast, Ethan's story is chaotic and without clear purpose: the pages of electronic spam, advertising and e-mail reflect the clutter both of his hard drive and his subconscious, but their inclusion appears to be haphazard. Ethan is aware that his world is contingent and unruly – '*Everybody* in my life is going random all over the place' – but, unlike his Seattle-based precursor, he displays no real desire to resolve this chaos (*JP*, p. 163).

All of Coupland's novels have explored the consequences of greed, lack of purpose and moral uncertainty in postmodern culture. The characters in *JPod* exist in a similarly compromised universe; the real difference, however, is that few, if any, of these thoroughly twenty-first century – and oddly likeable – people experience the ethical anguish of their fictional predecessors. Another arresting dissimilarity from the earlier novels is that the *JPod* crew appear to have read widely, if rather disdainfully, the work of their creator. After twelve pages of Coupland's trademark, non-linear, slogan emblazoned, pop culture sampling paratext, the novel's first lines of dialogue offer a withering acknowledgement of Vancouver's favourite literary son:

> '. . . I feel like a refugee in a Douglas Coupland novel.'
> '*That* asshole.'
> 'Who does he think he is?' (*JP*, p. 15).

This boldly – or dangerously – self-aware opening is a sign of Coupland's willingness to critique his own reputation and to mock the legacy of his fiction. It also marks a strategic rediscovery of the joys of irony. Later in the novel, his characters are both embarrassed by the whole Generation X phenomenon and claim that the real inheritor of Coupland's debut was nothing more radical than Aaron Spelling's trash-TV hit, *Melrose Place* (*JP*, p. 101). One character even suggests that the trendy beverage he is currently sipping would be used by Coupland as 'a device . . . to locate the characters in time and a specific

sort of culture' (*JP*, p. 191). While in *Microserfs*, Bill Gates appeared as
a spectral figure, in *JPod* it is Coupland himself who makes a series
of cameo appearances. Ethan meets 'Douglas Coupland' on a flight
to China. This appearance of the 'meta Doug' (so named by *Wired*
magazine) serendipitously echoes Bret Easton Ellis's *Lunar Park*
(2005) and a series of embarrassing encounters that Martin Amis sets
up between a writer named 'Martin Amis' and John Self, narrator of
Money (1984).[7] Like Easton Ellis and Amis, Coupland exploits aspects
of his public persona in this bizarre self-portrait, raising questions
about authority, identity and originality.

JPod operates less as a belated sequel than as a gleefully malicious
rewriting of *Microserfs*. The characters all have counterparts among
the extended 'Interiority' family who fled Microsoft in the mid-1990s.
For example, Ethan echoes Dan but shares a first name with
Microserfs' most cynical, amoral character. The libidinous Cowboy is
an avatar of Todd, the body-obsessed programmer, but the 2006
charmer lacks his spiritual ancestor's moral sensibility. In lieu of Dan's
encouraging mother, father and idealized, dead brother, Ethan has
two self-obsessed parents and a sibling whose business ventures
include people smuggling. These ironic inversions are part of the
novel's wider concern with the constructed nature of personality in the
twenty-first century. *Microserfs* cautiously welcomed the possibilities
of malleable identity – many of its characters experienced metamorphosis or spiritual change – but in *JPod* this instability is viewed less
optimistically. Kaitlin Joyce, occupying a similar space to Karla in
Microserfs as the novel's conscience, informs one colleague that he
has 'no character':

> You're a depressing assemblage of pop culture influences and cancelled
> emotions, driven by the sputtering engine of only the most banal form of
> capitalism. You spend your life feeling as if you're perpetually on the
> brink of being obsolete – whether it's labour market obsolescence or
> cultural unhipness. (*JP*, p. 100)

Kaitlin/Coupland's calm deconstruction of vacuous late capitalist
existence – and perhaps a self-reflexive challenge to the author seeking
to represent such a world – is met with an equally casual shrug of
indifference. The novel has a distinctively purgatorial atmosphere:
Kaitlin, the most recent and reluctant addition to the JPod anti-family,
casually suggests that her colleagues are like 'people damned forever'
(*JP*, p. 70).

This state of limbo is perpetuated by the narrative's use of a cartoon-like amorality. *The Simpsons*, once again, is a regular reference point and one character happily declares that an office argument is 'so *Pulp Fiction*' (*JP*, p. 71). At the beginning of the novel, Ethan is called by his mother who needs assistance in burying a biker she has semi-accidentally electrocuted – he had demanded a share of the profits from her burgeoning business in marijuana plants. The event is represented in a dead-pan style that is more reminiscent of the movies of Quentin Tarantino or Bret Easton Ellis's fiction than Coupland's previous work: 'Here's the thing: How *do* you get rid of a body?' (*JP*, p. 22). Ethan is bemused rather than appalled but he withholds judgement and the event holds only comic consequences: nobody is punished and the body is an inconvenience instead of a genuine source of remorse.

The unceremonious, guilt-free burial of a dead biker/business associate prefigures the novel's sly fascination with the evaporation of moral accountability in the era of globalization. Where Coupland's other Vancouver-set fiction has tended to emphasize the escalating influence of US cultural imperialism, *JPod* focuses on the rise of China in the global economy. In one bleakly comic set-piece, for example, Ethan is confronted by 'maybe twenty stick-thin Chinese people' hiding in his Chinatown house: these refugees have been smuggled into the country by his brother and a ballroom dancing obsessed gangster named Kam Fong. The dazed Ethan gives these exhausted and emaciated exiles his generically western clothes – including a Nine Inch Nails tour shirt – and pragmatically decides to start sporting their abandoned 'smuggling-wear': 'Voila! My new look' (*JP*, p. 82). The poverty of starving, poorly clothed illegal immigrants provides a middle-class Vancouverite with a distinctive new identity. This absurd sequence detailing an unlikely cross-cultural exchange embodies Coupland's moral-ironic approach to troubling, potentially over-whelming, political questions. In a related subplot, Ethan flies to China to rescue Steve, his erstwhile Ned Flanders-like boss, from slavery and witnesses the reality of global trade. Held prisoner in a factory and given an addiction to heroin by its owners, Steve is apparently 'clam happy, making fake Nikes on one of hell's more ghastly rungs' (*JP*, p. 273).

For a tale of such striking moral disorder, it is not surprising that *JPod* is the first of Coupland's novels to be bereft of even failed epiphanies. Although *Microserfs* is its most obvious precedent, *JPod* might have been subtitled *Life After God Too*. Spirituality is largely

marked by its absence but, in a muted echo of earlier work, the longing
for a genuine experience of the divine materializes in unexpected ways.
Ethan, for example, overwhelmed by a guilt that he cannot name, utters
an inchoate prayer 'that God would shake my Etch-a-Sketch clean
overnight' (*JP*, p. 134). Coupland's allusion to Thomas Pynchon's anti-
detective novel and paradigm of paranoid fiction, *The Crying of Lot 49*
(1966), in a subplot involving a piece of real estate (naughtily named
Lot 49), serves to intensify the sense of conspiratorial bewilderment.
Despite the novel's prevailing atmosphere of ethical haziness –
compared to the visionary fervour of *Girlfriend in a Coma*, for example
– it would be misleading to describe *JPod* as an amoral piece of
fiction. Indeed, Toby Litt claims that 'beneath' the novel's embrace of
experiment, technology and modish dissipation, Coupland remains a
'deeply judgmental' writer.[8] 'This is the Wretched Decade,' proclaims
one character, nostalgic for the certainties and comparative wealth of
the 1990s (*JP*, p. 198). Does Coupland view the first decade of the
twenty-first century as a failed vision of the future?

In a bittersweet echo of *Microserfs'* embrace of innovation – what
Dan calls 'Being One-Point-*Oh*' – *JPod* laments this as a lost possibility
(*JP*, p. 197). The recurrent trash motifs of his fiction and art, as
discussed in Chapter 3, might suggest that Coupland, like most of his
contemporaries, has abandoned the notion of originality and purity.
'All you ever talk about is junk', complains Kaitlin in a statement that
doubles as a piece of authorial self-critique (*JP*, p. 84). Certainly, his
work is interested in the failure of aura and the meaning of repetition;
he is an artist of an age in which mass production, replication and
universality typify everyday life. Fredric Jameson's argument that the
'great modernisms were . . . predicated on the invention of a personal,
private style, as unmistakable as your fingerprint, as incomparable as
your own body' apparently excludes Coupland's generation.[9]

Yet, beginning with the allusion to Salvador Dali's melting clocks in
Generation X (1991), Coupland's writing has flirted with symbols
and techniques that reiterate elements of Modernist art, particularly
those artists who sought to produce a tradition of the new.[10] In
Polaroids from the Dead (1996), Coupland stated that 'most of [his]
faith in the future – was invested, however wittingly, in the world of art,
and Modern art at that'.[11] Coupland has chosen to chronicle an era
of simulation defined by a ceaseless and passively consumed flow of
images – a world of endless choice and few responsibilities. However,
he is also working within a continuum of European and North

American Modernists, interested in generating fresh, defamiliarizing idioms and dislocating assumptions regarding literary form. In *JPod*, 'Douglas Coupland' becomes another junk artist: he bribes Ethan into surrendering his laptop which will provide the basis for his new novel: 'it's easier just to steal your life than to make something up', comments Coupland's evil alter ego (*JP*, p. 446).

The reverse iconoclasm of his recycled objects – in sculptures made from garbage and narratives that emerge from the waste of popular culture is – to borrow Jameson's phrase – a late flowering of the 'modernist aesthetic'. Even in a world that is filled with imitation, Coupland's work suggests that, despite Jameson's pessimism, art is able to 'generate its own unique vision of the world and to forge its own unique, unmistakable style'.[12] 'In a world in which stylistic innovation is no longer possible, all that is left is to imitate dead styles', claims Jameson, asserting that postmodernism 'will involve the necessary failure of art and the aesthetic, the failure of the new, the imprisonment in the past'.[13] Although Coupland has abandoned certain myths of absolute authorial originality, his work emphatically rejects both 'the failure of the new' and 'imprisonment in the past'. The writer's faith in the potential of the new – as opposed to home-sickness for a vanished era – is expressed in the Imagist-like chapter titles of *Girlfriend in a Coma*, one of which reads: 'THE PAST IS A BAD IDEA.'[14] 'Modernism, once about as alive as Walt Disney at two degrees Kelvin, is breathing and dancing', argued Coupland in the final year of the twentieth century, simultaneously lamenting those who continue to 'get all nostalgic for the past'. 'Crabbiness about the present allows us to live inside a static retro universe of brittle little *New Yorker* cartoons. Get over it.'[15]

In recent years, Coupland, the proto-Modernist, has participated in 'scenario building' with a 'futurology think tank' and is, apparently, highly frustrated that he will not 'see the second half of the 21st century'.[16] For example, in a visual art exhibition, *I Like the Future and the Future Likes Me* (2005), Coupland uses his 'favourite event horizon' of '1000 years' to imagine life in the year 3005 and, via traditional sci-fi images from the 1970s to the present, to re-examine contemporary ways of conceptualizing the future.[17] Nevertheless, this craving to witness the future is also experienced by a number of Coupland's characters in the earlier narratives. In *Miss Wyoming* (2000), John Johnson – producer of bad movies and failed nomad – remains instinctively optimistic about the world to come. 'I like to look at the numbers rev by on the gas pump', John explains to his long-suffering co-producer, because it allow him 'to pretend each number's a year':

> I like to watch history begin at Year Zero and clip up and up and up. Dark Ages . . . Renaissance . . . there's this magic little bit of time, just a few numbers past the present year, whatever it is. Whenever I hit these years, then for maybe a fraction of a second, I can, if not *see* the future, *feel* it . . . It's like I get to be the first one there – in the future. I get to be first. A pioneer.[18]

This description of an unconventional, improvised and, frankly, rather restricted mode of time travel exemplifies a resolute belief in progress. The confidently imagined rapid passage from 'Year Zero' to an unknown near future represents one strand in Coupland's compulsive futurology. This refugee from Hollywood identifies himself as an unconscious Modernist: standing in a petrol station – an emblem of technological advance, symbolic of both progress and environmental damage – John is eager for originality. Other characters, including *Generation X*'s cold war babies, Dag and Andy, are, however, plagued by a lack of faith in the future. Like John, Dag specifically associates a gas station memory with an optimistic future: as a child his father encourages him to inhale the fumes of spilled petrol: 'So *clean*. It smells like the *future*' (*GX*, p. 107). This odd sense-impression – 'the most perfect moment' – is Dag's happiest memory (*GX*, p. 108). Yet he has not retained the exalted optimism for the future embodied in that intense childhood experience.

Andy's waspish critique of his friend's quirky wardrobe – he dresses, apparently, 'like a General Motors showroom salesman from the year 1955' – identifies an alternative, contemporary propensity for avoiding the present and denying the possibility of a bright, creative future. Dag even confesses to envying his own parents, who married in the year of his alleged fashion fixation, their freedom from '*futurelessness*' (*GX*, pp. 96–8). *Generation X* is less sanguine than Coupland's later novels about the prospects for civilization. Indeed, as a set of overlapping stories that are heavily infused by the experience of growing up during the cold war and the quotidian fear of nuclear annihilation, this caution is not surprising. 'The possibilities of the future', notes one sombre critic, 'always include the possibility that there is no future.'[19] The theological implications of Coupland's penchant for end-time stories, discussed in Chapter 5, is always rooted in a more secular sense that, as Dag states, '[t]ime ... is ... running out' (*GX*, p. 36). Andy, concerned about his own parents' resistance to change, presents an incarnate image of the future as 'a horrible diseased drifter' with 'purulent green lesions' waiting to break into the fragile security of the static family home (*GX*, p. 167). Even Tyler, Andy's superficially confident younger brother, furtively confesses that he is unable to envision 'a future' (*GX*, p. 173). This private despair about the future disappears in the semi-sequel to *Generation X*.

In *Shampoo Planet*, the second of Coupland's swaggering characters named Tyler is keen to 'participate in the willful amnesia that propels' his fellow 'citizens into the sparkly and thrilling future that I desperately want to share' (*SP*, p. 10). When he scrawls a message on a dollar bill – 'You are unable to visualize yourself in a future' – it suggests that, like Tyler Palmer, his confidence is rather brittle (*SP*, p. 204). Uncertainties and hope for the future also haunt Coupland's older characters. In *All Families are Psychotic*, for example, Janet Drummond, born in the late 1930s, is happy to escape her peers in an internet café where she can be '*in a place with a few people who aren't scared by technology and who don't fear the future*'.[20] Janet's robust approach to the passage of time, however, is compromised when she becomes HIV positive: 'I stopped believing in the future – which is to say, I stopped thinking of the future as being a place . . . a place you can go *to*' (*AFAP*, p. 120).

Alan Bilton has argued that, despite Coupland's Canadian citizenship, there is 'something specifically American about this sense of being fleeced of the future'. The nation's unique emphasis on the right to the 'pursuit of happiness' in addition to 'life and liberty' is, he notes, 'predisposed toward the future, personal and social improvement, a dream of progress and perfectibility'. Members of the so-called X generation are, Bilton suggests, likely to be 'suspicious of what awaits them'.[21] There is certainly an explicit creative tension in Coupland's work between profound cultural pessimism and an equally marked sense of joy in the specifics of contemporary life. *Microserfs*, for example, both celebrates the possibilities of new technology and hints at the darker consequences of the digital revolution, including a subtle but perceptible erosion of interiority and human agency. Similarly, *Life After God* (1994) is simultaneously charged with the hope 'that beauty surrounds us – and that the world is knowable' and the annihilation fears common to those who grew up during the cold war (*LAG*, p. 256). *Hey Nostradamus!* and *Eleanor Rigby* feature narrators whose hopes for the future have been ruined by random violence or the ravages of illness. However, both novels end with a sense of hope for a different kind of future, one not dependent on perfect earthly happiness. *JPod*, by contrast, displays a more sceptical interpretation of the longed-for future – exploitation, moral carelessness and cruelty remain fundamental to human experience – but it offers a tacit challenge. What kind of world, if not the present one, might we live in?

'What of the future? The future can only be for ghosts. And the past.'[22] Jacques Derrida's statement reads like an uncanny description of *Girlfriend in a Coma*: the bleak future landscape of Coupland's fifth novel is littered by decaying remnants of the past and haunted by a single spectre. This strange, troubling fable, a sermon against the seductive complacency of consumer culture, suggests that a particular version of the future – as capitalist utopia – is no longer available. What Terry Eagleton has described as the conservative belief in the future as 'the present infinitely repeated – or, as the postmodernist remarked, 'the present plus more options' is derided in *Girlfriend in a Coma*.[23] One chapter title baldly states that 'The future is fake' and another suggests 'The future and the afterlife are different things altogether' (*GIAC*, pp. 218, 124). In this sense, Coupland is a *post*-modern author, who might 'harbor a revolutionary impulse: the impulse *to do things differently*'.[24] Nevertheless, in *JPod*, Coupland is able to write critically about wistfulness for lost futures and, in particular, the promise that technological progress will always be beneficial. Whatever the future of Coupland's writing, it is unlikely to be found in a retreat into the past. The twenty-first century landscape of his recent fiction is frequently troubled; it is marked by random violence, loneliness and moral ambiguity. But, the future is dynamically open. A comforting vision of the past holds no temptation for this writer of the ambiguous, dangerous, beguiling present and possible future: 'Nostalgia's *dead*.'[25]

Notes

1   Douglas Coupland, *Shampoo Planet* (London: Simon & Schuster, 1993), p. 54. All subsequent references will be given parenthetically as *SP*, followed by page reference.
2   Douglas Coupland, *JPod* (London: Bloomsbury, 2006), pp. 329–30. All subsequent references will be given parenthetically as *JP*, followed by page reference.

3   Fredric Jameson, *The Cultural Turn: Selected Writings on the Postmodern, 1983–98* (London: Verso, 1998), p. 3.

4   Fredric Jameson, *Postmodernism, or, the Culture of Late Capitalism* (London: Verso, 1991).

5   Mark Forshaw, 'Douglas Coupland: In and Out of "Ironic Hell"', *Critical Survey*, 12.3 (2000), 39–58 (53).

6   Douglas Coupland, *Microserfs* (London: Harper, 2004), p. 4.

7   J. K., 'A Tale of Two Couplands', *Wired* (May 2006), www.wired.com/wired/archive/14.05/posts.html?pg=6 (5 July 2006).

8   Toby Litt, 'In with IT crowd', *The Times* (20 May 2006), www.timesonline.co.uk/article/0,,23109–2186999,00.html (10 July 2006).

9   Jameson (1998), pp. 5–6.

10   Douglas Coupland, *Generation X: Tales for an Accelerated Culture* (London: Abacus, 1992), p. 8. All subsequent references will be given parenthetically as *GX*, followed by page reference.

11   Douglas Coupland, *Polaroids from the Dead* (London: Flamingo, 1997), p. 124. All subsequent references will be given parenthetically as *PD*, followed by page reference.

12   Jameson (1998), p. 6.

13   Ibid., p. 7.

14   Douglas Coupland, *Girlfriend in a Coma* (London: Flamingo, 1998), p. 189. All subsequent references will be given parenthetically as *GIAC*, followed by page reference.

15   Douglas Coupland, 'Nostalgia's Dead', *Architectural Record*, 187.2 (1999), 39–40.

16   Sheryl Garratt, 'Why is Douglas Coupland fascinated by garbage?', *Word*, 8 (October 2003), 24–5 (25).

17   'The Thousand-Year Plan', www.coupland.com/art/essay.html (15 February 2006).

18   Douglas Coupland, *Miss Wyoming* (London: Flamingo, 2000), p. 112. All subsequent references will be given parenthetically as *MW*, followed by page reference.

19   Werner Hamacher, 'Lingua Amissa: The Messianism of Commodity-Language and Derrida's *Spectres of Marx*', in *Ghostly Demarcations: A Symposium on Jacques Derrida's Spectres of Marx*, edited by Michael Sprinker (London: Verso, 1999), pp. 168–212 (p. 203).

20   Douglas Coupland, *All Families are Psychotic* (London: Flamingo, 2001), p. 36. All subsequent references will be given parenthetically as *AFAP*, followed by page reference.

21   Alan Bilton, *An Introduction to Contemporary American Fiction* (Edinburgh: Edinburgh University Press, 2002), p. 225.

22   Jacques Derrida, *Spectres of Marx: The State of the Debt, the Work of Mourning, and the New International*, translated by Peggy Kamuf (New York and London: Routledge, 1994), p. 37.

23 Terry Eagleton, *After Theory* (London: Penguin, 2004), p. 6.
24 Kevin Vanhoozer, 'Preface', *The Cambridge Companion to Postmodern Theology*, ed. by Kevin Vanhoozer (Cambridge: Cambridge University Press, 2003), p. xiii.
25 Coupland, 'Nostalgia's Dead', p. 39.

Bibliography

Work by Douglas Coupland

Novels (in order of publication; editions
listed are those cited)
Generation X: Tales for an Accelerated Culture (London: Abacus, 1992)
Shampoo Planet (London: Simon & Schuster, 1993)
Life After God (London: Simon & Schuster, 1994)
Girlfriend in a Coma (London: Flamingo, 1998)
Microserfs (London: Harper, 2004)
Miss Wyoming (London: Flamingo, 2000)
All Families are Psychotic (London: Flamingo, 2001)
Hey Nostradamus! (London: Flamingo, 2003)
Eleanor Rigby (London: Fourth Estate, 2004)
JPod (London: Bloomsbury, 2006)

Short stories
With Pierre Huyghe, *School Spirit* (Paris: Editions Dis Voir, 2003)
'Fire at the Ativan factory', in *Vancouver Stories: West Coast Fiction from
Canada's Best Writers* (Vancouver: Raincoast, 2005), pp. 223–34

Non-fiction
Polaroids from the Dead (London: Flamingo, 1997)
City of Glass: Douglas Coupland's Vancouver (Vancouver: Douglas &
McIntyre, 2000)
Souvenir of Canada (Vancouver: Douglas & McIntyre, 2002)
Souvenir of Canada 2 (Vancouver: Douglas & McIntyre, 2004)

Uncollected non-fiction by Coupland
'Foreword', Linklater (1992)
'Eulogy: Generation X'd', *Details* (June 1995), p.72.

'Agree/Disagree: 55 Statements About the Culture', *New Republic* (21 August 1995), 213.8/9, p.10.
with Kip Ward, *Lara's Book: Lara Croft and the Tomb Raider Phenomenon* (Rocklin: Prima, 1998)
'Nostalgia's dead', *Architectural Record*, 187.2 (1999), 39–40
'Introduction', *Vancouver Stories: West Coast Fiction from Canada's Best Writers* (Vancouver: Raincoast, 2005), pp. 1–5

Secondary sources

Abbott, H. Porter, *The Cambridge Introduction to Narrative* (Cambridge: Cambridge University Press, 2002)
Annesley, James, *Blank Fictions: Consumerism, Culture and the Contemporary American Novel* (London: Pluto Press, 1998)
Anthony, Andrew, 'Close to the Edge', *The Observer* (24 August 2003)
Attfield, Judy, *Wild Things: The Material Culture of Everyday Life* (Oxford: Berg, 2000)
Baudrillard, Jean, *America*, trans. Chris Turner (New York: Verso, 1989)
——, *Simulacra and Simulation*, translated by Sheila Faria Glaser (Ann Arbor: University of Michigan Press, 1994)
Bauman, Zygmunt, *Intimations of Postmodernity* (London: Routledge, 1992)
——, *Life in Fragments: Essays in Postmodern Morality* (Oxford: Blackwell, 1995)
——, *Globalization: The Human Consequences* (Cambridge: Polity, 1998)
Beaudoin, Tom, *Virtual Faith: The Irreverent Spiritual Quest of Generation X* (San Francisco: Jossey-Bass, 2000)
Bell, Daniel, *The Cultural Contradictions of Capitalism* (London: Heinemann, 1979)
Benjamin, Walter, *Illuminations: Essays and Reflections*, edited by Hannah Arendt (London: Jonathan Cape, 1970)
Bentley, Nick (ed.), *British Fiction of the 1990s* (London: Routledge, 2005)
Bibby, R. W., *Fragmented Gods: The Poverty and Potential of Religion in Canada* (Toronto: Stoddart, 1987)
Bill, J. Brent, 'Loneliness Virus', *Christian Century*, 117.31 (8 November 2000), 1150–2
Bilton, Alan, *An Introduction to Contemporary American Fiction* (Edinburgh: Edinburgh University Press, 2002)
Blincoe, Nicholas, 'A Modern Master' (Review of *All Families Are Psychotic*), *New Statesman* (10 September 2001), 52–3
——, 'Feeling Frail,' *The Daily Telegraph* (16 October 2004), 1–2
Blythe, Will, 'Doing Laundry at the End of History', *Esquire* (March 1994) www.geocities.com/soHo/Gallery/5560/crit1.html
Botting, Fred, 'From Excess to the New World Order', in Bentley, pp. 21–41

Brabazon, Tara, *From Revolution to Revelation: Generation X, Popular Memory and Cultural Studies* (Aldershot: Ashgate, 2005)

Brook, Susan, 'Hedgemony? Suburban space in *The Buddha of Suburbia*', in Bentley, pp. 209–25

Buechner, Frederick, *Listening to Your Life* (San Francisco: Harper, 1992)

Byrne, Eleanor and Martin McQuillan, *Deconstructing Disney* (London: Pluto Press, 1999)

Caputo, John D., *On Religion* (London: Routledge, 2001)

de Certeau, Michel, *The Practice of Everyday Life*, translated by Steven Rendall (Berkley: University of California Press, 1988)

——, *Culture in the Plural*, translated by Tom Conley (Minneapolis: University of Minnesota Press, 1997)

Clarke, David B., Marcus A. Doel and Kate M. L. Housiaux (eds), *The Consumption Reader*, (London and New York: Routledge, 2003)

Cowley, Adam, 'Prophet of Doom' (Review of *Hey Nostradamus!*), *New Statesman* (8 September 2003), 52–3

Craig, Stephen C. and Stephen Earl Bennett, *After the Boom: The politics of Generation X* (Lanham: Rowman & Littlefield, 1997)

Curnutt, Kirk, 'Generating Xs: Identity Politics, Consumer Culture, and the Making of a Generation', in Ulrich and Harris (2003), pp.162–83

Currie, Mark, *Postmodern Narrative Theory* (Basingstoke: Macmillan, 1998)

DeLillo, Don, *Americana* (London: Penguin, 1990)

——, *Underworld* (London: Picador, 1998)

Delvaux, Martine, 'The Exit of a Generation: The 'Whatever' Philosophy', *Midwest Quarterly: A Journal of Contemporary Thought*, 40.2 (1999), 171–86

Derrida, Jacques, *Spectres of Marx: The State of the Debt, the Work of Mourning, and the New International*, translated by Peggy Kamuf (London: Routledge, 1994)

Detweiler, Craig and Barry Taylor, *A Matrix of Meanings: Finding God in Pop Culture* (Grand Rapids: Baker Academic, 2003)

Detweiler, Robert, *Uncivil Rites: American Fiction, Religion and the Public Sphere* (Urbana: University of Illinois Press, 1996)

Dwyer, Victor, 'Puberty Blues', *Maclean's*, 106.34 (24 August 1992), 60

Eagleton, Terry, *The Idea of Culture* (Oxford: Blackwell, 2000)

——, *After Theory* (London: Penguin, 2004)

Edwards, Michael, *Towards a Christian Poetics* (London: Macmillan, 1984)

Eggers, Dave, *A Heartbreaking Work of Staggering Genius* (London: Picador, 2001)

Elliot, Michael, 'Global Whining: We're No. 1', *Newsweek*, 123.23 (6 June 1994), 69

Emerson, Ralph Waldo, *The Complete Prose Works of Ralph Waldo Emerson* (London: Ward Lock, 1898)

Ermath, Elizabeth Deeds, *Sequel to History: Postmodernism and the Crisis of Representational Time* (New Jersey: Princeton University Press, 1992)

Faye, Jefferson, 'Canada in a Coma', *The American Review of Canadian Studies*, 31.3 (2001), 501–10

Fiddes, Paul S. (ed.) *The Novel, Spirituality and Modern Culture* (Cardiff: University of Wales, 2000a)

——, 'Introduction: The Novel and the Spiritual Journey Today', in Fiddes (2000a), pp. 1–21

——, *The Promised End: Eschatology in Theology and Literature* (Oxford: Blackwell, 2000b)

Finnegan, Jim, 'Theoretical Tailspins: Reading "Alternative" Performance in *Spin* Magazine', in Ulrich and Harris (2000), pp. 121–61

Forshaw, Mark, 'Douglas Coupland: In and Out of "Ironic Hell"', *Critical Survey*, 12.3 (2000), 39–58

Franzen, Jonathan, *The Corrections* (London: Fourth Estate, 2002)

Fukuyama, Francis, *The End of History and the Last Man* (London: Penguin, 1992)

Fussell, Paul, *Class: A Guide Through the American Status System* (New York: Summit, 1983)

Garratt, Sheryl, 'Why is Douglas Coupland Fascinated by Garbage?', *Word*, 8 (October 2003), 24–5

Grassian, Daniel, *Hybrid Fictions: American Literature and Generation X* (Jefferson: McFarland, 2003)

Hamblett, Charles and Jane Deverson (eds), *Generation X* (Greenwich, Conn.: Fawcett, 1964)

Hamers, David, 'Having Arrived, Time to Move on: Coupland's Brentwood with Space and Time', *Environment and Planning A*, 33 (12), 2001, 2109–25

Haynsworth, Leslie, '"Alternative" Music and the Oppositional Potential of Generation X Culture', in Ulrich and Harris (2003), pp. 41–58

Heelas, Paul, with David Martin and Paul Morris (eds), *Religion, Modernity and Postmodernity* (Oxford: Blackwell, 1998)

Herod, Andrew and Melissa W. Wright, 'Theorizing Space and Time', *Environment and Planning A*, 33.12, (2001), 2089–93

Hornby, Nick, *About a Boy* (London: Victor Gollancz, 1998)

Horowitz, Helen Lefkowitz, 'Undergraduate Cultures', *Change*, 25.5 (September–October), 62

Howe, Neil and William Strauss, *13th Generation* (New York: Vintage, 1993)

Hutcheon, Linda, *A Poetics of Postmodernism: History, Theory, Fiction* (New York: Routledge, 1988)

Ingraffia, Brian, 'Is the Postmodern Post-Secular? The Parody of Religious Quests in Thomas Pynchon's *The Crying of Lot 49* and Don DeLillo's *White Noise*', in Westphal (1999), pp. 44–68

Irr, Caren, 'From Nation to Generation: The Economics of North American
     Culture, 1930s-1990s', *Canadian Review of American Studies*, 27.1 (1997),
     135–44
James, Victoria, 'Geographical Dossier: Rubbish', *Geographical*, 77.9 (2005),
     33–5
Jameson, Fredric, *Postmodernism, or the, The Cultural Logic of Late
     Capitalism* (London and New York: Verso, 1991)
——, *The Cultural Turn: Selected Writings on the Postmodern, 1983–1998*
     (London: Verso, 1998)
——, 'Marx's Purloined Letter', in Michael Sprinkler (ed.), *Ghostly Demarca-
     tions: A Symposium on Jacques Derrida's Spectres of Marx* (London: Verso,
     1999), pp. 26–67.
Jasper, David, *The Sacred Desert: Religion, Literature, Art and Culture* (Oxford:
     Blackwell, 2004)
Jay, Martin, *Force Fields: Between Intellectual History and Cultural Critique*
     (London: Routledge, 1993)
Jedeikin, J., 'Fiction for the post-boom', *Rolling Stone*, 597 (7 February
     1991), 1
Joselit, David, Joan Simon and Renata Saleci, *Jenny Holzer* (London: Phaidon,
     1998)
Jukes, Peter, 'Get a (digital) life', *New Statesman & Society*, 8.378 (10 November
     1995), 37
Kendall, Lori, 'Nerd Nation: Images of Nerds in US Popular Culture',
     International Journal of Cultural Studies, 2.2 (1999), 260–83
Keohane, Kieran, *Symptoms of Canada: An Essay on the Canadian Identity*
     (Toronto: University of Toronto Press, 1997)
Kermode, Frank, *The Sense of an Ending: Studies in the Theory of Fiction*
     (Oxford: Oxford University Press, 1967)
Klein, Naomi, *No Logo: Taking Aim At the Brand Bullies* (London: Flamingo,
     2000)
Klobucar, Andrew, 'The Apocalypse Will Be Televised: Electronic Media and
     the Last Generation', in Ulrich and Harris (2003), pp. 249–67
Kreitzer, L, Joseph, *The New Testament in Fiction and Film: On Reversing
     the Hermeneutical Flow* (Sheffield: JSOT Press, 1993)
Kröller, Eva-Marie, 'The City as Anthology', *Canadian Literature*, 169 (2001),
     5–10
Kunstler, James Howard, *The Geography of Nowhere: The Rise and Decline
     of America's Man-Made Landscape* (New York: Touchstone, 1993)
Lainsbury, G. P., 'Generation X and the End of History', *Essays on Canadian
     Writing*, 58 (1996), 229–40
Lambrose, R. J., 'The Abusable Past', *Radical History Review*, 77 (2000), 162–6
Landow, George P. (ed.), *Hyper/Text/Theory* (Baltimore: Johns Hopkins
     University Press, 1994)

Latham, Rob, *Consuming Youth: Vampires, Cyborgs, and the Culture of Consumption* (Chicago: University of Chicago Press, 2002)

Lehman, Daniel W., 'You Can See Nathan's from Here: Lobbing Culture at the Boomers', in Ulrich and Harris (2003), pp. 105–20

Levine, Joshua, 'Generation X', *Forbes*, 154.2 (18 July 1994), 293

Lewis, Peter 'Making Magic', *The Independent* (3 April 1993), 24–6

Linklater, Richard, *Slacker* (New York: St Martin's Press, 1992)

Loughlin, Gerard, *Telling God's Story: Bible, Church and Narrative Theology* (Cambridge: Cambridge University Press, 1999)

Lynch, Gordon, *After Religion: 'Generation X' and the Search for Meaning* (London: Darton, Longman and Todd, 2002)

Lyon, David, *Postmodernity* (Buckingham: Open University, 1994)

——, *Jesus in Disneyland: Religion in Postmodern Times* (Cambridge: Polity Press, 2000)

Lyotard, J. F., *The Postmodern Condition: A Report on Knowledge*, translated by Geoff Bennington and Brian Marsuni (Manchester University Press, 1984)

McCarthy, David, *Pop Art* (London: Tate Gallery, 2000)

McClure, John A., 'Postmodern/Post-Secular: Contemporary Fiction and Spirituality', *Modern Fiction Studies*, 41.1 (1995), 141–63

McGill, Robert, 'The Sublime Simulation: Vancouver in Douglas Coupland's Geography of Apocalypse,' *Essays on Canadian Writing*, 70 (2000), 252–76

McGowan, Todd, 'The Obsolescence of Mystery and the Accumulation of Waste in Don DeLillo's *Underworld*', *Critique*, 46.2 (2005), 123–45

McHale, Brian, *Postmodernist Fiction* (London: Methuen, 1987)

McQuillan (ed.), *The Narrative Reader* (London: Routledge, 2000)

Mills, Katie, ' "Await Lightning": How Generation X Remaps the Road Story', in Ulrich and Harris (2003), pp. 221–48

——, *Garden State* (London: Faber & Faber, 2002)

Moody, Rick, *The Ice Storm* (London: Abacus, 1998)

Needham, Clare, 'He's No Douglas Coupland: An interview with Julian Novitz', *Just Another Art Movement*, 22 (2004), pp. 61–7

Nehring, Neil, 'Jigsaw Youth versus Generation X and Postmodernism', in Ulrich and Harris (2003), pp. 59–78

Nicholls, Ashton, *The Poetics of Epiphany* (Tuscaloosa: University of Alabama, 1987)

Nicol, Bran (ed.), *Postmodernism and the Contemporary Novel: A Reader* (Edinburgh: Edinburgh University Press, 2002)

O'Rourke, P. J., *All the Trouble in the World: The Lighter Side of Famine, Pestilence, Destruction and Death* (London: Picador, 1995)

Palahniuk, Chuck, *Fight Club* (London: Vintage, 1997)

Percy, Martyn, *The Salt of the Earth: Religious Resilience in a Secular Age* (London and New York: Sheffield Academic Press, 2001)

Perlstein, Rick, 'Reality Bytes Cybergeek', *The Nation* (26 June 1995), 934–5

Redhead, Steve, *Paul Virilio: Theorist for an Accelerated Culture* (Edinburgh: Edinburgh University Press, 2004)

Ricoeur, Paul, *Time and Narrative*, translated by Kathleen McLaughlin and David Pellauer, 3 vols (Chicago: Chicago University Press, 1984)

Ritchie, Karen, *Marketing to Generation X* (New York: Lexington, 1995)

Rogers, Heather, *Gone Tomorrow: the Hidden Life of Garbage* (New York: the New Press, 2005)

Rushkoff, Douglas (ed.), *The Gen X Reader* (New York: Ballantine, 1994)

Smith, Ali, 'Amazing Grace', *The Guardian* (9 October 2004), 26

Soja, Edward W., *Postmodern Geographies: The Reassertion of Space in Critical Social Theory* (London: Verso, 1989)

——, *Thirdspace: Journeys to Los Angeles and other Real-and-Imagined Places* (Oxford: Blackwell, 1996)

——, *Postmetropolis: Critical Studies of Cities and Regions* (Oxford: Blackwell, 2000)

Star, Alexander, 'The Twentysomething Myth', *New Republic*, 208.1–2 (4 January 1993), 22–5

Tartt, Donna, *The Secret History* (London: Penguin, 1992)

——, 'The Spirit and Writing in a Secular World', in Fiddes 2000a, pp. 25–40.

Tate, Andrew, '"Now – Here is My Secret": Ritual and Epiphany in Douglas Coupland's Fiction', *Literature and Theology*, 16.3 (2002), 326–38

——, '"I am your witness": Douglas Coupland at the end of the world', *Biblical Religion and the Novel, 1700–2000*, ed. by Mark Knight and Tom Woodman (Aldershot: Ashgate, 2006)

Thomas, John D., 'All the Lonely People', *Publishers Weekly*, 251.46 (15 November 2004), p. 38

Thompson, Graham, '"Frank Lloyd Oop": *Microserfs*, Modern Migration, and the Architecture of the Nineties', *Canadian Review of American Studies*, 31 (2001), 119–35

Thoreau, Henry David, *Henry David Thoreau*, ed. by Robert F. Sayre (New York: Library of America, 1985)

Todd, Douglas, *Brave Souls: Writers and Artists Wrestle with God, Love, Death and the Things That Matter* (Toronto: Stoddart, 1996)

Turner, Chris, *Planet Simpson* (London: Ebury Press, 2005)

Twitchell, James B., *Lead Us Into Temptation: The Triumph of American Materialism* (New York: Columbia University Press, 1999)

Ulrich, John M. and Andrea L. Harris, *GenXegesis: Essays on Alternative Youth (Sub)Culture* (Madison: University of Wisconsin Press, 2003)

Vanhoozer, Kevin J. (ed.), *The Cambridge Companion to Postmodern Theology* (Cambridge: Cambridge University Press, 2003)

——, 'Theology and the Condition of Postmodernity: A Report on Knowledge of God,' in Vanhoozer (2003), pp. 3–25.

Virilio, Paul, *The Aesthetics of Disappearance*, translated by Philip Beitchman (New York: Semiotext(e), 1991)

——, *The Art of the Motor*, translated by Julie Ross (Minneapolis: University of Minnesota Press, 1995)

——, *Open Sky*, translated by Julie Rose (London: Verso, 1997)

——, *Desert Screen: War at the Speed of Light*, translated by Michael Degener (New York: Continuum, 2002)

Waldman, Diane, *Jenny Holzer* (New York: Guggenheim, 1997)

Ward, Graham (ed.), *The Certeau Reader* (Oxford: Blackwell, 2000)

Wasko, Janet, *Understanding Disney: The Manufacture of Fantasy* (Cambridge: Polity, 2001)

—— *Theology and Contemporary Critical Theory*, 2nd edn (Houndmills: Macmillan, 2000)

Westphal, Merold (ed.), *Postmodern Philosophy and Christian Thought* (Bloomington: Indiana University Press, 1999)

Wilson, Steve, 'Douglas Coupland', *San Francisco Review of Books*, 20.3 (July–August 1995), 32–3

Wolfe, Tom, *The Bonfire of the Vanities* (London: Picador, 1990)

Woodhead, Linda and Paul Heelas (eds) *Religion in Modern Times: An Interpretive Anthology* (Oxford: Blackwell, 2000) p. 376.

Žižek, Slavoj, *The Fragile Absolute – or, Why is the Christian legacy worth Fighting for?* (London and New York: Verso, 2000)

Internet sources

Brockington, Michael, 'Five Short Years: Half a Decade of Douglas Coupland', www.sfu.ca/~brocking/writing/couplong.html (7 October 2005)

Clark, Andrew, 'Finding true love in LA', *Macleans*, 17 January 2000, www.macleans.ca/shared/print.jsp?content=29187 (10 December 2005)

J. K., 'A Tale of Two Couplands', *Wired*, May 2006, www.wired.com/wired/archive/14.05/posts.html?pg=6 (5 July 2006)

Litt, Toby, 'In with IT crowd', *The Times*, 20 May 2006, www.timesonline.co.uk/article/0,,23109-2186999,00.html (10 July 2006)

Turner, Jenny, 'Top of the World', *London Review of Books*, 22.12, 22 June 2000, www.lrb.co.uk/v22/n12/turn03_.html (10 November 2005)

Vandrome, Frederick, 'Massage from the Dead', *Image [&] Narrative*, 4 (2002), www.imageandnarrative.be/gender/frederickvandromme.htm (7 October 2005)

Index

Lightning Source UK Ltd.
Milton Keynes UK
UKHW021259091222
413665UK00030B/279